LONGING FOR HOME

M. JAN HOLTON

Longing for Home

Forced Displacement and
Postures of Hospitality

Yale UNIVERSITY PRESS

NEW HAVEN AND LONDON

Yale University Press books may be purchased in quantity for educational,
business, or promotional use. For information, please e-mail sales.press@yale
.edu (U.S. office) or sales@yaleup.co.uk (U.K. office).

Set in Janson Oldstyle type by Newgen North America.
Printed in the United States of America.

Library of Congress Control Number: 2015955618
ISBN: 978-0-300-20762-0 (cloth : alk. paper)

A catalogue record for this book is available from the British Library.
This paper meets the requirements of ANSI/NISO Z39.48-1992
(Permanence of Paper).

10 9 8 7 6 5 4 3 2 1

*This book is dedicated to all displaced persons
whose hearts continue to long for a place called home.*

*In Memory
Betty Ann Holton*

CONTENTS

Acknowledgments   ix

Introduction   1

one Notions of Home   12

two Leaning into God   32

three Crisis and Forced Displacement   50

four Breathing Home   59

five Fleeing Conflict and Disaster   81

six War and Home—No Safe Place   107

seven Chronic Displacement and Persons without Home   135

eight Postures of Hospitality   166

Notes   189

Index   223

ACKNOWLEDGMENTS

I am deeply grateful to many for their time, support, and efforts of all kinds, which have made the writing of this book possible. The International Rescue Committee, Goma office, in the Democratic Republic of the Congo (DRC) offered valuable and kind hospitality during my initial fieldwork in the region. To Mading Arou, Achouth Kur, Pastor Othniel Mweniyamba, residents of the Wilson Inn, and the countless people I have met on roadsides, in fields, and at refugee camps—thank you for your trust and your stories; they are gifts beyond measure.

Many friends and family have championed this work during its writing and held steadfast when my own life was touched by displacement. Thank you, Nora Tubbs Tisdale, for envisioning with me what it means to lean into God and for letting me bear witness to the home you make along with your dear husband and my friend, Alfred Tisdale. Dale Peterson, you, too, have taught me, as I have witnessed your generosity and commitment regarding all things regarding home and the loving of family. I am grateful. Vida Maralani, Doug McKee, Roxana, and Ava, thank you for letting me be Aunt JanJan. Dawn Colapietro, dear friend and best cheerleader, I am deeply thankful for you. For my mother, Betty Holton, thank you for letting me share your story of a heavenly home that called to you and where you now rest. My entire family and many friends all have given in ways both small and large to advocate for me as I carried the heart of this work to its fruition. For all, I give thanks.

Kaudie McLean has traveled many roads with me and encouraged my voice at every turn. Rona Johnston Gordon has offered gifts toward this book's production of which I am simply in awe. It is a bonus to be blessed by your friendship. Carrie McDaniel has graciously helped me navigate two difficult Institutional Review Board (IRB) protocols at Yale University through their acceptances and numerous reviews. Willis Jenkins introduced me, almost quite literally, to the Batwa of Bwindi. Harry Attridge has been generous with his kindness; I am grateful for his support and leadership. Volney Gay has offered unwavering support of my work and career and, when asked, just the appropriate dose of practical advice. This book has been greatly improved by the many colleagues who have read drafts and offered comments. Yale Divinity School colleagues and friends Lisa Huck, Mary Clark Moschella, Grace Pauls, Carolyn Sharp, and Tom Troeger—thank you for accompanying me.

I am very appreciative of Jennifer Banks and Yale University Press for seeing promise in this work even in its early stages. My field research in Sudan and the Congo would not have been possible without generous financial support from Yale Divinity School and the Lilly Theological Scholars Grant. This book was published with the assistance of the Frederick W. Hilles Publication Fund of Yale University.

INTRODUCTION

I met Pricilla in Kakuma Refugee Camp in Kenya in 2003 while doing research with Dinka refugees from South Sudan.[1] *In 2008, after the end of the war, many of those refugees, including Pricilla, had returned to their home villages. Now, here I was in Bor, South Sudan, five years after our first meeting, sitting on a tree stump next to the sad little lean-to that was her home. She greeted me with a recited verse, 5:3 from the Gospel of Matthew.*

I was thrilled to find her familiar face. She was very generous to talk with me that evening. It was dusk, and she was standing a long and familiar vigil over her corn patch. It begins when the sun starts its decline and continues until night finally falls. I can still hear the distant "thp, thp" sound of the marble-sized mud balls she hurled at the birds perched to feed on her corn stalks.

In many ways Pricilla represents hundreds of people I have met in my many years of studying communities of violence and disaster. Having fled the war in Sudan and spent fifteen years of difficult life in a camp, Pricilla knows about loss of home and loved ones, suffering and grief. Like women from the Congo, Bosnia, Nicaragua, and elsewhere, she had great hope for her children when they were born, mourned the death of some during the war, and in its aftermath hoped that at least one of her surviving children might return to provide some comfort for her old age. Pricilla lives with the disappointment that her eldest son will not be the one to do this. He is now a U.S. citizen but suffers from alcoholism and is unable to send her money to buy food or supplies for building a house.

Still, she awakes each day with a faith in God and a sense of hope about what the future holds. Some days are bad, very bad. But she and millions of others like her get up every day and go about their lives—trying to feed children, care for neighbors, and worship God. They have survived awful events and yet continue to move through each day believing in something beyond the loss and suffering they have experienced.

I

It is with Pricilla and the others in mind that I write this book about displacement, forced displacement to be precise, and the costs it inflicts on the human spirit. Pricilla and others compel me to ask deep questions about home and homecoming, and why both are fundamental to our lives and our identity.

Blessed are the poor in spirit, for theirs is the kingdom of heaven.

—Matthew 5:3

Forced displacement is an urgent and global humanitarian concern that has deep theological and psychological implications. Due to war and poverty, more than 200 million people around the world are without home, and millions more live on the threshold of becoming homeless. Many social scientists and scholars examine the causes of homelessness and displacement. I do something different: I explore the psychological and theological impact of losing one's home place. I ask two questions: what is it about home that makes its loss so profound, and how should we think about this theologically?

The loss of home threatens how we make sense out of the world and takes away our feeling of belonging somewhere with regard to both people and place. Losing home jeopardizes intimate and sustaining relationships; it shifts one's status among the larger community. It also jeopardizes one's sense of physical and psychological safety. Home at its very best creates the conditions that help us trust in a benevolent world and its creator. It can help us lean into God, trust in a faithful God who bears us up during difficult times. Loss of home, then, can prematurely disrupt the nurturing of this relationship. All of these effects can impede the processes toward physical, psychological, and spiritual flourishing for the displaced.

The premise that home, or the home place as I also refer to it,[2] at its best is the ideal location from which to experience the conditions that help us lean into God creates an undeniable tension with which we must contend. For too many people around the world, home is not a place of flourishing. Violence, abuse, poverty, neglect, and any number of other conditions may impede the very notion that one can find any sense of meaning, belonging, security, or relationship in the home place, or that it helps one lean into God's presence. Too many under these dire conditions must find other resources that move them toward flourishing. I suggest that this reality does not negate my contention that home at its best is a worthy starting point, though it should hold us accountable to recognizing its limitations. Even home at its worst acknowledges these marks of flourishing by virtue of the longing it leaves in their absence.

In *Longing for Home*, I explore these outcomes from the perspectives of four groups that have suffered forced displacement. They are an indigenous tribe, the Batwa, in the Ugandan mountains; refugees and internally displaced persons (IDPs) in the Congo and Sudan; American soldiers struggling with post-traumatic stress disorder (PTSD); and homeless persons in the United States.[3] I describe my journeys into the Ugandan mountains, visits to the refugee camps in the Congo and Sudan, stories of American soldiers returning from Iraq and Afghanistan, and life in a transitional facility for the homeless. Through these intense, sometimes tragic encounters, I gained deeper insight into the psychological, social, and theological impacts of living without home. This book is an attempt to communicate the lives of those without home places and to provoke in readers and myself a deeper response to this common human dilemma.

The Obligation of a Caring Community of Faith

I offer a deep exploration of the effects of forced displacement and assert that the disruption of place—one's home place—is subsequently followed by a relational or social rupture that further embeds the ills of displacement in systemic structures. Physical displacement becomes social displacement. At its root both forms of displacement can compromise society's and even a community of faith's moral obligation to care for the displaced other. That we should and do have a moral obligation to care for the displaced other is an ethical assumption of this book.

Ultimately, my final aim is to unearth a set of guiding principles (or what I call postures) that reflect at least one particular way a community of faith can orient itself toward a moral obligation of care to the displaced others in our communities—local congregations, cities, even perhaps globally. I arrive at a pastoral theology of hospitality, relevant to both stranger and friend, as the frame that holds these postures. It is my deepest hope that others will come after me to challenge, expand, and explore these postures, especially as they relate to specific practices of care with the displaced.

Our task here is a challenging one. In order to better understand forced displacement and its effects we must move in two seemingly opposite directions. On the one hand, we must look at the particularities experienced by individuals and communities who have been forcibly displaced from their homes. But, if we linger only here, we fail to see how startlingly prevalent the experience of forced displacement is and the rather stunning and deeply entrenched social exclusion that is in direct response to and actively perpetuates such displacement. We start, then, with a broad look at notions of the home place, a theology of home, and a general overview of forced displacement. We then narrow our focus to four specific contexts of forced displacement before stepping back again to the broader concluding question of how a community of faith can best respond to a moral obligation to care for the displaced in its midst.

A Word on Method

In order to view a broad range of implications of forced displacement, I chose four different contexts, or case studies, in which I examine forced displacement as a situation that creates a significant loss of the functions of home—meaning, belonging, safety, and relationships for individuals and communities. In each context, I examine how it looks when *one* key function of home is lost. These are four very different settings, each with its own complexities. I chose them precisely because they are so different. Forced displacement is an issue not only for victims of war in Sudan or the Congo but also for the homeless in the United States and soldiers returning from war. I am not making claims that individuals or communities in all four contexts experience home or displacement in the same ways, or that I can define home for them, only that relationships, making meaning, a sense of belonging, and a sense of security—however these are defined—can be detrimentally affected by forced displacement. In spite of these situations, those who are displaced are also some of the most resilient people I have ever met, and I do not diminish the incredible efforts and successes toward thriving they accomplish. The complex differences between such diverse and vast groups joined with my claim that they experience similar losses resulting from forced displacement create a tension for us as we explore these categories of loss assigned to persons and communities living without home.

Although this contextual case study approach is clearly different from a case study of a single person, I use a familiar pattern of exploration that relies on: (1) experiences of the displaced told in their own voices, (2) my own experiences and observations gleaned from working with persons forcibly displaced from home places, and (3) research and theories of scholars from various theological disciplines and those in the social sciences. In some cases, the information within the case study was gleaned from my own ethnographic research projects—one in South Sudan and the other in eastern Congo. Other firsthand accounts about the experience of forced displacement come from within communities in which I have worked with those without home. In some instances I have drawn on firsthand accounts found in other research or public sources. Let me take a moment to highlight the methods and resources used for each of what I call the *core chapters*, which focus on four different contexts of forced displacement.

To begin, I focus on the Batwa, an indigenous tribe forced out of their mountain forest homes. I first became aware of the Batwa when a colleague and I taught a course (Refugee Ethics and Care) that culminated in a travel seminar to Uganda and Rwanda in the spring of 2012. To learn about conservation refugees, we engaged in an event called the Batwa Experience. While I have postcolonial critiques of this experience, which I address in chapter 4, the tour took a group of Western students far enough up into the mountains just outside of the Bwindi Impenetrable Forest National Park to make us aware that we were in a different world. This is how I began to learn about what home used to be for the Batwa. Two months later, I conducted interviews among displaced Batwa communities in Mugunga Camp for IDPs in Goma, Democratic Republic of the Congo.[4] I bring these interviews and observations into conversation with multiple disciplines to explore how traditional ways of making meaning from the forest have been threatened, as well as how hope nonetheless perseveres.

Next I examine a context of displacement frequently revealed to us through the news media: refugees and IDPs fleeing war. The refugee voices I bring to chapter 5 originate from my field research: 2003 in Kakuma Refugee Camp in northern Kenya, 2008 in South Sudan, 2011 and 2012 in the Democratic Republic of the Congo.[5] Here I bring together the voices of displaced persons I have interviewed with reflections on my own experiences learning about displacement in these areas. To this I add the work of other scholars who address the ways that *foreigner* serves as a category of social exclusion and threatens the sense of belonging—already at risk from displacement.

The next focus is, I think, the most challenging inclusion in this book—for reader and author alike. At times it seems to be an outlier, something that doesn't quite fit. Yet again and again it perseveres as a worthy, relevant, and important issue to address. Chapter 6 relies on narratives of U.S. soldiers returning from Iraq and Afghanistan. Here, I use first-person narratives told through social media. The level of detail that soldiers are willing to reveal to other soldiers (and the rest of us) in this fashion is quite compelling. In some ways, the internet has allowed soldiers to re-create a similar kind of supportive network otherwise found only in warzones. I put these narratives in conversation with reflections from my own experiences with soldiers from other cultures and thoughts from other scholars to ask questions about how PTSD and moral injury provoke a threat to one's sense of security and safety.

Finally, in chapter 7 I turn to the context of forced displacement we know as homelessness in the United States. For this case study, I use published narratives of persons without home and those in public housing to shed light on some of the complicating factors that lead to homelessness. I draw on my experiences as a staff person in residence in a transitional housing facility for women and bring all of these into conversation with the work of various scholars to examine categories used to objectify persons without home.

Through these case studies, I show that forced displacement compels a response from communities of faith whose members affirm that social justice—even more so, a relational ethic—grounds our moral obligation to care for the other. I argue that Christians in particular are challenged to live into becoming a hospitable community, to step outside of what is familiar to learn what home is for the other. This hospitality is modeled on the ministry of Jesus, who was a fierce advocate for the marginalized and displaced. He sacrificed home to move into the world, and in each act of his ministry offered himself in hospitality to all.

Distinguishing between Voluntary and Forced Displacement

Jesus was no stranger to a life of displacement. The infancy narrative in the Gospel of Matthew portrays Jesus as being born into the life of a refugee family as they fled violence and persecution to live for years in exile before returning to Nazareth.[6] For many Christian refugees around the world, and perhaps those of other faiths who see Jesus as a prophet, the historical accuracy of this narrative is of little consequence. Rather, they see in Jesus one who understands the fears and struggles of those forced by violence and persecution to flee their homes. It matters not that he was an infant—the refugee life is imprinted on him.

As an adult, Jesus surrendered a home life in answer to his ministry and role as the son of God—traveling and teaching until he was arrested and hung on a cross. He asked his disciples to leave behind all that they held dear in order to follow him. More than once he made it clear that the call to discipleship is to surrender the familiar, including home, in favor of a life dedicated to God.

How we parse these narrative events in the life of Jesus is less important here than the distinction between displacement that is *forced* due to threat and that which is *voluntary*. Even Jesus presumably spent his early years in Nazareth well acquainted with at least a relatively stable home place in the company of family and friends.[7] The call to discipleship and other forms of voluntary displacement show us that sometimes displacement can be a good thing that enhances life and provides better opportunities. But voluntary and forced displacement are two very different things. I begin here by separating the two so that we can enter into the case studies clearer about what makes forced displacement distinct.

Complexities of Displacement—Voluntary or Not?

There is nothing quite like working on a book about the fundamental importance of home and displacement to draw our attention to the many voices who claim that globalism and technology are moving us into an age in which we no longer require the same attachments to home and that, to some degree, we all live in a state of displacement. Virtual worlds have given some an alternative to believing we are attached to any one physical reality, even one called home. The best of globalization invites human connection and opens education and job markets around the world. We can now connect by FaceTime or Skype, allowing at least some level of freedom from the need to be grounded in any one home place. The digital age has introduced us to virtual worlds that challenge us with new rules about what community is and how we find a sense of belonging. How can this not help change the face of home? Perhaps, some claim, resisting the urge to be tied to a home place is the more courageous path.

As some borders become less defined because of ease of travel, and a culturally integrated world becomes the norm, we take less notice of the moments when we become displaced from our familiar world and move into the unfamiliar. Globalism has bridged gaps between cultures for millions. We are inclined though to forget that these opportunities are available only to those of certain socioeconomic strata. For those who live in poverty, the everyday world they encounter has changed very little.

A certain degree of displacement is a natural, healthy part of life. Every experience we have of leaving the familiar to move on to something new in life is a type of psychological, if not physical, displacement. The transitions we experience when we move out of the home place in which we were raised and move on to the beginning of our own first homes are usually voluntary, even if sometimes reluctant, displacements encouraged by our culture as successful progress toward adulthood. We should be mindful, though, that even these voluntary instances of displacement can bump up against contexts in which the displacement becomes forced.

For some this initial venture into the world begins gradually with a move to college; for others it begins with marriage.[8] In some cultures, parents arrange marriages for their children. This can be both an honor-bound tradition as well as a difficult transition. It may become particularly problematic for very young girls who are given in marriage but who are too young to safely fulfill the traditional sexual "duties" of a new wife, such as sexual intercourse and child bearing. In this case, a cultural transition moves from being a case of voluntary to forced displacement.[9] Some in the West begin having children in their early teens, while for others the first move from home comes with finding a job and then building a family. For millions of young black men in the United States, this natural voluntary transition is usurped by a justice system geared toward imprisoning them.[10] Economic circumstances in the United States beginning at the close of the 2010s have made this process of moving from home to begin an adult life much more difficult. Terms like *boomerang generation* reflect greatly altered progress in this regard for an entire generation of young adults who understand displacement in a new way.[11] The height of the economic struggles in the United States has seen the turn once again toward multiple generations living within one household. For many who live in poverty, multiple generations living together has often been the norm, as it is in many cultures across the world. For middle-class American culture, it more often marks a shift prompted by crisis.

Very little is new about the idea of displacement through migration—it has been ongoing throughout the history of humankind. While those in the very top tier of the socioeconomic strata may build homes across multiple borders, the poor continue to leave everything behind and migrate to new lands in hopes of providing even one for their families. Although poverty is seldom considered in the same category as the violence of war, when conditions are dire enough in a country, "economic refugees" flee in search of better opportunities elsewhere.[12] While this is an informal use of the term *refugee*, it reflects, I think, how fragile is the threshold between voluntary and forced displacement for these migrants. When a parent cannot feed his or her children, there isn't much choice in the matter of seeking a safer home where food is more plentiful.

Leaving home even if by choice does not shield a person from *all* of the emotional challenges associated with loss of home. These kinds of voluntary displacement can result in a variety of experiences, even quite difficult ones. Some who migrate by choice live with a lifelong sense of *never* belonging—always being a foreigner. Even as new generations of offspring dig deep roots in what is the only home they have ever known, these elders may still long for the home to which they will never return. This is made even more poignant if the reasons for leaving their home country were clouded by political unrest, retaliation, or fear. Nonetheless, others can experience the transition as quite positive, nurturing, and growth-producing.

Forced Displacement

Forced displacement comes at the hands of some compelling power that cannot be controlled by the individual or community. It can often be sudden, violent, and catastrophic. Natural disasters such as flood, hurricane, earthquake, tsunami, and fire are examples that come to mind; so, too, are wars and other types of violent conflict that descend on communities, leaving members to flee for their lives. Deeply embedded systemic practices influence social conditions that also create forced displacement, usually of a chronic nature, like homelessness in the United States and around the world. More immediate and individual crises erupt around issues of mental illness, addiction, social alienation (such as of lesbian, gay, bisexual, and transgender [LGBT] youth), and incarceration, which often deflect the larger systemic issues responsible for perpetuating the decline into displacement. No less than in situations of conflict or disaster, chronic displacement is often accompanied by physical injury, violence, trauma, loss, and grief.

Summary

As you read, I hope three main points become clear. First, I suggest that forced displacement can disrupt spiritual, psychological, and social flourishing by interrupting the central aspects of home (meaning, belonging, relationship, and sense of security). Second, I argue that those forcibly displaced from home are susceptible to social exclusion that becomes institutionalized in various ways. Third, I contend that it is the responsibility of the community of faith, as a just community, to respond with a particular notion of hospitality that attempts to repair social exclusion and alienation. Only then can hospitality turn toward discovering and honoring home as the displaced define it. This unique hospitality leans into the presence of God, leads toward flourishing, and celebrates God's vision of home for all.

Late in the night, I sat at my mother's bedside in the local hospital. She was recovering from an unsuccessful surgery during which the doctor attempted to repair her shattered hip. "I have to tell you," she began, "during surgery I felt God telling me it was time. I saw a house—a two-story house—like the one on Huddersfield Street or on Rockfalls Drive [houses where I grew up]. There were windows and a door, but the door was closed. I didn't see anyone . . . not daddy or Mimi or Andy [her parents], but I felt God and it was so peaceful and I wanted to go but I wanted to stay too."

Having just been displaced, perhaps permanently, from her home by injury, my mother recalled to me her image of God's invitation to her heavenly home. The notion of heaven as *home* is familiar to many. Indeed, for people of faith, recognizing our home in God celebrates a knowledge that we are intimately bound to the God who created us, in whose image we are formed, and to whom we return when our early life is done.

But my mother's experience reveals more than just how she imagines heaven might be for her after death. In it is reflected many of the ways that home has helped her, perhaps like many of us, lean into God throughout her life. While a house is a common enough symbol of home for many, especially in the middle-class, Western context, this was not just any house. The two-story structure in her dream or vision was an amalgamation of two of the most important places in her adult life, built structures where she, as a wife and mother, made home for her family. Like many women of her generation, home-making and all that it represented was her generative act—how she gifted the world. Home is still the lens through which she makes meaning from her experience in the world. Not only was home the place that gave her the greatest sense of belonging; it was also where she created belongingness for the children she raised and the husband she loved. It was the place where she felt safest and lived with purpose. The powerful connection to the relationships that made home for her became the linchpin for her staying or leaving—living or dying—and would remain so throughout this crisis.

Most of us either intuitively or from our own experience know that the home place is different from all other places, do we not? Yet pinpointing precisely how it is different and why it moves us so is a difficult task. Phenomenologist Alfred Schutz has suggested that home is different not necessarily because of the place itself or because of the people we find there but because of how that particular place makes us *feel.* He wrote,

> Home is not merely the homestead . . . but everything it stands for. The symbolic character of the notion "home" is emotionally evocative and hard to describe. . . . It means, of course, father-house and mother tongue, the family, the sweetheart, the friends; it means a beloved landscape, "songs my mother taught me," food prepared in a particular way, familiar things for daily use, folkways, and personal habits—briefly, a peculiar way of life composed of small and important elements, likewise cherished.[1]

Indeed, for most of us home is the place that helps give form to the most intimate experiences of human life and relationships, and can function in particular ways to move us toward physical, emotional, and spiritual flourishing.

The lifelong influence of home, and the impact of being displaced from it, affects us because of the place, the relationships we encounter in it, and all the experiences it gives us. Decades ago, preeminent geographer Yi-Fu Tuan, specializing in humanist geography, wrote about the relationship between humans and the places they inhabit. Contrary to the notion that place can be known without also understanding the human experience of that place, Tuan introduced the term *topophilia,* or love of place, to describe "[all] of human being's affective ties with the material environment," in other words, the ways people are bonded to place.[2] Home has a shielding aspect and is a place of nurturance and refuge; as Tuan noted, "To be forcibly evicted from one's home and neighborhood is to be stripped of a sheathing, which in its familiarity protects the human being from the bewilderments of the outside world."[3] The home place matters to us in a unique and irreplaceable way. In its absence it leaves a deep, deep longing.

Home, or the *home place* as I name it frequently throughout this book, is a complex notion. Home is a deeply personal phenomenon and its impact can ultimately only be measured subjectively. Nonetheless, I move forward with a working definition that allows us to set a direction for the rest of the book. Home is the *experience* of one's physical, spiritual, and emotional relationship with (1) family, biological and chosen; (2) the physical environment, both natural and built, in which one dwells and engages in the practices of daily life; and (3) God or the sacred. At its best, home serves to nourish and nurture a sense of meaning, belonging, security, and relationship building in and with the surrounding world. Home, therefore, includes the geographic area and/or environment, the relevant relational system, the spiritual and sociocultural environment, *and* the much more abstract and difficult to articulate experience that results when all of these come together.

In order to better understand displacement, I begin in this chapter to explore the notion of home as place and how it influences us. Place-identity theory offers a frame for understanding the deep emotional connections we have with places dear to us as well as for considering how the places we inhabit influence us. Once we come to understand more about how we become attached to places, we can see that our sense of the home place extends outward from house or dwelling in a radius of significant places and people. We look at these circles of home to help us appropriately expand our sense of home. Next I bring to the foreground four key functions that I propose emerge from the experience of home which together enhance our possibility of moving toward human flourishing. It is the complicated nature of home that often keeps us living in a tension between imagined ideals and beloved memories of the past. It is helpful then to briefly consider how forced displacement compels our notion of home to waver between these extremes of idealism and nostalgia. Finally, I give attention to the social significance of home, or more particularly how displacement influences social exclusion.

Emerging Identity

My assertion that home is, in the best of circumstances, the place where most of us first learn to make meaning from the environment around us, to experience a deep sense of belonging, to develop a sense of relative security within place and relationships, and to build lasting relationships with others is built on the notion that home is where our self-identity begins to form.[4] We are born fragile creatures that require significant care and nurture to survive, grow, and thrive. In the best of all cases, this caregiving is provided in the first home place. While the effectiveness and degree of emotional and spiritual flourishing toward which these caregiving relationships lead are always compromised by finite abilities and resources, their impact on our notion of self and home is essential. Meaning relates in part to how we learn to appropriately interpret our experiences in the surrounding environment. A sense of belonging begins when we are able to form significant attachments to others yet only if we can also see ourselves as different from these same others. The possibility of security evolves from an early sense of trust in others including a predictable environment, and relationship building requires interpersonal skills—the seeds for all of which begin to whatever degree of sufficiency in the first home place.[5]

Home is especially significant because it is the place where the developing infant and then child learns to negotiate various successes and non-traumatic failures in her social world and, to various extents, in the surrounding environment. That there is a normative process of psychological growth and maturation toward a cohesive self-identity is the basic premise of Western psychological developmental theory. I turn briefly to particular aspects of theories from psychoanalysts John Bowlby, Erik H. Erikson, Margaret Mahler, and D. W. Winnicott in later chapters not as normative guidelines for identity development but as starting points for conversations from which suggestions and critiques based on other cultural experiences might emerge. Many are helpful in that they also emphasize, at least in some small way, how the surrounding environment and closely associated social systems impact infant and child development.[6] Over the decades, many scholars have offered critical postmodern engagement with psychoanalytic theory that examines the role of context—gender, sexuality, race, culture, and class among other things—and its influence. Numerous sub-disciplines in psychology and the social sciences have evolved to focus on the in-depth exploration of just these particularities. Only a few have considered the role of "place" as context.

Although most psychoanalytic theories do not ignore entirely the impact of the physical environment on the developing psyche, they seldom attend to how place itself directly influences one's developing identity.[7] Clare Cooper Marcus, in her book *House as a Mirror of Self*, which examines the psychological impact of home on the self, recognizes this absence when she writes:

> As we change and grow throughout our lives, our psychological development is punctuated not only by meaningful emotional relationships with people, but also by close affective ties with a number of significant physical environments, beginning in childhood. That these person-place relationships have been relatively ignored is partly due to the ways in which we have chosen to "slice up" and study the world. Psychologists whose domain is the study of emotional development view the physical environment as a relatively unimportant backdrop to the human dramas of life. Those who are interested in people-environment relations—geographers, anthropologists, architects, and . . . environmental psychology—have for the most part ignored issues dealing with emotional attachment.[8]

Of those who do study the impact of place, there are a few who examine the connection between place and human emotion and attachment.

Environmental psychologist Harold M. Proshansky and his colleagues in a seminal article propose that people develop a *place-identity* in addition to a self-identity. They write, "The development of a self-identity is not restricted to making distinctions between oneself and significant others, but extends with no less importance to objects and things, and the very spaces and places in which they are found."[9] Proshansky and colleagues suggest that not only do significant relationships impact us but places themselves influence our identity. They define place-identity as "a sub-structure of the self-identity of the person consisting of, broadly conceived, cognitions about the physical world in which the individual lives. These cognitions represent memories, ideas, feelings, attitudes, values, preferences, meanings, and conceptions of behavior and experiences which relate to the variety and complexity of physical settings that define the day-to-day existence of every human being."[10] They suggest that place-identity is very relevant to how the home place contributes to the creation of who we become particularly in relation to meaning making, identifying the places that are safe and creating a sense of place belongingness.[11]

Social psychologists John Dixon and Kevin Durrheim strongly critique Proshansky and colleagues' understanding of place-identity as being too cerebral and individual. They specifically note that, "[The] overall problematic that informs a variety of approaches [to place-identity], [is] a problematic that defines place-identity as a specific kind of phenomenon: individualistic, mentalistic, uncontested and apolitical."[12] Instead, Dixon and Durrheim propose a discursive approach to place-identity that complicates and honors the way that people together, especially communities, participate in the messy negotiation of creating and contesting place. While Proshansky's idea of place-identity, they claim, "is a predominately cognitive structure to be discovered in the heads of individuals," a discursive approach

reconstitutes place-identity as something that people create together through talk: a social construction that allows them to make sense of their connectivity to place and to guide their actions and projects accordingly. . . . It acknowledge[s] the relevance of places to their collective senses of self, but it also highlights the collective *practices* through which specific place identities are formed, reproduced and modified. . . . Language becomes the force that binds people to places. . . . It is through language that places themselves are imaginatively constituted in ways that carry implications for "who we are" (or "who we can claim to be").[13]

So, is place-identity primarily a construction of an individual cognitive process or a collective endeavor that emerges through communal discourse? I suggest that both have characteristics which are essential to the understanding of home. Dixon and Durrheim presume that it is "through language that everyday experiences of self-in-place form and mutate."[14] Tuan agrees, noting, "Speech is a component of the total force that transforms nature into a human place." He points to the biblical creation narrative, in which speech brings forth creation, as an example, especially for those in the Judeo-Christian tradition, of that which might help us understand the "creative power of words."[15] As he writes, "Although speech alone cannot materially transform nature, it can direct attention, organize insignificant entities into significant composite wholes, and in so doing, make things formerly overlooked—and hence invisible and nonexistent—visible and real."[16]

Yet we can emotionally or spiritually *feel* affected by place in ways that cannot be fully transferred to language. Pastoral theology has long contended with aspects of the unconscious and mysterious, neither of which can be fully articulated but both of which can add deeply to the substance of who we are. So it is with place, especially the home place. There is much that defies language and cannot fully be shared. Most theorists agree that place-identity is a psychological structure that includes aspects which remain beyond our conscious awareness, though Proshansky and colleagues resist the term *unconscious* in favor of "not in awareness." Journalist Roger Cohen poetically describes the mysterious relationship between the place of our childhoods and the process of emotional bonding that defies articulation in our youngest years when he writes of the fondly remembered landscape of a childhood home: "It was the landscape . . . of unfiltered experiences, of things felt rather than thought through, of the world in its beauty absorbed before it is understood, of patterns and the sounds that lodge themselves in some indelible place in the psyche and call out across the years."[17] This deeply felt but largely unconscious belongingness is one of the reasons, Proshansky and his fellow authors suggest, that emotions can be so overwhelming when a person returns to a place after a long absence.[18]

Often it takes some form of crisis to bring to awareness these deepest feelings of attachment to places most important to us. We may not realize how much the place we identify with home means to us until we are faced with the magnitude of how much it has changed. This can create a sense of displacement that Dixon and Durrheim suggest is a "dis-location of identity brought about by a sudden transformation of valued places. From this perspective the sense of loss they express is not only a loss of place but also, more profoundly, a loss of self."[19] As we see in the coming chapters, to whatever degree displacement creates a loss of self, it also creates a vehicle for social exclusion of the displaced other.

Dixon and Durrheim become most helpful to us in understanding how these points of crisis might serve to create communal narratives that help negotiate, even change, contested places. Displacement, the loss of the home place, creates narratives that emerge from within the community or are projected on the community from others. This is especially recognizable in refugee communities, which often have overarching meta-narratives about the conflict that displaced them and which then form new narratives of identity as displaced persons within the places they come to inhabit. Dixon and Durrheim are particularly insightful in naming how people together, that is, a community, can participate in negotiating meaning—especially in relation to a contested place. Dixon and Durrheim examine this discursive approach through four narrative excerpts from a larger discourse from the period of desegregation of South African beaches. Not surprisingly, discourses about place in this context reveal the sociopolitical dynamics of place, even home place, and the manner in which ongoing discourses can change our relationships with places.

Dixon and Durrheim as well as Proshansky and his colleagues focus their attention on the affective attachments of persons to *any* significant places in daily life. They tend to home merely in a secondary manner mentioning it only sparingly. Even so, I consider these attachments to be fundamental to our connection to the home place as the central place of daily life.

Expanding Circles of the Home Place

Thus far I have held the spotlight on the immediate physical location of the home dwelling. We start here because home is, as Tuan wrote, "a bounded center of meaning" for us.[20] But, as most of us know, our sense of the home place and our attachment to the people in it can extend well into the surrounding area and beyond. A second level of engagement occurs in the larger communal environment. It includes the broader geographical area of neighborhood or village.

Place and relationship come together in a home place in different ways from the beginning days of infancy through childhood as one develops and grows, then into adulthood and old age. We might consider the home place as geographic regions with overlapping social systems that begin in the small dwelling(s) into which one is born and move outward. For most, the sense of home increases (geographically and relationally) as the individual grows and is able to experience and perceive the importance of meaning for each "circle" of space. Perhaps we can think of the home place in terms of these concentric circles extending outward. The relatively smaller systems I identify as the *immediate relational*. The smallest circle I reserve for the primary place experienced by the child in the beginning years of life.[21] Although a very young infant may only be aware of a primary caregiver and of having basic needs met, as the child grows, so does her awareness and mastery of the surrounding environment. As one ages and mobility decreases, the lived home place and one's social circle once again become more concentrated, even though one's mental notion of both may continue to encompass larger memories and visions of the home place. These are artificial boundaries, to be sure, for once one has outgrown the limits of his circles of influence, that person may look back nostalgically with a sense that it is all home.

From the outset, this inner circle of home appears to be a very Western notion in which sits a house or apartment. But I also make room here for other ideas of what may exist in the center of this circle. For example, in Sudanese Dinka culture, family systems into which a child is born include one or more co-wives and siblings who live in a compound with multiple dwellings. Home is not one but many dwellings within the defined space of a family compound. These descriptions do appear to presume some level of permanence. I suggest, though, that there is room within these circles for understanding a broader defined area. Even nomadic cultures have somewhat predictable, even repeated, patterns of movement that one might consider as this inner circle. The main point is that the areas of the home place increase for most over time and as one becomes aware of allegiances to larger social systems.

At the smallest level, the home place is the relational (biological or otherwise) system set in a particular, limited geographical space. This is what we would know as the family unit, be it an immediate or basic family unit (including two-parent, single-parent, and blended-family units), the extended family that lives together, or the combined families of polygamous unions. Here the family system creates its own interpretations of the world and processes of meaning making. The physical location of the home, including the dwelling place, land, community, and general environment, can become intimately attached to the meaning systems created by the family system.

The second set of circles is the larger *communal environment*. It includes the broader geographical area that is often limited by access, safety, and interest as a child grows. Within this area is another set of relations that include friends, neighbors, and perhaps additional family members. Here the home place can also be the larger community, clan, or tribe. For some, this is the small town or village; in larger

cities, perhaps it is the neighborhood. I think here of my own up-
bringing in Richmond, Virginia. While Richmond is my hometown
and I have fond memories of many places around the city, something
shifts in me when I come near to my neighborhood. As with most
children, certain boundaries were established as I grew. Most were
marked by limited access (an acceptable distance by bicycle), safety
(limited traffic and other rules), and interest. On occasion, two of
these would come into conflict. For example, playing by the river
or the quarry, which were both an easy distance from my house, was
strictly forbidden, the first prompted by the drowning of many who
became caught under the ever-alluring rocks and the second because
it had a no-trespassing sign in front of it. In these cases, the rules
usually won out. What I realize now when I return after a long absence is that I begin to feel home when I cross these neighborhood
boundaries of my childhood. Driving down the steep hill that was
out of bounds, I feel *almost* home; driving up the street where I rode
my bicycle so often, I *am* home.

In my years interviewing South Sudanese refugees who became
known together as the Lost Boys, the young men would tell me many
stories about their role in tending cattle—the main task of Sudanese
boys ten to twelve years old.[22] While doing fieldwork in South Sudan, I finally got to see the range of space the young boys would
cover in order to care for the cattle. The two miles or so from the
village to the camp where the cattle were gathered for the night were
about the same distance from my home to the swimming pool where
I rode my bike every day during the summer. Neither the terrain nor
the purpose could be more different, yet we both know home when
we enter that space.

In South Sudan, the clan or those who live in the village act as the
extended relational set for a home place. In a similar manner, when
I travel back to my neighborhood, though my family no longer lives
there, I still feel a strong emotional connection thanks to the continued presence of two neighbors, Mrs. Bern and Mr. Mays. Mr. Mays
"rescued" me through the bedroom window at age six when the lock
got stuck on my door. They have known me my whole life. Not only

did they know me as a child, but they are part of my memories of "home" as I grew and my parents aged, through my father's illness and ultimate death, and even as my mother moved away. They remain there still. I am aware that as time moves on, and ultimately as these beloved folk move on as well, something in the nature of my relationship to this place will shift and change. My attachments will become grounded in memory instead of people.

The circle of relatedness that is home eventually expands still further outward to include a sense of place in a city or nation state, a homeland. All we need do is cross a foreign border, especially as refugees in search of safety, to be reminded that in one place we are home, in another we are strangers. Patriotism to one's homeland and love of one's local cities can be deeply abiding. We call all of these places, at some times and under some conditions, home.

Functions of Home

Geographers James Duncan and Nancy Duncan, writing about Tuan's work, argue that "topophilia suggests not only that there is an affective response to place but a practice that can actively produce places for people."[23] To carry this into our context of home, we can say, in other words, there is between humans and their home place a mutual ability to influence each other. We make home and home makes us.[24] As with development of the self, meaning making, belonging, security, and relationship play a significant role in the development of one's place-identity.

Does the home place have a particular role in creating the meaning by which we interpret and understand the world of which we are a part? I contend that it does. Just how the home place serves in this manner is one of the leading questions of this book. Meaning is the interpretation an individual or community gives to experiences common and foreign as they encounter those situations. Meaning does not develop in a vacuum. Rather, it is nurtured in the context of an individual's perception, a community of people, a social setting, an ethnic tradition, a physical environment, or, for some, a faith orientation. An individual perceives the world through embodied experience. Cultural and ethnic traditions within the individual's community lay claim to the particularities of meaning transferred from one generation to the next as embedded in rituals, myths, and narratives of transition and transformation. These inherited interpretive systems establish parameters as to how the individual gives meaning to his perceptions, though he may at any time choose to alter or reject these parameters. Further, as embodied creatures, humans are, consciously or unconsciously, influenced by the physical environment. It is a powerful shaper of perception and memory, and offers perhaps the most visceral channel for human experience and its meaning. Faith orientation, for those who adhere to religious or spiritual practice, is often the frame within which all these other categories are considered. This is especially true for those experiences that fall outside of or find no acceptable place in other interpretive categories. The sacred has long provided a context of meaning for those experiences that otherwise defy interpretation and understanding. God can give meaning to the very places of mystery and contradiction that seem to defy meaning. All of these factors together shape the ways we make meaning in our home place.

At a recent public lecture, I invited the audience to consider the difficulties of defining meaning—what does meaning, well, mean— and to offer any additions they thought helpful. Afterward, a young mathematics professor offered a perspective. Meaning, he said, is externally and objectively verifiable such that one can judge its validity. In the field of mathematics, this must be true. The meaning of an equation must have a verifiable outcome—one that can be proven again and again. Yet meaning created from human experience is seldom verifiable in the same objective manner as a mathematical equation. Rather, meaning is often drawn from something deep within us, relationships, and the environment that constitute the home place— each of which teaches us to understand and interpret.

It is easy to see in this attempt to pull at the strings of defining meaning that experience is the linchpin which connects meaning and interpretation. I can interpret what I see when my neighbor's home has been destroyed by a tornado. I can even try to offer a meaning for such destruction and suffering. But if I *experience* the complete destruction of my own home from a tornado, the difference in how meaning is both sought and constructed is paramount. Only I can interpret meaning for my experience, but I always do so within the context of a complex web of social systems, traditions, physical environments, and faith considerations. It is within the home place that we first learn how to negotiate these systems and to make meaning from our encounters with others, the world, and God.

Home is the place where one can feel a deep sense of belonging. For evolutionary purposes, belonging to a particular group was fundamental for physical survival, as it continues to be for emotional thriving. The home place is where a common language in all its nuances and particularities binds a group together. Growing children develop their *identity* both as a part of a community of others and as individuals in the central and extended home place. The successful home environment helps individuals grow to maturation through embracing home and then rejecting it so that they can leave in order to create their own homes. A deep sense of *longing* often accompanies thoughts of the home place when one is absent, home is compromised, or one has never been able to successfully identify with a home place.

The home place is where we have the first opportunity as infants to discover what security and safety can feel like. In its absence, it is to the home place that we return again and again in the effort to find this security. For many reading this discussion of the home place, a "yes, but . . ." may come quickly to mind. For all of the wonderful images and descriptions of a constructive and nurturing home, we can find an equal number of stories overshadowed by destructive, abusive, and painful home settings from which some barely survive and others bear lifelong scars. Policies on housing, healthcare, childcare, education, and justice (especially concerning drug rehabilitation over and against incarceration) all shape possibilities and limitations for the home place for millions of people in the United States. Political influences are sometimes difficult to articulate and often affect those of lower socioeconomic status more than the wealthy. Internationally, the lack of effective political structures and national safety deeply influences home for millions around the world, such as those living in eastern Congo.

Yes, the home environment—relational and physical—can have a disastrous impact on one's sense of security, as well as a positive one. This strengthens my argument. The home place is so powerful, especially to the developing psyche, that for good or ill, it fundamentally shapes how an individual perceives what is safe and the ability to feel secure in a sometimes unpredictable and threatening world.

Throughout this book, I refer frequently to the "home place." As suggested above, it is clear to me, though, that place and relationships can be closely related when it comes to our notions of home. We are relational creatures. We are born helpless and require other humans to nurture, protect, and teach us until we are able to do so for ourselves. This intense work requires endless hours of selfless dedication from primary caregivers. Over time we have discovered that it is not just enough to offer food, safety, and education—there is something fundamental about being in relationship itself. Love and trust, at some level, are required to develop healthy human adults. Our ability to create and sustain relationships with others becomes a marker for mental and emotional health. The first and most influential relationships we have are with those caretakers and others who make relationships within our home place.

The home place as the center of this system of caregivers and others is fundamental to learning to create relationships with self (ego development), other, and God. Although relationships are central to the very definition of home and family (openly defined) and to success or failure in this regard, my sole focus is not on family systems at this point. Rather, I ask, what is it in the home place that is fundamental to human relationships (both family and community)? I suggest it is the ability to trust, the development of altruism, and the engagement in shared acts of naming what is just, which requires empathy, that most benefit, relationally, the individual in the home place.

Visions of the Ideal Home

When closing up my family home five years ago, I was packing books from the long-untouched living room shelf. I ran across a book of etiquette printed in 1923. Among its pages, I could find every possible example of appropriate behavior that persons of a certain socioeconomic standing strictly adhered to but that others used to measure an unattainable ideal. An entire section is devoted to building the home, expectations of children, and appropriate roles of wives and husbands. I have used this book countless times in the classroom to show how rituals of home life (and death) are subject to the social influences of our times.

I would dare to say that many a counselor and pastor has heard from the mouths of those to whom they offer care the long-held conviction: "Well, home *should* be . . . " There is no shortage of resources to feed a vision of the ideal home. It is constructed by influences from the personal, social, cultural, religious, and political structures of which we are a part. The families into which we are born or in which we grow and learn to trust offer the most significant personal influences on our understanding of the home place. Socially, public media have an overwhelming influence. Whether images come from the glossy pages of a magazine, the episodes of our favorite television show, or the big screen in the movie theater, every image shapes our impression of what can or should be the home place. New social media sources are emerging daily to add to the slew of possibilities that can shape our image of home. From my research with women and men in Sudan and the Congo, I have found in these contexts very specific traditions associated with creating home that differ from those in the United States—even among those from the same ethnic origins now living in America. The home place is as much a cultural creation as anything else—and a powerful one. The political ideology of the American Dream came under tremendous threat in the first decade of the twenty-first century but has held a tenacious grip on those who refuse to abandon the hope of "rising" to a middle-class, suburban home life. Even further, nearly every religion has parameters that function as either guidelines or strict laws, depending on the tradition, for creating a home in keeping with a spiritual ideal. All these elements suggest the significance of the home place across cultures, even if differing in the specifics. Ultimately, these factors—the personal, social, cultural, political, and religious—come together in unequal and sometimes surprising ways to create an often unattainable image of what the home place should be. Many of us carry these ideal visions of home with us throughout our lifetimes.

The ideal of home comes not only from a place of possibility (albeit sometimes an unreasonable possibility) but also from what once was. Nostalgia for home is the deep longing for the past—even if we no longer have an accurate vision of what used to be. The power of the home place to draw us toward a lifelong search either to replicate the memory of the home we once had or to create the home we always longed for is profound. Often these two longings fall at opposite ends on a spectrum of the ideal. Both the nostalgic and ideal, however, have something important to tell us about our own relationship with the home place.

The etymology of *nostalgia* means quite literally pain, or longing, to return home, or homesickness. As the title of this book suggests, those who are absent from home, especially those forcibly displaced from it, often long to return. But even those who leave home for much less drastic reasons can become quite homesick in its absence. A common understanding of nostalgia is a sense of longing for the way things used to be in the past. Freudian thought understands nostalgia to be a longing for a past that never really existed. Why quibble over the difference? To long for a return to home implies that one is removed from it and can in a physical sense return (even if return is only proximate to the region). To already have a home yet long for a different way of being in the home place is another matter. One implies a physical return, the other a philosophical and emotional one. Yet again, both indicate the symbolic value we place on the notion and reality of home.

Social Significance of the Home Place

The Western ideal of a permanent dwelling or structure as the home place toward which people strive has long been the standard of a so-called civilized and progressive society. As a permanent structure and part of the built environment, a home is set apart from and assumes a level of advancement—even dominance—over the natural world. Such a structure serves a functional purpose by adding a layer of protection against most natural external threats such as weather or predators of the wild. Even more so, psychologically and perhaps existentially, it encourages a sense of relative control over unpredictable and chaotic forces. Of course, the problematic nature of imposing this standard on other cultures is seen in many of the colonizing assumptions and practices found throughout the historically colonized regions of the world. It has been especially damaging to those peoples who have traditionally lived with deep respect for and in a cooperative relationship with nature, especially in Africa.

In the United States we have a particular attachment to houses as places of home. They are culturally mythologized as a key aspect of the American Dream—owning a home of one's own and perhaps a parcel of land to go with it. It remains at least one standard measure of success for the middle class and has remained so even through the most severe economic challenges.[25] Although ingrained in American culture in this particularly unique manner, a home is a dream and mark of success in many lands throughout the world. And, in all parts of the world, permanence is relative.

Much to the dismay of development advisors and government officials who planned an orderly system of land distribution, in 2006 displaced persons in Bor, South Sudan, long having dreamed of a return to their homeland, flocked to patches of land remembered from yesteryear to stake squatters' claims on places for home. They too desired a sense of permanence in the structures they built. In reality, however, the relative permanence of the built structure depended on the materials available and the financial means to acquire them.

For some, like Pricilla in the opening narrative of the introduction, it was a lean-to made of blue plastic and wood scraps. Others built traditional mud-walled houses with thatched roofs. Only those with plentiful resources could afford to purchase bricks fired from a local business.

Habitation of home and property, whether through ownership or means of legal agreement, extends a sense of control to a social level as well. The relative permanence inferred in the home place serves to legitimize a person's social presence and provides an entryway into social acceptance and participation. Even when social presence, acceptance, and participation are distorted and maligned through racism and other forms of discrimination, lack of a home place exacerbates the circumstances and results in social exclusion. Having a home sets a boundary that determines a place is mine and not yours. It offers, even at a minimum level, a barrier of security literally and figuratively. Refugees from conflicts around the world who have returned to towns and villages to find others inhabiting their homes and using their belongings understand how fragile is the contract of ownership in times of forced displacement.

The home place as a minimum standard affects not only how we understand our own place in the world but also how we judge others. A person with a home place elsewhere is frequently received as a visitor in the neighborhood, a stranger with purpose who likely only raises curiosity. A person without a home, however, may be perceived as a wanderer, a stranger without purpose, and very often a cause for suspicion. How do we know if someone is "homeless" or not? Each culture has its own unwritten rules used to determine who belongs and who is suspicious, and these rules are often influenced by social perceptions regarding ethnicity and class. Having a home place, or the perception of it, is a marker of one's social place in the community, for accepting or rejecting the presence of the other. Rules of hospitality inherent in many cultures and most religions are based on the need to protect the stranger from harm associated with this rejection. But even these customs are not ultimately strong enough to hold back the manner in which this rejection has become embedded in social structures and further legitimized through political and legal means.

Summary

We are embodied and thus emplaced creatures; the *place* we call home and our relationship to it can have a remarkable impact on us.[26] But our connection to the geographical location or physical space called home is much more than a mere attachment to the material or even to practices we embody or demonstrate. Home also includes a deeply connected web of *relationships*—beginning with those we need in early life to survive and extending toward others, both kin and friend. Even when we bring together the impact of place and relationship, there is something much more abstract and difficult to articulate that forms the core of home. It is the *experience* of these together that leads to the powerful and lasting impact home has on us. Home—place, community, and experience—together help us define ways of making meaning, belonging, security, and relationships that move us closer toward flourishing. Only when we understand the power of this home place can we begin to comprehend the impact of losing home through forced displacement.

As I approached my old neighborhood, every turn held a memory, most quite mundane. This home place filled with memories both dear and dreaded seemed to know me as much as I knew it. As I drew near to the house, memories of my grade school bus route and neighborhood bike rides to my best friend's house came flooding to mind. As I passed a favored but all too steep hill where I left a considerable amount of skin from a bicycle accident at age twelve, my knee ached in response. It seemed every tree had a story it could tell. The old, once-yellow house—now a dark gray—was the center of these swirling memories, and it was disconcerting to feel it beckoning yet know that it was no longer a space of welcome waiting just for me. The surrounding houses reminded me of a village of family and neighbors who walked with me through childhood. The experience of home came flooding back to me.

In 2008, I traveled to South Sudan to conduct field research in a small rural town called Bor. My translator, Mading Arou, a former refugee who fled from Bor during the war seventeen years before, was returning home for the first time. His homecoming was in some ways similar to my own. He too felt the familiarity of home beckoning to him miles before reaching the town itself. For the Bor-Dinka, his tribe, home was one of at least two locations depending on the season, the small summer village on the Nile where crops of corn and peanuts flourished and then Panchad, further inland, where sorghum was the mainstay in the winter months. Both home places held deep memories of family and community. Even though Mading was only a young child when he fled, the waters of the Nile, the oil well that marked the place where his village once stood, the sights, sounds, and smells—all announced that he was home again.[1]

Our oldest, most sacred stories have tried in various ways to tell the tripartite story of home, displacement, and return. The Judeo-Christian creation story moves toward creating a place of habitation and flourishing for humankind.[2] The ultimate place for this flourishing—the garden called Eden—depicts the first "home place" in the Judeo-Christian tradition. Whether one believes that this narrative represents the first human moral failing or mortal creatures' acting out of their limitedness, banishment resulted in the ultimate displacement from the one place where these humans experienced God most intimately. This story seeks to explain the desire for belongingness and to be in relationship with each other, with a meaningful place, and, especially, with God. It tells a tragic story of the first forced displacement.[3]

Expulsion from this garden, and the grief and longing that ensue, begins a long succession of stories in the Hebrew Bible perpetuating both exile from a home place and broken relationships between humans and the Divine Heart. Stories throughout the Hebrew Bible reflect humankind's interminable efforts to find our way back—mostly with disastrous results. Alienation from God results in human alienation from each other and the land—from home. Violence, greed, and hopelessness creep into the narrative with only the exceptional story of commitment, faith, and love that actually move humans toward God.

God uses the stories of displacement and return to home to demonstrate the power and faithfulness of a loving God. They are stories that so resonate with the experiences of Christian refugees across the globe that stories like the freedom of the Exodus or redemption from the Exile are often lifelines of hope for the displaced and disempowered. Even for those whose experience of physical exile from home is less of a tangible reality, the emotional or spiritual separation from a home place has resulted in a plague of spiritual displacement. The resulting spiritual longing is for the same God of promise and hope to lead them out of bondage and exile.

Longing for a place that is uniquely our own is both inherent in and frustrated by the human condition. This longing is for both the physical place that we can claim as our own and that place to which we feel we belong as no other. Theologian Paul Tillich named finitude of place as one of the four categories of finitude against which all humans struggle as creatures of God. He wrote,

Every being strives to provide and to preserve space for itself. This means above all a physical location—the body, a piece of soil, a home, a city, a country, the world. It also means a social "space"—a vocation, a sphere of influence, a group, a historical period, a place in remembrance and anticipation, a place within a structure of values and meanings. Not to have space is not to be. Thus in all realms of life striving for space is an ontological necessity. It is a consequence of the spatial character of finite being and a quality of created goodness.[4]

Of course, for Tillich the ultimate inability to have a space that is truly our own, ontologically speaking, leads to an existential anxiety against which humans always struggle to some degree. He noted, "Finitude means having no definite place"; we can never have any place that truly belongs to us—we will leave it one day and with it "lose being itself."[5]

Tillich's definition of the *space* for which we yearn includes both physical and social space.[6] Even further, it is that we *belong* to this space, or place, and that this space of longing and belonging helps shape meaning in our lives which make it indispensable to human flourishing. To stave off the insecurity that accompanies the reality of our limitedness, humans create complex systems to secure and protect the space we acquire.[7] We defend the notion of owning and acquiring land—space or a place that will be here long after we can no longer claim it—as a sign of progress and civilization. For Tillich, it is a temporary and ineffective solution, for only through turning toward the courage found in God can one overcome this anxiety.

Psychotherapy and its sub-disciplines, environmental psychology in particular, approach human relationship to the home place in psychodynamic terms.[8] Leading theories on object relations or place attachment, for example, focus on attachment to human relationships in the home or attachment to the place itself. Others focus on the home environment as it adds to or detracts from the functioning of the family as a whole. Psychological approaches on their own, however, have a difficult time evaluating human flourishing in spiritual terms, that is, what moves us closer to an intimate relationship with God.

For many around the world home is deeply connected to the sacred. For some, women in rural South Sudan for example, it is the acts of child bearing and home making that are necessary to garner God's blessing.[9] I suggest that home at its best can invite us to lean closer into glimpses of God, in Christian contexts and otherwise. But what does it mean to lean into God? Many of us have had the experience of feeling despair or joy that causes us to lean deeply into the arms of a friend or loved one. Children do it often. Even our canine companions, when feeling safe and content, have been known to offer a slow, steady lean into the leg of a beloved human.

Leaning into God means that we are willing to decenter ourselves as the source of "balance" or grounding—to trust that God will bear us up. We trust God will not pull away unexpectedly but remain faithful to us. We give over our self-centeredness and "take in" a sense of belonging to and relationship with God. That which is life-giving—strength, compassion, and love—comes to define the essence of what is safe. When we lean into God's faithfulness, whether in anticipation or resignation, we find the frame, as Christians, for making meaning from our experience in the world.

Functions of Home

To understand the parts of making a home place that lean toward God requires that we explore how home in the world (1) frames our shared ways of making meaning, (2) creates in us a sense of belonging, (3) names the places that are safe, and (4) teaches us to create relationship. All home places vary in their successes in these four categories. And though the categories may seem arbitrary, they reflect in so many ways, I think, what societies on a larger scale have attempted to do across the ages.

On a physiological level, a primary place, a home place sufficient for the meeting of fundamental needs, has always been a basic evolutionary necessity. This is enhanced by a group of supportive others that help us move toward physical survival if not flourishing. But home is more than a basic evolutionary stopping point. When home helps us lean into God, we move closer toward spiritual flourishing as well.

Meaning

The home place that leans into God is where events ordinary and extraordinary, tragic and joyful, and everything in between are interpreted through a lens that sees more broadly than the self, family, community, or culture. It frames experience through an understanding of a faithful God who longs to be in relationship with each of us. Meaning and hope are intricately bound.

I suggest that this meaning making leans into God when it reaches toward an embedded faith narrative that anticipates a cooperative relationship between the human and divine, that encompasses the larger community including the saints of the past from whom we have learned, and, finally, that anticipates God's faithful transcendence in our experience of the world. All of these engage us in the process through which we discover sacred purpose. It inspires and invites a response of gratitude often enacted in service to others.

One of the greatest challenges to meaning making is that there is no objective measure for its veracity. Unlike scientific meaning, the validity of spiritual meaning is based on internal measures of experience framed by belief in a faithful God and the traditions of a long lineage of ancestors in faith. Ultimately, this type of spiritual meaning cannot be imposed upon nor gifted to another.

Meaning emerges from reflecting within one's experience, not looking for meaning in the event as if it is something that just happens "to us." For example, meaning comes not from cancer itself but from the experience of how one moves through the illness. So meaning making does not reflect a causal event set forth by God through experience for the purpose of manipulation or teaching that is ultimately limited to the interior spiritual world of an individual.[10]

Rather, it emerges from practices of reflection, the ability to tolerate ambiguity, and engagement with the sacred.

Meaning making happens in the home place in mundane and unspectacular moments of life. But we notice it most in times of crisis. Pastoral theologians Siroj Sorajjakool and Bryn L. Seyle note, "The need to create meaning as an essential part of ontological structure, becomes much more obvious when a person is confronted with crisis. Crisis questions the meaning of one's existence and complicates his/her concept of life."[11] Some of the most important lessons learned about meaning making come in the face of great adversity or by those who have suffered deep and terrible loss. Many find ways to offer support and care to others and find in the process their own sacred purpose and a balm for grief that brings glimpses of hope back into their lives.

Those who do meaning making well and habitually, however, live with an orientation toward seeing sacred purpose in the everydayness of life, not only in times of loss or crisis. The experience of something as simple as a setting sun evokes God's purpose in creation and a posture of thankfulness in response. Seeing the blazing light of the sun drip into the pink and orange as it melts into the horizon, for example, is seldom just a sunset to those oriented toward sacred purpose. They see more than just the sun but a moment of God's glory that compels in us a response of gratitude—this is meaning that leans into God.

Belonging

To whom do we *ultimately* belong? Home leans into God when it moves us toward recognizing our place of belonging in the God who claims us. Sacred stories in the Judeo-Christian tradition tell us repeatedly and in no uncertain terms of God's declaration: "You are mine . . . you are precious in my sight . . . and I love you" (Isa. 43:1, 4). God searches for—even pursues—us so that God's beloved ones can live into this unbreakable bond of belonging.[12] This belonging is fundamental to sustaining both spiritual and relational flourishing.

The language of belonging is faithfulness. Leaning into God reminds us that focusing only on our own ability to be faithful—in all its limitedness—is misleading. Indeed, God's unwillingness to be thwarted by human rejection and infidelity is contrary to all human expectation and practice. Receiving such an unrelenting faithfulness requires that we practice a reorientation of belief. Focusing on God's faithfulness and recognizing our place as precious and beloved can then act as a strong balm for the internal narratives of people of faith, especially women and the marginalized, long weaned on feelings of self-failure and worthlessness. In this struggle with the self, many are likely to believe that God has no interest, cannot hear, or will not listen because they carry such feelings of worthlessness and shame. But to feel precious in God's sight is to understand a value of self measured differently from the social norms of our culture or the potential distortions of self and others. Feeling one's belongingness to God is a real and urgent need for many. Practical theologian Mary McClintock-Fulkerson names just this struggle when she describes the theological deliberations of those at Good Samaritan United Methodist Church located in a small southern city. She writes:

> Even as God's abundant promises were celebrated . . . discussion quickly turned to the risks that come with experiencing God's love. . . . Proper dependence upon God requires heightened self-scrutiny. . . . Letty confessed to a guilty self-doubt that added even more torture to this piety of risk and difficulty. Her self-abrogating fears that God cannot even see or hear her add a particularly female-gendered dimension to the sense of worthlessness so often attached to Christian repentance. Christian life—dependent upon a covenanting loving God, say these believers—is an ongoing struggle within the self.[13]

The appropriate response to a loving God is . . . love. But this comes with some risk. Loving back means loving not only God but other people as well. McClintock-Fulkerson continues, "The struggle of faithful discipleship has a social character. The nature of Jesus' love . . . compels you to risk; and risking is doing. As Beatrice put it, love your neighbor as Jesus has loved you. And for this community, the neighbor turned out to be the social 'Other.'"[14] When we can actually "take in" a sense of belonging to God, we can begin to draw on our identity as children of God. Recognizing our belonging in God allows us to live more fully into human relationships and the belongingness of home.

Security

Security is not the absence of fear but rather comes to us as a particular kind of courage. Home that leans into God teaches us to be bold and courageous as we learn how to distinguish between at least three types of fear. First, we experience fear as a God-given gift intended to preserve life, the fear we feel when our physical or emotional self is at risk of harm. I share here the story of Marika, a remarkable woman I met in a small village forty miles from Goma in eastern Congo. Marika was forced to watch as rebel soldiers murdered her husband and two children in a horrific manner. She was then brutally raped. As often happens in this region, her extended family subsequently rejected her because of the sexual nature of her injury. Fear can be presented in moments of actual threat, such as Marika experienced, or as mental aftershocks through flashbacks, dreams, and other physiological representations. All are equally valid as sources of fear.

Second, fear can be evoked by individual or collective authority, power, and control. Eventually, this can become institutionalized in order to preserve its function over the long term. This fear, then, occurs when an individual or system (not mutually exclusive) attempts to manipulate others—often with real-life consequences. As colonialism, racism, homophobia (or heterosexism), and all the other "-isms" reveal, this fear can be as life threatening as any other threat for those in the margins.

Finally, fear can also be the first thing we feel when God is asking us to learn and grow by moving into unknown or unfamiliar territory. True, fear is not nearly as distinct or exclusive as represented here. Nonetheless, home at its best can teach us how to discern differences between the three and empower us to move more boldly toward not just surviving but thriving. This way of discerning fear acknowledges that unjust systems use fear to create and maintain power. The more we recognize fear and its sources, the more God invites us to recognize an alternative source of power in God. How this knowledge changes larger systemic challenges may remain unknown, but it holds the possibility of transforming our inward and outward responses to the day-to-day threats that surround us.

Nowhere is it more important or difficult to negotiate fear of all types than in the context of forced displacement, particularly when armed conflict is involved. Marika and many other remarkable women like her have found a way to live boldly into the fear in order to live into all that God asks of them. In spite of all she had endured, after she recovered from her injuries Marika managed to build a home in another village. Refusing to hide in shame, she opened her doors to other women victims of rape and rejection. Convicted by her faith and called by God to offer help, Marika faced her own fears by walking back through the mountains filled with the very soldiers who had so brutally attacked her to retrieve women in need of care. Even after being raped at least once more, Marika continues to bring women over the mountain to find home again. There are few better examples of how a home leaning into God helps one to find courage in the face of fear and in the process discover a new sense of security in an unsteady world.

Relationship

Home that leans into God is one that gives rise to love of self and others as we seek to live in relationship with one another. It teaches, in essence, appropriate narcissism—love of self that grounds love for the other. It hardly seems possible that Western culture could benefit from becoming *more* narcissistic. What I consider here, though, is not the type of narcissism that acts as a defense against feelings of inadequacy and shame—such as what might garner a psychological diagnosis. Rather, it is one that recognizes God's createdness at work within self and others. Home that leans into God encourages the self to gain feelings of self-worth through a loving God that measures value very differently than do most cultures in the world. Appropriate narcissism allows us to truly engage in a love of self that celebrates being enough in a world which constantly tells us we are inadequate. It finds humor in foibles and lovingly accepts limitations of self without shame, thus freeing us to embrace the same in others. It celebrates giftedness. Love of self makes empathy possible, compels altruistic care, and nurtures a love of neighbor that names a just world as one that resists exclusion of all kinds. It is this self-love that rests at the root of the great commandment: "You shall love the Lord your God with all your heart and soul and mind, and love your neighbor as yourself." Love of neighbor cannot come without appropriate love of self.

This love of other is a response of thankfulness. An expression of this doxology, David H. Kelsey suggests, comes in the form of wonder and delight as the appropriate response to the other. Kelsey writes, "Learning to wonder at fellow creatures involves both a conceptual discipline and an aesthetic discipline that together capacitate one to pay sensory attention to fellow creatures in their concrete actuality without assimilating them to preformulated types. . . . Wonder at fellow creatures involves a curiosity about them that is committed to their well being."[15] Of delight he notes, "Learning to practice delight also involves learning to love properly the objects of our delight. . . . [It is] a love born of need . . . rooted in all of the ways in which human persons are needy because of their relative dependence on fellow creatures and radical dependence on God."[16] Relationships that lean into God are best enlivened in the Christian community by a just community that takes seriously its moral obligation of care toward the other. Love is both the basis from which this moral obligation of care emerges and the horizon toward which it reaches. Theologian John Wall writes of this moral love, "Moral love is not reducible . . . to the merely reciprocal give-and-take in which I should return what I receive. It requires the self to decenter to others with the radical degree of responsiveness."[17]

Of course, not every home place will provide these aspects—meaning, belonging, security, and relationship—in the same way or even in a manner that always leans toward God. Even naming *home* at its best as a marker for where we find meaning, belonging, security, and relationship risks creating an unattainable ideal that places an overwhelming responsibility on those working hard every day to create the best home place they know how. It likewise risks dismissing moments of grace found in even the most damaging experiences of home. Such risks are especially relevant when we face the challenge of understanding how this theological notion of home place that leans into God applies in cultures very different from the Western, particularly American, context in which I write.

So, how do we sort out, without legalizing, when home place works and when it does not do as well? When I first considered this question, I thought in typical linear terms with failure on one end and success on the other, but I now find this spectrum to be incomplete. Failure encompasses those home places mired in violence, abuse, and neglect. But they are only the most obviously negative ways to distort the power of home. It is also possible to distort home at what appears to be the positive end—to such a degree that it is not really positive at all. Let's take a moment to consider both ends of failure then pursue what realistically might lie in the middle.

Home Gone Wrong

At every turn in the writing of this book, I have been aware that the claim that home leans into God is difficult—if not downright alienating—for those whose experiences of home are heartbreaking rather than life-giving. For many, leaning into God has come *in spite of* their home place, not because of anything they ever learned or experienced there. The most common reasons that this is so are violence, abuse in its many forms (physical, sexual, emotional, or verbal), and neglect.

Such home places most often distort belongingness by falsely limiting one's sense of belonging—one belongs to no place. External violence turns inward. Self-identity becomes ensconced in failure, shame, low self-esteem, and self-loathing. One's ability to belong to larger communities or to develop an appreciation for belonging in contexts other than violence can become compromised. Home relationships become fused in cycles of violence, and, without intervention, future relationships run the risk of perpetuating the same. Relationships wither from lack of trust. Not only is the home place unsafe, but violence, abuse, and neglect risk distorting perceptions of other places—thus making no place safe. Suffering from violence, abuse, or neglect is senseless and makes the process of finding meaning all the more difficult. Meaning constructed only from within the limited scope of this type of home place risks seeing a meaningless world or meaning only in suffering itself.

Looking toward the other end of the spectrum, failure can occur from over-engagement as well as neglect. One's sense of belonging may become fused to particular relationships, especially those that elicit positive emotions, through enmeshment, making it difficult for the individual to emerge and stifling the underlying relationship.[18] One may have difficulty distinguishing among self, other, and God. In this home place, a false sense of what is safe based on the overdependence of others emerges, distorting the true nature of security. Meaning struggles to tolerate uncertainty and is threatened by any interpretation that does not strive to uphold an ideal as the ultimate goal.

In spite of the failed nature of these kinds of home places, however, grace can and does break through. When all else fails, God can still become the frame for belonging, meaning making, relationship building, and security. It is a challenge that highlights resilient possibilities in the face of harsh realities. Because God remains faithful to us in spite of our failures in home, nothing is impossible, though it may remain quite inexplicable.

When we consider the human endeavor of creating the home place in contemporary times, we must view its successes and failures within a wide range of possibilities that move us either farther away from or closer to the face of God—the intimate place of belonging with the Divine Heart. Here linear models fail us. Estrangement can result from either the home place filled with fear and neglect or over-engagement with the other that ceases to nurture love. Realistically, most families are a messy mix of successes and failures of all kinds. Somewhere in this mix are the home places that, though not perfect, do nonetheless encourage love, hope, and nurturing that lead to flourishing. We live in the hope that through attained skills and some genuine gifts, each generation will move closer to the place of flourishing and, for people of faith, back toward the face of God.

Flourishing

Home is the place that we hope leads toward appropriate physical, psychological, social, and spiritual flourishing of individuals and communities. Home places that are able to provide sufficient food, water, and shelter and contribute, in their own cultural contexts, to the ability to develop significant relationships based on trust, love, and respect, among other things, are included. The resilience of human emotional and physical flourishing is helped significantly by the presence of spiritual flourishing, which may look a variety of ways depending on one's traditions. I momentarily separate human flourishing and spiritual flourishing only for the purposes of our discussion, though as embodied creatures, we cannot truly divide the spiritual from any of the other dimensions of flourishing. In the Christian tradition, spiritual flourishing sits on the horizon through which we are fed and nourished in God through Jesus Christ toward the good of other, self, and community. Pastoral theologian Barbara J. McClure uses flourishing as a metaphor for "the well-being of the kin-dom of God" and as the starting point for defining "salvation, health, and well-being."[19] In terms of the home place, the greater the degree to which our flourishing finds sustenance in God, the more we are able to loosen our grip on our fixed need for home to be the source of belonging, relationship, safety, and meaning, and paradoxically the better we become at creating each. As with all things human, we do this in proximate ways, with each effort enhancing and encouraging the next, yet we are seldom able to give ourselves over completely.

In his theological anthropology, theologian David H. Kelsey finds flourishing to be both the expression of God's glory and human beings' (what he calls "personal bodies") response to God through faith. He writes, "Hence, it is precisely in faith that personal bodies flourish as the glory of God."[20] I find Kelsey most helpful for the manner in which he attempts to hold the tension between flourishing in its "ultimate" and "proximate" contexts.

These proximate contexts address aspects of flourishing that relate to human temporal, embodied, and relational needs. McClure suggests basic elements of flourishing that include "having fundamental needs such as food, shelter, and love, opportunities to live out one's deepest values (for example, through good work), as well as developing a relationship with the Divine."[21] Flourishing must also include a relational and social good toward which humans move. We are creatures whose lives are interwoven with others. McClure infers that interrelatedness is a primary aspect of flourishing and further that "life-giving institutions are necessary for human flourishing."[22]

If we equate notions of flourishing with aspects of well-being such as wholeness or health, we may be tempted to imply an all-or-nothing definition. Can one be a little bit whole? Is there such a thing as a small amount of health? What about partial flourishing? If only examined on the surface, flourishing, wholeness, and health are usually seen as antithetical to suffering and distress. Kelsey recognizes the problematic tendency to ally flourishing only with health and other notions of the functional good. Although he acknowledges that health is always preferable to unhealth, even persons with failing bodies, and other failings of mind and spirit, may find flourishing by virtue of God's glory.[23] He writes,

> [They] express God's glory in virtue of the minimal degree of functioning life they still do have as the condition, as it were, of their profound dysfunctions. So long as they do physically live in virtue of God self-expressively relating to them, those suffering extreme unhealth

also are in their own ways the glory of God. The index of their flourishing as God's glory is not any sort of health, but simply the fact that God's creative relating to them is inherently self-expressive of God's own glory. In all the ambiguity of their dying lives, as God's creatures they express God's glory.[24]

If we locate flourishing in health and physical well-being alone, we deprive others who suffer, such as the displaced, of the possibility of finding even glimpses of flourishing until the circumstances of their suffering have ended. I am unwilling to stake such a claim. Flourishing is relative. For Kelsey, to flourish is to "blossom" and "thrive"; even so, he notes,

> What counts as any particular personal body's flourishing [is] relative to her particular range of powers, it is also at any given time in her life a matter of degree. The degree to which any particular personal body may take itself in hand ("thrive") so that it is able to manifest the beauty of the emotional, intellectual, and social grace of which it is capable and is able to nurture both companions and descendants ("blossoms") may vary considerably.[25]

My experience of human resilience, especially among the displaced, has taught me not to underestimate the powerful drive to overcome one's circumstances to whatever degree possible and find moments that transcend suffering and move into flourishing.

How in our notion of flourishing do we contend with the reality of ongoing suffering that comes in so many forms, not the least of which is displacement? Is flourishing something we all live toward without the possibility of actualizing? Or, because of the reality of human suffering, must we move true flourishing to a horizon beyond this life? I suggest we give in to neither of these temptations. Flourishing can take hold in even the most unlikely, devastating, or tragic of life circumstances—even if only seen in fits and starts and broken glimpses. Counter-intuitive though it may seem, human flourishing is not utterly thwarted in the absence of complete satiation of everyday human needs. If our definition of flourishing does not reflect a spectrum of what flourishing can be in the lived reality of multiple life contexts and circumstances, we risk making the idea of flourishing a measure of success—relevant only for those with means and power.[26] Or, even worse, we relegate it to becoming a trite and idealized concept, applicable to few and worthless to all.

It is due to the resilience of human creatures that sometimes beyond all expectation, with merely good enough resources—and sometimes even no resources at all—humans can thrive in the midst of adversity. So it is with the idea of home. Kelsey points out that "human flourishing is something quite different from utopian life in a paradisiacal setting free of social and physical stresses and conflicts."[27]

If we name flourishing as *only* that which can be found in home at its best, then we take away from the incredible resilience of all those who flourish to some degree in spite of a home that did not live up to its best measure or even no home at all. And yet, should we not hope for home to be just that—the place where humans find their first glimpses of what it is to flourish? So we sit in this uneasy space striving for a horizon of flourishing in all the best ways and grateful for the ways that God pulls us across the absence thereof to make up for the distance.

God, Home, and Displacement

I began this chapter asking what it means for home to lean into God. Ultimately, though, this book examines the effects of forced displacement, asking what is at risk when the home place is irreparably lost.

Forced displacement can threaten these functions and the emotional and spiritual lives of those left without home. But even in the face of the worst circumstances, many are able to draw on resources of spiritual, psychological, and cultural resilience to bridge at least a temporary path toward spiritual sustenance, if not flourishing. Each of the following core chapters reveals in some depth just how this happens. However, these chapters also reveal that something else rather striking occurs. Persons *with* place often succumb to participation in collective and systemic responses of social exclusion toward those without place. This social exclusion renders those without a physical home place to be without a social place as well. Paradoxically, those with place who participate in social exclusion to whatever degree risk their own opportunities for flourishing. Displacement ultimately puts at risk the spiritual flourishing of both those without home *and* those in the larger society who participate, individually or systemically, in these acts of social exclusion.

The home place, in whatever form it is found around the world, has become a practical and social standard. From the Western perspective it is part of human entitlement—a universal human right—to be part of a family, to own land, and to have the protection of citizenship, all elements of home around the world. In the West it is the symbolic place where many attempt to carve out our own small pieces of utopia, or perhaps redemption. Although it may be a right, it is far from guaranteed.

Once the loss of home, its causes, and its remedies become embedded in sociopolitical systems, the loss of the sacred prompts a profound act of social exclusion by the larger community. For those of the Christian tradition, perhaps it is one more in that long line of narratives describing how we act out the primal loss when first we felt alienated from the face of God in that garden called Eden.

This particular tragedy of social exclusion occurs when we fail to see the face of God in those without home. Social evil is one perspective on the causes and effects of social exclusion, especially as we see it played out in the coming chapters. At least one of the problems of concepts such as social evil, of course, is how to understand the relative responsibility of the individuals within the system and the collective power of the system itself. The sum of the whole is greater than any individual yet never separated from the individual. We are left with the challenge of how to parse accountability for the social disaster of forced displacement.

Theologian Edward Farley suggests that there are two streams that feed what he terms "social corruption"—social infection and collusion. First, he points out that there are no isolated individuals, rather always persons in community with others. Communities carry forward to the next generation their social needs, concerns, and fears through language and other symbols of meaning. *Social infection* occurs when distorted fears and acts of discrimination, or what he calls "dynamics of idolatry," spread into the larger meaning-making structures of society.[28] The second stream is *collusion*, the aim of which is to "do whatever is necessary to establish and defend" what Farley calls the "absolutized enemy."[29] Racism is a prime example of such collusion. The coming chapters offer examples of how the loss of home, particularly the forcible loss of home, results in a similar absolutizing of the unwanted other—the foreigner or the homeless, for example—and becomes a social trigger for relational and spiritual alienation.

Walk Gently

For people of faith who spend a lifetime leaning into the spaces of everyday life looking for glimpses of God, there is something powerful to be found when we bring notions of home and God together. Yet claims such as "our true home is in God" may ring hollow and risk a cold reception from those displaced from their beloved homes. Rightly so, I think, for it seems too easy an answer that glosses over the devastation, loss, and tragedy of losing home as we know it. We would do well to tread with caution when transplanting such faith ideals into the lives of those living in the wake of natural disaster, violent conflict, mental illness, or resettlement into refugee camps. Given what is at stake for the displaced around the world, as we move forward, let us walk gently into the discussion of home and God.

I make no claim that the experience of home always ushers in the experience of God. As we have seen, home, for many reasons, is the place where we are often the most vulnerable and where human relationships have failed us most deeply, leaving lifelong wounds. But it is precisely because of the power home holds over us that I am compelled to pursue this connection—to push and pull at the corners—in the effort to better understand how home binds God and the human heart.

During field research after Hurricane Mitch in 1998 in Nicaragua, I met families who watched homes and loved ones perish as a great wall of mud washed away the side of the mountain on which they lived. They lived on deforested and consequently dangerous land, past its point of commercial use, which had become the site of hundreds of makeshift homes for those who could afford no other place to live. This is hardly an isolated example. Whether it is a bare mountainside in Nicaragua, poor housing in an inner city in the United States, or a rural village on the frontlines of conflict in the Democratic Republic of the Congo (DRC), these are leftover spaces where the poor are left to dig out a home and life. Both the spaces allowed to them and very often the political systems that perpetuate the poverty that grips them greatly increase the likelihood of forced displacement in situations of natural or human-made disaster.

The efficacy of both short- and long-term responses to forced displacement is, likewise, impacted by the ability of larger systems (such as nation states) to absorb or respond to the needs of those caught in the throes of the crisis. Such crises can illuminate operating biases and failings, even in the most stable and self-sufficient governments. The United States' federal, state, and local government responses to Hurricane Katrina are an excellent example. The Katrina event will, unfortunately, forever be notorious for the loss of life, large-scale damage, and legacy of failure in government response to the most vulnerable citizens in New Orleans.

Personal resources, including social capital, are thin and desperate for those who live in poverty. For them, hope for recovery once displaced, like in the case of Katrina, depends on aid received from others. In other cultures, especially in rural areas, where many depend on a combination of cattle raising and farming, displacement often means destruction or abandonment of livelihood. Refugees from eastern Congo must leave fields and animals when they flee from home with only what they can carry.

Of course, people and communities of means also encounter forced displacement through war and natural disaster. Ultimately, though, the financial and social resources available help determine the nature and length of their displacement. It is not my intention to belittle the impact of displacement for those who have the means to overcome it. On the contrary, forced displacement can be the source of a deep and mournful loss for anyone. Nor do I imply that contrary to the poor, who live in spaces more vulnerable to disaster, those with means live in protected spaces. Ironically, some of the most desirable and least desirable spaces share the high risk of vulnerability to natural disaster. Expensive ocean-front property on the East Coast of the United States sells at a premium, but like the bare mountainsides of Nicaragua, living in either area places one at extreme risk when facing the forces of a hurricane.

Still, the reality remains that all things are not equal in times of disaster. The greater the resources, financial and social, the less likely that those left homeless by unexpected events risk permanent displacement. For people with adequate resources, displacement is most often a difficult but temporary condition to be endured while insurance matters are settled and contractors hired. Temporary shelter can be found with family or friends, in hotels, or at other temporary locations. Indeed, displacement can be emotionally devastating and stressful in any number of ways, especially when loss of life is also involved. But resources such as continued employment, family, and insurance, even if these are minimal, can make the difference between recovery and long-term homelessness.

Forced Displacement

National governments, aid agencies, and academics alike find it useful to separate into stages the overwhelmingly complicated circumstances of disaster and conflict events that displace communities.

The stages that follow are based on my experience in the field with refugees and, in a limited respect, with aid agencies. They are similar, though, to those constructed by others in the field of disaster response.

My purpose here is to give the reader a glimpse of the complicated nature of large-scale displacement events and some indication of the types of resources needed to navigate such events. While these stages focus on community displacement, I also suggest that chronic issues of individual crisis and displacement follow a similar pattern.

Crisis

Crisis is another one of those malleable, overused words that creeps into our descriptions of life events which upset expected norms. Even as we attempt to use it in the service of understanding the stages of displacement, we may resist the boundaries of definition. Nonetheless, it is necessary and even helpful to construct a frame for understanding the process of displacement and consequential emotional and spiritual impacts.

If we try to delineate a timeline for crisis for the purposes of definition, let us say crisis for a community, in the context of displacement, begins in the moment of realization that people, families, and homes are under *imminent danger* of death or annihilation. The crisis period continues through *flight* from the force of threat to the point at which individuals are outside the range of immediate harm from that particular force. I include in this stage the *post-event waiting period*, depending on context, for rescue or initial assistance to meet post-flight needs: safety, treatment of injuries, food, water, medicine, and shelter.

Large-scale communal displacement of a forced nature is, clearly, precipitated by some type of event—natural disasters and armed conflict are two examples. In some cases, the crisis may include a warning period of some duration. For example, large storms off the coast of the United States are monitored well in advance. While the ultimate impact of a storm may be difficult to gauge, measures of wind and speed can help determine *possible* consequences. Based on this information, some communities may even be evacuated in the effort to save lives. Sometimes this is done in massive proportions, like in the cases of Hurricanes Sandy and Katrina—though the latter is remembered more for the failure to actually facilitate the evacuation of the most vulnerable. Earthquake prediction is much less accurate, but communities are at least likely to know that the area in which they live is prone to earthquakes, thus enabling people of means to make whatever preparations possible. Ultimately, however, the timing of the event itself and its severity is known only at the moment it occurs.

Some communities in the paths of advancing armies or rebel groups may have a degree of warning. While doing research in Goma, the Congo, we were informed by cell phone contact, quite prevalent even in remote regions, of rebel movements through the surrounding villages. But advanced warning is relative in the context of active conflict zones. Unlike sophisticated weather modelling that can predict dangerous weather systems days in advance, a phone call that rebels are near may leave villagers fleeing with only moments to spare. In 2012 I encountered hundreds of families milling about in a schoolyard on the outskirts of Goma only hours after fleeing their village. In spite of the advanced warning and of being in a safer place, the fear remained palpable. It had been a close call. In some cases, there is simply no warning, such warnings never reach the community at large, or there are no means with which to make such knowledge actionable. In the end, advance warning does not fully mitigate the crisis, but it can influence the resources—emotional and other—at hand during and after the event itself.

To be caught unaware in the throes of a massive storm, flood, or earthquake; to flee your home under threat of live gun and mortar fire; or to have soldiers storm through your house, killing indiscriminately, setting fire to you and your home—these are the things crisis is made of. On all accounts, it involves senseless and sudden loss of property, loss of life or injury, and deep, deep fear.

We often forget that when entire communities are displaced, they are also displaced from their worship spaces, religious leaders, and sometimes even the local community of faith itself. Refugees in Sudan on the run from bombings in their villages recalled how they lost contact with their pastors in the confusion. The extended crisis that came with weeks of walking toward safety caused them to choose new pastors from among their elders. Crises can have varying effects on the personal faiths of individuals but almost always challenge them to ask difficult questions of where and how God's presence can be felt when life is most dire.

Crisis, of course, does not end when one flees the immediate threat. Most assuredly other threats loom in the aftermath. In the initial stages of crises, this is true almost regardless of the context. Villagers running from rebel troops in the Congo must find safety, shelter, food, and medicine as did the residents of New York and New Jersey or New Orleans. What differs to some degree is how quickly, or if at all, these needs can be met.

Short-Term Stabilization

This stage does not indicate resolution of the crisis or even elimination of subsequent threatening conditions. It begins when the threat from the initial, precipitating crisis event diminishes. For example, when superstorm Sandy passed through the Northeast in fall 2012, flooding came not only with the storm surge during the height of the storm but again at a high tide enhanced by a full moon. In spite of these additional threats, efforts at stabilization were already in progress.

Immediate post-event efforts at triage and stabilization after a large-scale disaster or conflict almost always feel slow and inadequate. I imagine this is true for survivors as well as emergency responders and humanitarian aid workers. I have not met any on either side who did not wish more could be done faster. Regardless, there is a point for survivors at which some semblance of a daily life routine—even though inadequate—begins. This is a transition from minute-by-minute chaos to more predictable, though not certain, movements and efforts of daily life. Getting water, tending children, finding food, navigating aid agency bureaucracy—all become a new normal. Although this is a stabilization period to those in the field of disaster and crisis recovery, for survivors this is still a miserable time when crisis seems the only fitting description of what they are going through. Many feel forgotten and desperate to return to "normal life."

Of course, when this post-event period is met with inadequate resources, the risk of a shift into a new crisis phase is possible if not imminent. Illness or death from lack of medicine, food, or water, and a lack of security that invites violence from armed groups or thieves can threaten the community. The displaced are constantly living within a horizon of renewed crisis that leaves them negotiating the edge of chaos on a daily basis.

In the United States, we are appalled to see responses to large-scale disasters taking up to five days for full-scale coordinated federal and volunteer responses that sufficiently transition survivors to a stabilization phase. A similar time frame was seen in Japan after the earthquake of 2011. Realistic or not, we have an expectation and, to some degree, a sense of entitlement to the immediate relief of life-threatening conditions and emotional despair. We are shocked that in spite of all our abilities to control our environment, even the most technologically advanced countries can still be brought to their knees by natural disaster and acts of human violence. We want immediate relief and find it difficult in the midst of our own suffering to understand the logistical challenges of assessing, mobilizing, and distributing aid under difficult conditions.

In other contexts where crisis and displacement are common events due to ongoing conflict, an even greater delay is common. Not only are goods and services less likely to be available but the problems are further exacerbated by massive challenges regarding transportation to regions of the world that lack sufficient infrastructures or by difficulties in reaching survivors in hostile territories.

Then there are other matters to consider. For example, while I was doing research in Goma, DRC, ongoing fighting in the region north of the city sent civilians fleeing into the outskirts of Goma. This is not the first time displaced persons have fled to Goma. In fact, a former refugee camp on the northwest fringe of the city that once housed refugees from the Rwandan genocide is now used as an internally displaced persons (IDP) camp. Instead of going to this camp, however, the villagers planted themselves on the other side of town in what are called "spontaneous IDP camps"—taking up shelter in schools and churches while others spill over into the open spaces.

In spite of the chaos and fear, once they have made camp, these groups attempt to organize themselves. They choose leadership, negotiate with local leaders for resources, and work with local government agencies and nongovernmental organizations (NGOs), when they eventually arrive, to obtain water and means for sanitation and register civilians for food and medical treatment where needed. In spite of this organization, during my visit, over five hundred newly displaced families in Kibumba, outside Goma, waited more than eight days before the first aid agency arrived from five miles away. To some degree, this delay is, dare I say, intentional. Logistically, NGOs have systems already in place in the established camps and so must walk a fine line that resists encouraging spontaneous camps while also responding to humanitarian need when other options are closed. It is somewhat like those who refuse to heed evacuation warnings in the United States, then complain when help does not arrive quickly enough to get them out of a jam. It is a dilemma. On the one hand, we want to applaud every effort at maintaining agency when all else is stripped away, but the fact remains—aid does not always come on our own terms and conditions.

Long-Term Stabilization

Stabilization occurs when one of two directions is taken: survivors are returned to the location of their home place, even if this is among destruction, or they are relocated to long-term shelters. Examples of the latter include refugee camps, trailers provided by the Federal Emergency Management Agency (FEMA) in the United States, or even less formal housing options such as living with family members in another village or city. Long-term shelters imply that the crisis event, or threat thereof, in the original location of displacement continues or has created such damage that it is no longer habitable. Stabilization in this instance refers to the degree that aid agencies can predict and meet needs. It should be noted that stabilization is a relative term. It does not imply that all needs are adequately met. For example, in some long-standing refugee camps, availability of food fluctuates or other factors interfere, thus leaving rations below the recommended caloric intake for each refugee. Such circumstances do, indeed, push the situation closer to the edge of a secondary crisis.

Restoration or Systemic Displacement

The next level is restoration. For those who have fled their homeland, this could mean repatriation or resettlement in a third country.[1] For others fleeing disaster, it includes the final steps of rebuilding or relocating to a new home. Restoration should be interpreted according to context here. Restoration from disaster in the Western context likely means a restored or new home place. In some cases, it may mean permanent relocation. For those without the means to fully restore their home place, there is risk of becoming part of a long-term systemic response represented by refugee camps or the chronically underhoused or homeless in the United States.

Looking Forward

The case studies in this book reveal glimpses of multiple stages of displacement. For each there is a crisis event that initiates a forced loss of a home place. Each case also shows how, over time, particular forms of displacement becomes systemic and social exclusion emerges in association with that displacement.

The crisis event for the indigenous tribe of Batwa in Buhoma, Uganda, occurred fifteen years ago when the Batwa were removed from the Bwindi Forest. Other crises over many decades were responsible for displacing thousands of other Batwa living throughout the Great Lakes region. Through a colonialist lens, some might argue that the Batwas' standard of living has not only been restored but exceeds their previous life in the forest. Viewed from another perspective, however, it is not possible to restore their previous home, and they have instead been absorbed into the larger system of poverty navigated by millions in this region of Central Africa.

Although the shape of the crises vary, most refugees and IDPs have experienced all the stages of displacement introduced here. Some who have been forcibly displaced make their way into the urban centers of neighboring countries and seek safe harbor there. But most refugees and IDPs have, at one point or another, ended up in refugee or IDP camps run by the United Nations High Commissioner for Refugees or other aid agencies. Some refugees around the world spend their entire lives in a camp. These camps, intended to provide temporary places of safety and stabilization, are becoming permanent dwelling spaces in some troubled areas around the world. Refugees who cannot be repatriated or resettled find themselves caught in systemic displacement created by circumstances and the good intentions of international aid.

U.S. soldiers returning from war in Iraq or Afghanistan rotate through these stages of displacement more than once but would probably use different language for their experiences. For example, shipping out for active duty is not the same as a crisis, yet entering a combat zone may bear some similarities. One must reorder everyday existence to a new normal in a warzone. The heart of the displacement, though, centers on the emotional and spiritual struggle of post-traumatic stress disorder (PTSD) and moral injury. The psychic displacement incurred under these circumstances is no less daunting than that originating from hurricanes or other disasters.

Homelessness is largely focused on individuals. But even so, most homeless persons and their families can look back to a single event or series of crisis events that precipitated the displacement. The chronic nature of homelessness in general speaks to the largely systemic nature of the services that both offer aid and perpetuate the circumstances of displacement.

four

BREATHING HOME

When my father was alive we could get honey and meat from the
forest. We gave local people firewood and they would give us sorghum
to make our local drink with; or we would get honey and sell it to buy
clothes and food. Our food was meat. When the forests were taken
away, we were stopped from entering the forest and given nothing.
. . . The white people said it is a game reserve and game reserves
are under white people. The park said we want to eat Gorilla, but
we are not interested in that. Even if we could only go back into the
forest once a week that would be better.[1]
Without this forest we do not have our lives—everything
we need comes from the forest. We have to stay here
because this is our forest, this is our home.[2]
—Batwa living near Mgahinga National Park, Uganda

The Batwa originated in the Great Lakes region of Central Africa and through their plight offer a poignant example of the suffering experienced by thousands of other indigenous people, or "first
peoples," around the world who become displaced from their homes
due to land development, conservation, or other marks of what is
commonly deemed "progress."[3]

I have chosen the collective experience of the Batwa people, found
throughout central Africa, to examine the first of the four functions
of home, meaning making, and how it is disrupted by displacement.
I point to the natural environment, the community that forms the
Batwa relational core, and their relationship with the sacred as aspects of the Batwa home place that are particularly significant to the
process of meaning making.

Understanding the effects of displacement begins by seeking to understand the home place that a community has been forced to leave.

Home for many across the globe, like the Batwa, includes a deep connection to the natural world. When refugees from rural African areas describe their lives of farming, cattle herding, or forest living, they are not just describing what they do—as we might describe our profession. Rather, they are offering a glimpse into how they define home—the place from which they draw meaning and to which they dream of returning.

Together the Batwa in the Great Lakes region of Central Africa number perhaps only a few hundred thousand.[4] The specific timelines and experiences of displacement for the Batwa vary from region to region, but the resulting poverty and marginalization is nearly uniform. The history of Batwa displacement, like that for many indigenous groups, is long and complex, and understanding it is helped by bringing multiple perspectives into conversation with each other to gain a more comprehensive view. Accordingly, in this chapter I combine what I learned from my encounters with Batwa living in dire circumstances in Goma with information I gleaned from a Ugandan Batwa tribe and their historical performance of pre-displacement life in the forest. I weave these together with other historical and contemporary narratives, including scholarly sources, to create a larger picture of who the Batwa are as an indigenous people, what life once looked like when they lived in the forest, and how forced displacement has affected their ability to make meaning. The Batwa in Goma, who have been twice displaced—first from their forested home decades ago and again more recently as a result of war—help provide a glimpse into life as it exists today for many Batwa living throughout the region, as well as how they are perceived by others. The historical reenactment of everyday life before displacement performed by Batwa elders in Uganda helps us move closer to understanding a time when the forest was home. All Batwa tribes were at some point forest dwellers, but the Ugandan Batwa provide an especially helpful perspective because they are among the most recently displaced from this natural home and teach about this life from firsthand experience.

Meeting the Batwa

Walking along the road bordering Mugunga Internally Displaced Persons (IDP) Camp, I was on my way to meet a group from the Batwa people. I rendezvoused with a woman called "Apostle" Miriam, so titled for her leadership position in the local Pentecostal church. She was a warm and welcoming woman whose wide smile invited me easily into an embrace of greeting. Making our way over the sharp lava-covered road was quite arduous. Two men joined us—they were dressed in clothes quite worn and simple but clean and clearly their best offering for a special occasion. One man was very small in stature, four feet tall or so, and the other only a bit taller. These gentlemen were the elders from the Pygmy community and leaders in their local church. Today in Uganda, Rwanda, and other countries in the Great Lakes region, Pygmies are social outcasts relegated to the most impoverished margins of cities and rural communities. In the Democratic Republic of the Congo (DRC), Miriam tells me, they are considered to be filthy and ignorant with a reputation for stubbornly adhering to old traditions. While most "primitive" Pygmies refuse Christianity, according to Miriam, some have been open to conversion. This day I was invited to see the site of the Pygmy church—a small plot of land without any building. Nearby was a small wooden shack in ill repair in front of which was a group of women and children. The men, seated in the front, rose to greet me as I arrived. These were a gracious and kind folk whose appearance made clear they were also a long-suffering people.

Although the Batwa, or Twa, people in the Congo are considered to be among the first inhabitants of the forest—the original people of the DRC, these Christian Batwa currently live along the edges of Mugunga Camp in Goma, a complex of former refugee camps remaining from the Rwandan influx during the genocide of 1994.[5] Home in this camp consists of small shelters erected in an area that is quite inhospitable, made so by excessive layers of lava rock deposited during the 2002 eruption of Mount Nyiragongo a dozen or so miles away. The Batwa are particular targets of derision and violence in nearly every community of which they are a part and have been for many decades. During the Rwandan genocide they became a targeted population along with the Tutsis, resulting in the slaughter of over 30 percent of the Batwa population in Kigali.[6] Although there were surely no clear boundaries for anyone in that killing spree, the Batwa were murdered by those on both sides of the conflict—Tutsis and Hutus.

First Peoples

Like indigenous peoples around the world, the lives of the Batwa in the Congo and throughout the Great Lakes region provide a window into the devastating results of forced displacement from a home place that has long shaped a meaningful world. The story is a familiar one. The American Indian, the aborigines of Australia, indigenous tribes of the Amazon throughout South America—to name only a few—all have suffered a similar plight as the Batwa.

Like other "first peoples," the Batwa have fallen victim to politics and so-called progress, neither of which recognizes their culture or historical claims to lands much coveted by those in power. As we heard from Miriam, traditional customs are often devalued and mocked as backward and uncivilized, particularly because they are rooted in the natural environment.

Scholars have attempted to uncover the ancient history of the Batwa and the veracity of the traditional claim that they are the aboriginal people of the Great Lakes/Central African region. While there is no archeological evidence that this is so, ethnographic studies in the region do reveal linguistic and narrative evidence in favor of this view.

Africa historian Kairn A. Klieman suggests that Europeans first discovering Central Africa in the mid- to late nineteenth century projected onto the Batwa much evolutionary baggage suggesting a less than human status in the notion of the ancient Pygmy.[7] Because of this diminished status, little attention was paid to the rich, complex particularities of the Batwa's own history. Klieman accordingly turns to the historical narratives of the Bantu to close the breech of knowledge about the Batwa, and in the process has uncovered an estimable people who create meaning in the world through rich traditional practices and life drawn from centuries living deep within the forest.

Far from being a people isolated within the forest and resisting contact with the outside world, however, over time the Batwa became closely associated with the local Bantu people, a primarily agrarian ethnic population of mixed origins who cover a large swath of Central Africa.[8] The Bantu had a long tradition of trading with the Batwa—depending on them for meat and other goods foraged from the forest. As first comers to the land, the Batwa were revered as religious "experts"—mediators and intercessors with the natural and spiritual world. The oral traditions of several tribes in Central Africa credit the Batwa with "not only the introduction of fire and iron, but with cooked food and prohibitions against incest as well." The literal truth of these contributions is less important here than the civilizing theme of the myth, which is often reserved for "those with extraordinary supernatural powers."[9] This is especially ironic, or perplexing, considering how the Batwa are held in such social disdain today. Klieman suggests this social marginalization is a relatively modern development that began as early as the slave trade and escalated with colonial rule.

Pygmy versus Batwa

Apostle Miriam's description of the social distinction between Pygmies and Batwa notwithstanding, sorting out the historical difference between the two terms is challenging. From Miriam's description, we have a sense of the Pygmy as a primitive people living wild and naked in the forest, holding a near mythical place in the history of humankind. Klieman, using a method she describes as "comparative historical linguistics," offers keen insights into the ancient history of the Batwa and a compelling theory of the notion of the Pygmy in general. She suggests that "the idea of the Pygmy has been one of the most enduring root metaphors of Western culture. . . . The power of the idea lay in its role as a commonplace referent to the non-western or nonhuman 'other,' one that was readily and freely evoked by both the masses and intellectuals alike."[10] She continues, "These ideas can be traced as far back as Aristotle's *scala naturae* and the Medieval Great Chain of Being, for mythical Pygmies are situated between apes and humans in both. Associations between semi-human status and the idea of the Pygmy influenced Western thinking well into the modern era, providing a conceptual model for the development of the Missing Link paradigm, evolutionary theory, and scientific racism."[11]

This Western view of the Pygmy as primitive raises a curious observation. Pygmy populations have certainly coexisted with the people of the Congo for centuries. So, it is not the coexistence itself but a different kind of "civilizing" theme, that is the need to civilize this non-Christian native people, that emerges from Miriam's story, which is most remarkable and may indicate a residue of colonialism.[12] Does her perspective reflect the deeply embedded European structures used by King Leopold and the Belgians to oppress and colonize the Congolese that are now being projected onto the indigenous of the region by Congolese who are in positions of authority, such as herself? Anthropologist Axel Kohler suggests this is possible, stating that the "civilizing mission" of multiple waves of colonization, including Christianity, embedded itself in particularly strong ways in the last half of the twentieth century so that at least among his study group, the Bantu, "new ideas of being 'evolved' and 'civilized' took root."[13] Is this such an example? Trying to identify and understand important points of influence when cultures and beliefs differ is a precarious task at best.

I am aware that for me to suggest this as a critique of Miriam's experience risks offending her position as one of authority in matters of the Pygmy population. Again, I raise the matter not in the attempt to make a judgment but to name some of the assumptions and complications that arise when a white American attempts to analyze the plight of Congolese, Pygmy, or Batwa people. What is clear, however, is that Miriam has spent many years working with the Pygmy and Batwa populations, as she defines them, and has authority within these groups and great wisdom to offer us and others as our teacher.

The Forest Home

The Batwa tribe now residing in Buhoma, Uganda, were displaced from the Bwindi Impenetrable Forest National Park in the early 1990s. The overall timeline for their banishment differs slightly among various accounts of Batwa throughout Uganda. Generally, the Batwa were first removed from their nomadic forest living when Bwindi was given "reserve" status under British colonial rule in the 1930s. Batwa tribes moved out toward the edge of the forest close enough to regularly venture into the forest whenever food, herbs, or other natural supplies were needed. When Bwindi became a national park and World Heritage Site, these regular movements within the forest were halted.[14] All access to the park was monitored and carefully managed by park authorities. Batwa living near the park reported, "Going back into the forest is completely out of bounds. . . . Sometimes we get honey, but illegally because they always fear we will burn out the forest and take the bamboo. Some time back I used to go back, but ever since they started imprisoning people I have stopped."[15] Limited access was granted to some groups who could negotiate the government requirements, but most Batwa communities apparently lacked the necessary political "sophistication" to advocate for themselves and thus lost all access to their beloved forest.[16] Today, Bwindi Forest is best known for the endangered mountain gorillas living there.

The Buhoma Batwa are often categorized as *conservation refugees*, but the term is misleading. Although indeed displaced due to conservation efforts to provide a habitat for the mountain gorillas, these Batwa people most assuredly are afforded none of the rights or protections of refugees as officially designated by the United Nations. Like the Goma Batwa, they are denied official classification even as IDPs, thus making them ineligible for large-scale humanitarian aid. Rather, they live in a social and political "no man's land," a space between borders—neither here nor there, claimed by none.

Until relatively recently everyday life for the Batwa in Buhoma was so imbued with that of the forest and their embodied connection to the natural environment that it formed perhaps the most deeply informative dimension—the frame or lens—through which they learned about their world and how to make meaning in it. A group of Batwa from Kitahurira, a town near Buhoma, describe life and the forest in this way:

> Our parents used to go with us to the forest where they would teach us names of plants, hills, valleys and swamps. That's why even today, though we live outside the forest, we still know much about our forest, plants and animals. While in the forest, we were taught how to track bees (*okutara enjoki n'obuhura*) in search for honey. We were also shown how our forefathers used to live in caves and to worship the gods especially after hunting. We were taught how to make fire by rubbing sticks together. Back home in the village, boys would sit around the fire place with their father and listen to him as he narrated about the names of plants, animals and places especially those he had been to for hunting. Likewise, the girls would be with their mothers learning how to cook and to prepare traditional medicine. Boys and girls were taught how to weave mats, baskets, winnowing trays and to mould and repair clay pots. We also got to learn from our parents about the legends, tongue twisters, poems, riddles, folklore, songs and dances. We were taught to respect elders.[17]

Now, the absence of this environment, the forest, in their lives offers us a rather bracing example of how utterly devastating it can be for a people, an entire culture, to lose the point of reference that framed everyday experience and gave a sense of meaning and purpose in the world.

Home as the Natural Environment

Climbing high into the forest in Buhoma near Bwindi Forest National Park in Uganda, my lungs ached as the world around me subtly began to change in ways that my senses could not quite translate. I had taken my position on the trail behind the students and others. We were being led along a well-hewn path by a group of Batwa elders up into forested space similar to what once was their home.[18] We began our trek from a field in the middle of a community center, then moved through the heavy, weepy leaves of the banana groves and past a few small huts with smiling children shouting their greetings. Leaving behind the sounds of chickens and a lone cow mooing in the distance, I felt the incline gently increase. We were moving in a slightly upward direction but not too steeply—it still felt as though we were moving *into* something.

My lungs registered both the climb and the altitude. Before long, I noticed that the trail now hugged the earth to one side with a significant rolling drop to the right. Occasionally, I glimpsed our Batwa hosts on the forward section of the trail winding above us. Dressed in traditional garb they were leading us into a replicated clan dwelling site in the mountain forest. Here, through historical cultural performance, the elders would teach our group of Western students about life and ritual in the forest.[19]

As I moved up the mountain toward the Batwa Experience, I could see beauty and wonder in the forest that surrounded me, but it remained radically other.[20] I certainly did not see it with the same familiarity as did the Batwa. My feet were slipping on the moist dirt and moss long before I could cognitively acknowledge that the filtering of the light through the dense branches made the earth more damp than earlier on the trail. My watch warned when evening was approaching, yet the filtered light made it difficult for me to accurately sense how quickly darkness was falling. Our Batwa hosts seemed to know quite clearly how much time remained. How was the wind shifting and moving differently? The air was thinner. I inhaled oxygen, but the Batwa were breathing *home*. I became acutely aware of how little I was able to truly understand about home for the Batwa but also how irreplaceable is a home so closely tied to the natural world, which shapes meaning in such a unique way.

Yi-Fu Tuan asserts that we humans do indeed shape places but that places also shape us.[21] This is a helpful starting point to connect with the Batwa and how their relationship with the forest fosters meaning making. Many of us in Western culture approach our use of space as something to be owned, shaped, molded, or designed to fit our tastes and desires. Even pseudo-natural spaces, such as yards, gardens, playing fields, and the like, exist for our pleasure and enjoyment. It is true, especially in the last decade or two, that we have recognized the need for and given a greater respect to preserving natural spaces that are unmarred by human interference. Some individuals instinctively live with this inclination. Even so, financial gain continues to be a driving force for drastic harm to the environment. We are only beginning to recognize the damage our manipulation of the natural world has inflicted and hope against hope that the resilience embedded in nature is stronger than our destructive capacities.

The Batwa, on the other hand, are a people with a culture whose perception of the natural world is not that of something to be conquered but a gift to be respected and lived with cooperatively. Social anthropologist Axel Kohler notes that the idea of aboriginal life, as "a people living in social harmony with each other and in ecological harmony with their forest environment," is right in line with academic views that have dominated at the turn of the twenty-first century.[22] Aboriginal life certainly also seems appropriately reflective of a growing ecological perspective that attributes an indwelling sense of reverence for nature to those who depend on it, aboriginal groups especially. But harmony and respect, though clearly essential, do not seem to fully reflect the depth of relationship the Batwa we met in Uganda have with the forest.[23]

According to the stories the Batwa shared, they lived in a *partnership* with the natural environment. The forest provided shelter, sustenance, and healing. Shelter could be found under the ledges of large stones or in the hollows of tree trunks. Huts were built high in the trees or on the ground in clan groupings. One middle-aged Batwa remembered, "I saw how my grandparents had lived [in] permanent houses in [the] form of caves. They also had temporary houses in [the] form of fallen trees where they occasionally slept."[24] The Batwa were expert hunters whether using bows, spears, or snares. Honey found in treetops or underground was a prized source of food and medicine. Batwa characteristics that helped them so keenly adapt to finding resources in the forest have become nearly mythical. For example, Emmanuel Turyatunga, a Ugandan researcher, recounts one such story about the extraordinary eyesight of the Batwa: "A Mutwa [singular form of Batwa] is able to see a honey ant (tiny as it is) and follow it for several miles until it lands on the ground and then he/she goes on the exact spot and extracts honey from there."[25] He attributes this astonishing characteristic to the Batwa diet of vegetables, fruits, and game gleaned from within the forest.

As with many other indigenous populations, it is difficult to accurately gather or assess information about Batwa health so many years ago when they still lived in the forest. Those Batwa living today who do remember life under the forest canopy suggest that, indeed, food from the forest kept them in good health while herbs and other plants soothed and cured the body when necessary. Although a long tradition of trading with non-Batwa exposed them to some degree to outside diseases, many Batwa believe that it is only since expulsion from the forest have they become susceptible to malaria, sexually transmitted diseases, and other illnesses. Some studies suggest that belief in traditional medicine continues to trickle down through the generations so that even youngsters doubt the effectiveness of modern medicine over and against traditional forest medicine.[26]

The loss of forest game, food, and healing sources was more than a shift in resources. Traditional healing methods required a distinct wisdom about forest life that is now deemed irrelevant by the practices of modern medicine. Hunting was a rich tradition that crossed boundaries of mere sustenance to bind the living community to their ancestors through hunt rituals and narratives.

The natural world itself is for the Batwa an extension of the human community and vice-versa. Kohler applies the concept of a "cosmic economy of sharing"—a phrase coined by anthropologist Nurit Bird-David—to the Pygmy tribes of northwestern Congo.[27] Kohler describes this as "relations among humans, animals and plants [that] are perceived and experienced as on an equal footing and within an undivided cosmos." This relationality "extend[s] beyond inter-personal exchange relationships to include more or less the whole environment."[28]

The Batwa were known to move in small settlement groups throughout a defined region of the forest, never staying so long in any one place as to strain its resources. Their relationship is a cooperative one. Bird-David suggests that various hunter-gatherer tribes express a similar perspective:

> In the traditional Western view, nature and humankind have been "seen" as detached and in opposition. Furthermore, they have been viewed within a "subject-object" frame: nature "seen" as a resource to be utilized, controlled, possessed, dominated, managed, and (more recently) looked after by humankind. In the . . . tribal cases, however, nature and humankind are "seen" within a "subject-subject" frame as interrelated in various forms of personal relatedness. Since these tribal peoples share an intimate and time-proven knowledge of their respective natural environments, their representations cannot be dismissed outright in favour of the Western one.[29]

Rather than deplete the resources of any one space in the forest, the Batwa would move, allowing for nature to replenish what has been given toward their needs. The cultural traditions of the Batwa reflect this same power of nature to reclaim and replenish its own. Death rituals of the Batwa demand the burial of human remains on the forest floor—one comes from nature and returns to nature in death. To them, home is a natural and sacred space within the forest that honors the cyclical movement of nature itself.

Notions of the Sacred

The world of the sacred in the company of communal ancestors is a fundamental aspect of meaning making for many indigenous peoples, including the Batwa. It is likewise important for Christian and other faith communities, though in slightly different ways. In their displacement, many Batwa have declared a commitment to Christianity or Islam.[30] But traditional beliefs continue to undergird the ways the Batwa understand human relationships, the ethics of a just community, and their relationship to the natural world.

The traditional narrative of how the Batwa came to dwell in the forest is told with variations among the differing Batwa tribes of Central Africa. From the Batwa in Buhoma, I heard a version somewhat like this: The Batwa tell of their ancestral encounter with God, to whom they said, "You have given the most fertile farmlands to the white people and the remaining farmlands to the black Africans. What have you to give to us? So God thought for a moment, looked around, and said: 'To the Batwa I will give the forests.'"

It seems clear that this narrative is a "revised" version from the one contemporary Batwas' ancestors might have told prior to colonization and is revealing for several reasons. First, we can see that this myth attempts to make some distinction between the races here signified as black, white, and Pygmy. In her research in Central Africa Kairn Klieman notes several examples of primordial myths of creation that show evidence of similar attempts, some of which are "eloquent example[s] of the way oral traditions can be used to explain the realities of modern day. Having only recently emerged from the colonial experience when these myths were collected, [they] tended to highlight stories about the origins of races and conflicts between Black and White."[31]

Second, the myth gives stewardship of the forest to the Batwa. But, more than that, it also reveals a *just* world in which there is room enough for everyone—a point made by the Batwa during our meeting in Uganda. This is a view of compromise and abundance that is reflected in the Batwa approach to life within their own community as well as with those living on the edges of the forest. Social anthropologist Jerome Lewis notes the manner in which this sense of justice impacts the day-to-day life of the community. He writes, "An individual who has more of something than they immediately need is under a moral obligation to share it without any expectation of return."[32] The result is a community with a remarkable lack of inequality between genders and between the young and their elders.[33] They even apply this sense of sharing to the problem of protecting the gorillas. The Batwa I encountered appreciate the need to protect the endangered gorillas but believe that there is room for all to have their place. As the Batwa elder said, "We could have just a small section of the forest and the gorillas could have a section. It would be enough."

Finally, the narrative expands the notion that coexistence is possible for all—colonizers (whites), Africans, and the Batwa. But the Batwa are left instead with a paradox. While they are acknowledged by others in Central Africa to be the first people of the land, they are considered set apart from other Africans. Even their own narrative places them last among those to take their place in God's created world.

Ultimately, like Native Americans and other indigenous peoples, the Batwas' innate respect for the land and unwillingness to dominate or claim ownership over it became one of the key elements used under colonialist agendas to maintain power, usurp land, and actually displace the Batwa.

Love of Nature

Many indigenous groups have deep, binding connections to the natural world and find life in, near, and around nature not only a good toward which to strive but also something essential for life itself. In the mid-1980s, Edward O. Wilson proposed the Biophilia Hypothesis, which suggests humans are driven by a biological need for nature in order to find psychological and physical flourishing. All humans began, like the Batwa, as hunter-gatherers. Stephen R. Kellert, a scholar in forestry and environmental studies at Yale University, argues that this hypothesis suggests that "human identity and personal fulfillment somehow depend on our relationship to nature. The human need for nature is linked not just to the material exploitation of the environment but also to the influence of the natural world on our emotional, cognitive, aesthetic, and even spiritual development."[34] Humans need nature.

As human societies "developed" from hunter-gatherers to agrarian to industrial to technological, humans have found different ways to connect to nature, whether literal or symbolic.[35] There is a reason Central Park exists in the sea of concrete we call Manhattan. We visit zoos and take nature hikes when life becomes too stressful. Those readers who were raised in a family that made its life both on and from the land—in whatever fashion—likely have an intimate understanding of this connection.

In the world of global cities and virtual reality, there are others who find the claim of such a connection to nature to be contrary to the notion of a developed and progressive society. Kellert has developed a typology of nine ways that humans value nature based on a biological (evolutionary) connection to nature, the last of which is the "negativistic experience of nature . . . characterized by sentiments of fear, aversion, and antipathy toward various aspects of the natural world."[36]

From an evolutionary perspective and a modern one, there are reasons to fear some aspects of nature as well as to love it. Particularly in Western culture today, the relative distance from any actual experience with nature for some may evoke a kind of fear or, at the very least, disregard for it. In a similar vein to biophilia, *biophobia* proposes that there are biological reasons humans have certain fears of nature. Robert Ulrich, for example, suggests that "both the rewards and the dangers associated with natural settings during human evolution have been sufficiently critical to favor individuals who readily learned, and then over time remembered, various adaptive responses both positive/approach responses (biophilic) and negative/avoidance (biophobic) responses—to certain natural stimuli and configurations. This perspective explicitly recognizes that the natural habitats of early humans contained dangers as well as advantages."[37]

I would not be the first to suggest that fear of nature, especially the unknown in nature, sits at the root of colonialist violence in the "conquering" of the jungles of Africa. Notice here how Joseph Conrad describes the forest and river in his novella based on his time in the Congo under King Leopold: "We were wanderers on a prehistoric earth, on an earth that wore the aspect of an unknown planet . . . men taking possession of an accursed inheritance, to be subdued at the cost of profound anguish and of excessive toil."[38] Similarly, Klieman notes that in the nineteenth century, when Africa was portrayed by Europeans as "a hostile, primeval environment, a green hell where humans could do nothing more than survive, the forest came to take on anthropomorphic attributes in the minds of Westerners. As such, it was used to explain not only the tragedies induced by the European presence in the region, but the perceived lack of civilization among Central African peoples as well."[39]

Colonialism

The devastating impact of European colonization on Central Africa has laid the groundwork for Western engagement ever since. As Klieman suggests, to Westerners, Pygmies have long been considered less than civilized—less even than human. A case in point is King Leopold of Belgium's armies, which conquered and ruled the Congo in a particularly violent and brutal manner, plundering natural resources and terrorizing her people. African life, and Pygmies in particular, were reduced to spectacles of entertainment for the curious. Nearly three hundred Congolese—including two Pygmies— were shipped to Belgium and put on display at the 1897 World Fair in Brussels. In the United States, a former Presbyterian minister turned businessman promoted a "Pygmy exhibit" in the Bronx Zoo in New York in 1906. Ota Bena "was displayed in the monkey house . . . [with] an orangutan. . . . Visitors ogled his teeth—filed, newspaper articles hinted, for devouring human flesh."[40] In the end, a group of black ministers eventually rescued him, though he committed suicide ten years later.

We cannot say that the circumstances of the demise of Batwa culture occurred in exactly the same ways in every specific context throughout Central Africa due to the presence of different colonial entities. Nonetheless, various groups of Batwa currently appear to experience similar states of poverty, social exclusion, and lack of political power. The rise of European colonization and later Western involvement increased deforestation due to agriculture, which threatened the Batwa way of life in general. Jerome Lewis writes, "Each colonizing group put increasing pressure on the original forest, turning most of it into farmland, pasture, commercial plantations and, more recently, protected areas for game parks and military exercises. And, as Klieman suggests, each colonizing group consequently increased the disregard—even utter disdain—with which the Batwa have come to be treated. Although the Europeans have left, decolonization remains an issue for the Batwa."[41]

Over time it has been the Batwa's deep connection to and respect for nature, and their *unwillingness* to harm or claim ownership over it, that has contributed to the tendency of various cultures to dismiss the Batwa as a civilized community and their rights to land tenure, especially in the forest. Like many other indigenous groups, the Batwa did not possess formal title to any portion of the forest though each clan, through mutual agreement with others, "owned," for lack of a better term, a particular part of the forest. Freedom of use was understood and granted between clans as each moved around as limitations of the environment required. The fact that the Batwa do not have the tradition of constructing permanent dwelling places in the forest, having chosen instead this more nomadic existence, prompted the ease with which governmental and international agencies could (and continue to) dismiss claims of ownership or rights of habitation within a particular environment. It further feeds into the justification for keeping the Batwa classified as an uncivilized population relegated to the margins of society.

With such a complex love-hate relationship to nature, some in the West may struggle to connect with the nature-bound experience of the Batwa or even sympathize with their displacement. Western "civilized" society has dismissed the traditional hunter-gatherer lifestyle of the Batwa as primitive, but scientific research is now revealing an inherent value in nature, even—or especially—for modern life. Science, a "proper" language for the "civilized" world, is saying what the Batwa have likely known for centuries—we all have deep connections to and need for our environment.[42]

Christian Mission and the Batwa

It is difficult to number the ways displacement has changed life for the Batwa. Once removed from the forest that was given to meet their every need, the Batwa now live in a constant state of need. Once living as a community in the forest, they are now dispersed and isolated in cities, unable to always identify clans from which they once hailed. The God that moved daily in the forest has now been replaced by a God who seems to move only through churches that offer handouts or NGOs that offer programs for the needy.[43]

During my interview, Apostle Miriam shared that many years ago she was called by God to go into the forests of North and South Kivu in search of the Pygmies. There, says Miriam, they ran naked and ate raw fruits from the forest. They feared outsiders and would flee at the slightest hint of an intruder. To seem less the outsider, Miriam's first trips into the forest were gentle excursions during which she, like the Pygmies, was naked except for bands of cloth for modesty that covered the private parts of her body. Her message to the Pygmies was that as the first people of this country, God wants you to become leaders, by which, she later explained, she meant they needed to become "civilized" and Christian. She is very proud of her ministry and the conversion of many Batwa and Pygmies to Christianity.

Scott and Carol Kellermann, former medical missionaries, have helped Batwa in Buhoma, Uganda, to create a truncated narrative of their life in the forest long ago. This narrative also helps frame their role as victims of conservation displacement and social decline. This narrative and the performance nature of its telling in the Batwa Experience are valuable tools for preserving for their children (and a few outsiders) a vision of life as it once was and the traditions and rituals that gave it meaning.

Both the Kellermanns and Apostle Miriam recognize the deep meaning of the Batwa status as first people of the forest. The Kellermanns have purchased land so that the Batwa can preserve their culture while also promoting a healthy Christian settled life as both the social reality and, perhaps, higher good. Apostle Miriam recognizes that Pygmies once held a place of great esteem and value as the first people of the Congo and are due a certain level of respect as those who have roots in the land longer than any other tribe or political force.

Most development agencies and even a few scholars have suggested that the Batwa are making the necessary steps toward development, even civilization. This line of thinking believes that the advantages of education, healthcare, and increased productivity in the civilized world are benefits worthy of the loss since the Batwa can no longer live in their first choice of home, the forest. Even if these groups' motivations are well meaning, organizations that attempt to assess the progress of the Batwa in their adapted environment by using markers such as formal education, farming, and healthcare are at risk of missing the deeply embedded markers of identity and meaning disrupted by forced displacement from the forest.[44] The question becomes, can these colonial markers of "progress" that end in poverty and social exclusion truly claim a higher value? Can we leave them unexamined over and against a once flourishing life in the forest? I suggest that we cannot.

What judgments can we make about the suffering and subsequent loss of meaning endured by the Batwa simply from leaving the forest? This question is actually quite complex. For the Batwa, the forest home cannot be approximately replicated. All of the ways that everyday life was enfolded and enriched by the forest were lost. All referents to interpreting their experience in the world changed. What is the cultural, spiritual, and psychological impact of living with this irreplaceable loss of home? Dwellings made in or under the forest canopy, the thin air high in the mountain forest, the rituals of death and burial in the forest floor, the freedom to move the community to fresh forest spaces when custom or nature demands—all became memories. How does one recover from such profound, irreplaceable loss? How does the culture absorb the disintegration of its source of meaning making? And, at what cost do they survive thereafter? How does this loss affect the long-term life of the Batwa, and how are we as a community of faith to empathize with the loss of an environment and its associated meaning when our ability to articulate or perhaps even to perceive the physical effect of the forest experience might be woefully limited?

Resilience and Hope

One of the most significant tasks of theology is to fine-tune the lens through which we are able to envision with others how hope moves in the world. Theology also helps to reframe what hope looks like when conditions of injustice, oppression, poverty, violence, and suffering distort or obscure the ways we are accustomed to seeing it. How do we see God breaking through?

Pastoral theologian Andrew D. Lester suggests that an ability to imagine a future story is a fundamental aspect of hope for all of us —Ugandan forest dweller or Western urban professional alike. Creating a future story, according to Lester, requires imagination. One must be able to imagine the possibilities of that which is not yet realized. Ultimately, Lester proposes that, theologically, hope is "a person's trusting anticipation of the future based on an understanding of a God who is trustworthy and who calls us into an open-ended future. This God keeps promises of deliverance, liberation, and salvation."[45]

In his stunning book *Radical Hope*, Jonathan Lear, though not addressing Lester specifically, rightly identifies the challenge of such a future story by asking how one is able to hope when one cannot imagine what the future will look like.[46] For communities like the

Batwa, how do they follow meaning into the future when there is no vision for it—when all familiar points of reference are gone? Lear describes the Crow Nation, and I would add other first peoples, in this predicament as "living at the horizons of their world." He goes on to write, "For if a people genuinely are at the historical limit of their way of life, there is precious little they can do to 'peek over to the other side.' Precisely because they are about to endure a historical rupture, the detailed texture of life on the other side has to be beyond their ken."[47] How do a people find hope when the vision for a future is literally beyond their imagination?[48]

To step forward into a future that you cannot imagine requires an extraordinary kind of courage. As Lear so poignantly asks, how is it that a community can grasp a future story when a way of life is destroyed? The problem with imagination is that we are somewhat limited, at least in regard to familiar concepts that are based on past experience or those we have heard about. Lester and Lear both understand that hope must be rooted in reality. This makes hope for first peoples, indeed, a radical hope, as Lear so rightly names it. He notes, "So if there were to be such a thing as a courageous response to these radically altered circumstances it would seem to require a transformation of the psychological structure with which we 'face up to reality.'"[49]

I suggest that for people of faith such a courageous response is aided by a God who reaches across the limits of our horizon to pull us toward that hope-filled future even when we cannot imagine it ourselves. God's vision of the future is broader than anything we can hold, and, indeed, all that we envision is encompassed by God's faithful presence and participation. Our sacred stories tell us of when God reached across the horizon to Hagar in the wilderness, to the Israelites as they followed Moses into freedom, and again as they left Jerusalem in exile. God reached further still across this horizon in the birth of a refugee child and yet again in an empty tomb. Each of these stories reflects a moment when those displaced by violence and oppression have stood at the threshold of an unknown and unknowable future. In each, God has closed the distance.

I offer these theological reflections without the intent to impose them on the Batwa, or the Crow, for that matter. While some Batwa have become Christians and others Muslim, I write for the broader communities of faith who may recognize the sacred as it moves toward an unfolding future of hope and possibility.

Lifting the Veil

As our group made the way slowly back down the mountain trail from the Batwa Experience in Uganda, we could hear the soft conversation of the tribe elders as they followed. We were progressing rather slowly—the steep downward grade the cause for our timid movements. They were remarkably patient with our slow progress down the unfamiliar slope. They were close on our heels until we reached the lower quarter of the trail, at which point they were able to branch off onto a parallel track. As I looked to my left fifty feet, I saw our hosts now dressed in everyday clothes having changed out of the indigenous costumes used for the presentation an hour earlier. Others followed carrying the pots in which they had prepared food for us in the forest.

The veil was lifted—any illusion I had of the Batwa climbing into their huts built in the treetops, tucking in for a night at peace in the forest, was quickly shattered as I watched them walk across the field toward life as it exists now.

After the performance, it was difficult to imagine any place but the forest as home for the Batwa we had met. Now, there was a deep sadness in watching them transition from this forest "home" to their lowland one, the mountain forest receding into the dusk as they moved toward a smattering of mud-walled and thatched roof houses.[50] In my mind's eye, the delight I saw in the faces of the elders as they reenacted life among the trees seemed to be replaced by the sad and wearisome reality of perpetual loss and displacement.

FLEEING CONFLICT AND DISASTER

It was 9 a.m.; already the temperature was over ninety degrees Fahrenheit and I had a fine layer of red dust covering my skin—a remnant from the forty-minute trip to the reception center at Kakuma Refugee Camp in northern Kenya. Refugees generally enter the country through one of three points: Lokichogio, Kenya, at the border of Sudan, the eastern region of Kenya bordering Somalia, or the westernmost region bordering Uganda. If they seek help from UNHCR [United Nations High Commissioner for Refugees], their process will begin at one of these points. If then assigned to Kakuma, they will be transported to the camp and delivered to this reception center. New arrivals are sorted into communities according to nationality and tribe to which they belong. If a minor is unaccompanied, then the community will seek a foster family for that child. This morning we met Mary, who was tearful and quite distressed:

MARY: *"I ran to Southern Uganda because of the killing and kidnapping in my home in the North. Everywhere I went people were suspicious of me because I was from the North. One of the leaders there put a curse on me because I was a foreigner. Now the curse causes me to become very nervous and upset, it takes over my body until I am paralyzed and cannot move. I can't care for my baby. Please, you must help me!"*

JACKSON *(intake officer):* *"Are you a Christian? Then we must pray to God for help."*

—Field notes, Kakuma Refugee Camp, 2003

Belonging is a deep feeling within us of connection to community and place that helps us answer the question: who am I? In this chapter, we move toward understanding this sense of belonging, the second of our four main functions of home, through the context of refugees and internally displaced persons (IDPs) like Mary. When we begin to break down what belonging really looks like, we start with the four characteristics that I think emerge from narratives like hers and others to help guide us. Belonging helps shape our identity. It is *reciprocal*, it *orients us* toward place and people, it is *dynamic* in nature, and it requires a *practice of remembering*. With these characteristics as guides we can explore how we develop and maintain a sense of belonging to the places important to us, especially beginning in the home place during childhood; how we recognize our "belonging-ness" to God; and, finally, how development of these characteristics is thwarted when the displaced become categorized as the outsider or "foreigner."

Characteristics of Belonging

One possible way of understanding Mary's experiences of paraly-sis might be as the affective result of a symbolic rejection from the witchdoctors in her home of Uganda where she once claimed a sense of belonging. In order to have a sense of belonging, we must not only have our own feelings of deep attachment to people and places. Something more is needed. Whether we understand her states of paralysis as significant episodes of witchcraft or symptoms of anxi-ety that we might rather diagnose using Western psychotherapeutic models, her despair is *real*. My culture will likely interpret it one way and hers another, but from either perspective, metaphorically and literally, she feels rejected and cursed because she is an outsider. Yes, we must claim the places to which we belong, but people and places must claim us as well. *Belonging is reciprocal.*

Our sense of belonging to a home place has an orienting effect on us by acting as both anchor and compass. In other words, the places and people to which we belong both give us firm ground to stand on (anchor us) and act to orient us (like a compass) to the familiar and safe as we move through life. They help remind us of who we are. By employing anchor and compass, I am using somewhat contradictory metaphors. I do so because the belongingness of home can be some-what paradoxical. It often serves to both hold our identity in place and simultaneously propel us outward into the world toward growth and change. *Belonging orients our identity.*

Our sense of belonging has a dynamic nature to it. Even if war or disaster never displaces us, we are born and raised in a particular community located in a particular place, but we grow and change, as does the sense of where we belong. The less than 1 percent of refugees from Kakuma who are eventually relocated to a third country for permanent resettlement face the difficult transition to a new culture and eventually the question of defining a new home and a new way of belonging.

During my years working with Catholic Charities Refugee Resettlement in Nashville, Tennessee, I met many of these refugees from across the world, each struggling to reconcile the ways that the place they called home had changed for them. They carried a deep longing for the home left behind yet also worked hard to live into the new home they struggled to understand. Now, more than ten years later, most have two places of belonging—two places that anchor them— one in their homeland of origin and the other in their adopted homeland. Friends from South Sudan continue to honor their elders by seeking advice and sending remittances. They visit family in Sudan and work toward peace and development in their beloved country. But they have also married, had children, and put down roots in the United States. They will not forfeit citizenship in either country nor surrender the right to call both home. Nira Yuval-Davis, director of the Research Center for Migration, Refugees, and Belonging at the University of East London, reminds us that, as these resettled refugees show us, belonging has multiple dimensions: individual or emotional, communal or social, and political. She notes, "Even in its most stable 'primordial' forms, . . . belonging is always a dynamic process, not a reified fixity."[1] *Belonging is dynamic.*

The many thousands of other refugees and IDPs who remain in camps around the world, sometimes for decades, hope for the chance to return to their homeland but cling in the meantime to memories of home as it once was, memories woven together with the threads of daily life. For my Sudanese friends, conversation is filled with deep longing for all that was left behind—the cool waters of the Nile River, crops of peanuts and sorghum, and grazing herds of cattle.

In Kakuma Refugee Camp, youth performed traditional dances on Sunday nights in the hope of preserving Dinka culture for children born in the camp and perhaps also of providing some comfort of home for themselves. Passing these ritual dances on to the next generation was a way of handing down the tribal memory and binding them forever to a "home" the children had yet to see. South African practical theologian Amon Eddie Kasambala reminds us that in Africa, "the past is the focal point for the present."[2] Like the notion of home itself, belonging looks to the past, sinking its roots as deeply toward ancestors, tradition, and history as toward future survival and flourishing. *Belonging requires practices of remembering.*

Learning to Belong—Separation, Attachment, and Reflexivity

Learning to belong requires certain psychological processes usually experienced through the course of normal development and growth. From these we learn how to receive love and care as well as form a sense of attachment to others. Just how this looks depends much on cultural context. Most Western theories of human psychological development propose that at a significant point in infancy, a child begins to recognize him- or herself as separate from parent/caregiver. In other words, there is an "I" and that which is "not I." From that point on, through the natural process of childhood and adolescence and, perhaps, likely for a time thereafter, he or she will put great energy into differentiating from parents. The concepts of individuation and differentiation speak to the development process essential to Western culture in which the development of the individual is so highly prized.

It may seem ironic to some that in Western psychodynamic theory, the ability to effectively separate is essential to the subsequent ability to form healthy relational attachments throughout life (i.e., in human relationship or in a sense of belonging among others).

But it is a reminder that these processes never happen in isolation; the larger community, especially the familial one, is necessary to the process.[3]

Psychoanalyst Margaret Mahler, a pioneer in the study of "normal" (Western) childhood development and more specifically the separation and individuation process, highlighted the biological development and recognition of the outside world as essential to the intrapsychic development of the infant. In particular she notes the value of physical mobility, writing, "The motor phenomena are correlated with intrapsychic events. This is particularly true in the first years of life."[4] Psychoanalyst Harold P. Blum emphasizes the degree to which Mahler recognized this value of locomotion to ushering in the separation-individuation process. The literal moving away of the infant encourages the exploration of the surrounding world, "paving the way for intrapsychic separateness and, eventually, individuation, identity, and autonomy."[5] This theory is fitting, of course, for environments conducive to such exploration by an infant. I recall, however, a visit to one of the slum areas in Nicaragua in the mid-1990s. As is frequently the case in tightly packed slums in many locations around the world, raw sewage flowed beside the main walking paths. I met a lovely young couple and their child, who appeared to be between eight months and a year old. For the several hours we were together, the mother held the child in her arms. The child did not struggle to free herself or insist on moving to the ground. It became clear that the surrounding conditions prevented free movement from being in the child's best interest. Such freedom was not something the young child was accustomed to experiencing. I began to wonder how a child who is held continuously learns to crawl, walk, or eventually separate herself emotionally from her mother. And yet, as surely as American children who follow patterns described here, or African children growing in communities with multiple mother figures, grow and become mature adults, so too do children in a vast number of other contexts who develop through perhaps slightly different patterns of attachment and separation.

In many tribal cultures, the objectives of personality development likely reflect culturally specific nuances. In the Dinka tradition in Sudan, many children are raised with the influence of two or more mothers, co-wives in the same household, where commitment to the larger community is paramount. Here, emphasis on and expectations of kinship systems and community take precedence over the individual. My research in Sudan, the Democratic Republic of the Congo, and Uganda suggests this is certainly so. Instead of discovering the "I" and the "not I," the developmental trajectory for the child is "I exist because you exist"—in other words, the individual is always intimately tied to the community's existence.

In both contexts, one's sense of belonging begins in childhood with the culturally appropriate concept of who I am in the midst of others—caretaker and community. African religious philosopher John S. Mbiti describes the African community as having vertical as well as horizontal understandings of relatedness. In other words, a person's connection to God is directly related to her connection to other humans. Regarding the horizontal relatedness, he writes, "Each person in African society is related to other people so closely that he has literally hundreds of 'fathers', 'mothers', 'brothers', 'sisters', and so on even if there is no immediate blood or biological link. . . . Each person exists because others exist."[6] Theologian Augustine Chingwala Musopole comments further on Mbiti's notion of horizontal relatedness: "This network of kinship relationships is greatly valued. To be human is to relate positively to others. It is to belong."[7] Musopole goes on to examine Mbiti's underlying philosophy of this kinship network and proposes that it serves to control social relations, govern marital customs, guide inter-relational behavior, endorse communal solidarity, and extend relationality horizontally through the totemic system and vertically through the spirit world and to God.[8]

Few have written more on the psychology of separation and attachment in children than John Bowlby. In 1950, he was a consultant for the World Health Organization called in to evaluate the mental health of children who were homeless.[9] His conclusion was that early separation of children from their mothers leads to significant difficulty in the young children (and even in later life), which led to his advocating for nurturing continued relationships between mothers (or substitute caregivers when necessary) and children. This early observation of displaced families in turn led him to explore the psychological structures surrounding the powerful process of attachment.

Early on he suggested that like most creatures, humans tend to prefer the familiar environment to the unfamiliar one. This is not really a surprising observation. From an evolutionary standpoint, familiarity increases likelihood of survival—if for no other reason than the dangers, as well as comforts, are known. Bowlby wrote, "Since two of the natural clues that tend to be avoided are strangeness and being alone, there is a marked tendency for humans, like animals of other species, to remain in a particular and familiar locale and in the company of particular and familiar people."[10] Roy F. Baumeister and Mark R. Leary, writing on the psychology of belonging, suggest that "the need to form and maintain at least a minimum quantity of interpersonal relationships" is innate in human beings.[11] These relationships form the context of our belonging and help us feel comfortable in the world. But feeling more comfortable is not all there is to attachment; otherwise, we would never leave that first home environment. Part of human growth and maturity compels us to widen our circle of familiarity and sometimes choose a different place altogether to call home.

Belonging implies that one has a deep sense of attachment to both a community of people and a place. Think about where you feel that you most belong. Of whom are you most fond in this place? What about place? As embodied creatures, we exist in particular places that in and of themselves become a part of what makes us feel we belong. Part of this is related to the comfort of the familiar—the place, community, and environment where we can be our most relaxed selves.

As I suggest in chapter 1, the feeling of being "at home" or the sense of belonging includes a circle of people within a defined place.

For me, when I return to my "growing up home," it includes my immediate family, though they no longer live there, but also a community of family friends who have known me my whole life. As years have passed, the circle has grown wider to include my own friends from childhood and then those from adulthood. All of these persons are physically associated with a place. Remove the people from the place and home feels different.

On the one hand, our attachments and sense of belonging are something we don't really need to think about—we just know. But in order to exercise the dynamic characteristic of belonging, we must be able to reflect back, even on a cursory level, to what makes us feel we belong in the first place. In other words, we can feel a deep affection and belonging "in the bones" without ever giving a moment's thought as to why. But if I move to a new town, or a refugee resettles into a new part of the world, it is beneficial to have some sense of what is missing in order to make changes necessary to create a new place of belonging. Sociologist Anthony Giddens notes, "The capacity to use 'I' in shifting contexts, characteristic of every known culture, is the most elemental feature of reflexive conceptions of personhood."[12]

Belonging to God

From a Christian perspective, belonging to God is as simple as it is complex. That we belong to God is a continuing promise throughout the Old and New Testaments: "I have called you by name, you are mine" (Isa. 43:1b) and "Nothing can separate us from the love of God" (Rom. 8:38). God is quite attached to humans, who are precious and beloved. God pursues us and is always faithful to us. In relation to God, faithfulness and belonging are intertwined.

But let us ask the question: is our relationship with God one in which *we* feel a sense of belonging? This is a difficult question based on the criteria or characteristics set out in this chapter. While God may be deeply attached to us, is it reciprocal? When the question of discerning attachment rests on human shoulders, it becomes quite complicated. Fear and anxiety more easily overcome us when our lives are threatened or we are forced to flee our homes. In a crisis, God can feel very far away or intimately close. Indeed, we are as likely to feel God's abandonment as God's faithfulness. I met with a group of Congolese men and women at Nakivale Refugee Camp in Uganda. Sitting in the shell of an old church with crumbling walls and only the sky for a roof, one brave man admitted that his difficult journey fleeing war had caused him to question God's faithfulness. Yet a woman sitting nearby said that because her life was spared and she survived the journey, she now believes in this Christian God. It is an imperfect reciprocity that holds together our sense of belongingness to God. By faith, we attach ourselves to God; by promise, God is faithful to us.

A community of faith can be the compass that helps orient us toward God when all else has failed.[13] While African and Western cultures may differ on the characteristics of individualism and even one's personal relationship with God, a community of faith in either context can provide the sure heart of love and comfort that can hold someone steady in times of crisis. This may be exactly why churches and other sacred sites, the gathering places of the community, become targets in times of conflict and war. Before the Sudanese war, churches, much like those in other parts of the world, were built as the center points of villages. It did not take long, though, for the northern forces to realize that bombing a church would surely destroy many people and dwellings nearby. The mud-and-thatched-roof churches now stand quite a distance from the centers of the villages.

Nyamata Church, on the outskirts of Kigali, Rwanda, another place of gathering, is now a memorial to the ten thousand Tutsis and others who were slaughtered inside and around the building after fleeing there for protection during the Rwandan genocide. The community, still together, now lie bone to bone in the crypt behind the church.

In refugee camps and along roadsides, in fields and in vacant buildings, those forced to flee from their homes find places to gather as groups of faithful strangers who become, in that moment, communities of faith—seeking to reorient and sustain themselves, even in the midst of fear and despair, by knowing they belong to God.

We experience evidence of God's participation in our lives that enhances a sense of belongingness to God through transcendence, that is, God breaking through into our daily life to effect change. Although God's faithfulness to us itself never changes, how we experience God's breaking into everyday life is dynamic—ever evolving and growing. In times of crisis, particularly when all that is familiar has been stripped away, we become ever more vigilant to the signs of God's participation in our lives. In the immediacy of losing or fleeing home, displaced persons search for God to break through in the minute to minute and hour to hour of survival.

Ritual brings all of these aspects of belonging to God together in moments of remembrance when refugees and other displaced persons gain strength and courage not only from the gathered community but also from a host of ancestors who have gone before. Even we in the West call on the "saints"—family members who have died but are held close in memory. The entire Christian community, through scripture and the Eucharist, calls into presence the family of Christ from all ages to shore us up in times of difficulty.

Displacement: No Place to Belong

Refugees and IDPs, victims of violence, war, famine, or disaster, are probably those who first come to mind when we hear the term "displaced." When conflict or famine covers a large region of the country, citizens not only flee home, village, or town but also cross national borders in search of safety. Leaving behind one's homeland is a desperate measure and often results in long-term displacement. What is the difference between a refugee and an IDP?[14]

Angelique, an IDP in Goma, DRC, longs for her place of belonging—for the very people who have rejected and ostracized her after being raped by a gang of eight rebel soldiers one day while working in the fields. As is the frequent and unfortunate custom in rural areas of eastern Congo, rape has caused Angelique's husband to reject her—refuse even to receive her back into the home or allow her to see her five children. Her extended family and community have likewise cast her out. She is now without home, family, or any means of livelihood. She has no place where or people to whom she belongs.

Deng, an elderly refugee from what is now South Sudan, describes his home in his village of Panchad. In contrast to the dry dust of refugee life in the camp in the Kenyan desert, he longingly speaks of the cool waters of the Nile, the white clouds reflecting off its still smooth surface, from which he fished and in which he learned to swim as a child. Simply the idea of so much water in a desert where water is rationed is enough to understand his longing. The crops of peanuts and tall corn in Panchad were plentiful. Memory brings to mind the lush and green places of his homeland as well as the people he loves—a large family and a village of familiar people. For Deng, the deep and lasting loss of belonging came when his land and the home that held memories and meaning were taken away.

The term *refugee* is often used in very broad ways. We might use it to describe generally those in the scenarios above who have been displaced from their homes due to war or violence. Closer to home we can recall hearing about refugees from Hurricane Katrina in the United States who were sent to various places outside of Louisiana for emergency shelter. In a similar way, we referred to the survivors of the 2011 tsunami in Japan as refugees. I discussed the term "conservation refugees" in chapter 4 to describe people displaced due to the conservation of a natural habitat for the mountain gorillas of Uganda. All of these examples are both entirely accurate but also somewhat misleading.

Refugees

The distinguishing factor between refugees and IDPs, as implied in the definition of a refugee, is the loss of a homeland.[15] In the global context, a refugee is defined by the United Nations, or more specifically the UNHCR, which is responsible for care of displaced persons around the world, as one who "owing to a well-founded fear of being persecuted for reasons of race, religion, nationality, membership of a particular social group or political opinion, is outside the country of his nationality, and is unable to, or owing to such fear, is unwilling to avail himself of the protection of that country."[16] *Refugee* is a legal and political term. Individuals must apply for refugee status in order for it to be determined that they fall under the rule of "well-founded fear" and are thus eligible to receive the rights, humanitarian aid first among these, to which they are entitled. Nation states often use the terms *immigrants* and *migrants* to speak of persons fleeing over their borders in search of safety who have not yet obtained status as refugees. In the face of the legal ramifications, this makes some sense. Unfortunately, it is also a shift in language that is misleading and can serve the political agendas of governments that are unwelcoming of newcomers. Immigrant and migrant may move by choice; refugees often endure tragic and fatal consequences because even the possibility of life elsewhere is better than the near certainty of death at home. One may choose to be a migrant; no one chooses to be a refugee.

Implicit in the definition of refugee, and made explicit in the UN Universal Declaration of Human Rights, is the responsibility of nation states to equally protect all of their citizens. But, as I write these words, I am reminded of George Orwell's *Animal Farm*. The famous quote from this novella is perhaps the underlying reality for "equal rights" in terms of equal expectation of safety in the home nations of many of the world's refugees (adapted it for this context): All citizens are equal but some citizens are more equal than others.[17]

Internally Displaced Persons

Like Angelique, persons who flee their immediate home place (house, village, town, city, etc.) but remain within their nation of citizenship are considered by the United Nations to be IDPs and due appropriate care from the nation in which they reside. As is often the case, however, the ability or willingness of nation states to respond is limited or at least complicated by the magnitude and scale of a disaster, corruption, lack of resources, and violence, among other factors. In such cases, aid is sought from the United Nations, nongovernmental organizations (NGOs), and the international community.

The plight of IDPs is a complicated matter. As a loose frame with which to begin our discussion, let us separate IDPs into three categories: long-term, brief, and intermittent. Each carries its own set of difficulties, unique impact on the community, and understanding of belonging. Long-term displacement within the country of origin often occurs in conditions of natural disaster, including drought and famine, whether caused by human or natural factors. Citizens may move from one region of a country to another in an attempt to find resources lacking in their home area.

If the situation is dire enough, it can become a national issue, forcing citizens to flee across borders into neighboring countries, at which point IDPs become refugees. Internal displacement of this nature is seen frequently in the developing world where subsistence farming or the raising of small herds of cattle remains the primary food source for individuals and communities. Recurring drought and violence in Ethiopia and southern Somalia consistently displace hundreds of thousands—millions over the years—causing people to flee to refugee camps both within and outside of their countries.

The tsunami in the Indian Ocean in 2004 and even Hurricane Katrina in 2005 in the United States are examples of long-term internal displacement in other parts of the world prompted by natural disasters. We cannot overlook the fact that the abilities of national governments to respond to disasters that befall their citizens vary considerably, though, as we saw in the case of Katrina, even when resources are plentiful, they may not always be used well or efficiently. Both scarcity and incompetence can result in devastating consequences for the most vulnerable, who face displacement.

Conflict is another primary cause of long-term internal displacement. Two such contexts in which I have particular experience are South Sudan and eastern Congo. Many refugees in Sudan were displaced by the war for over fifteen years. Even after repatriation by the UNHCR beginning in 2006, thousands stayed in refugee camps because conditions for life continued to be so dire in Sudan. In spite of repatriation assistance from the UNHCR, most among those who did return faced substantial limitations of food, medicine, and shelter, a situation that was complicated by the limited presence of NGOs to which to turn for assistance.

During my recent visit to Goma in eastern DRC, an upsurge in rebel conflict swept through North Kivu creating a new wave of thousands of displaced villagers. The spontaneous IDP camp in Kibumba, mentioned in chapter 3, emerged as a result of this influx. The scarcity of resources to meet basic needs and constant chaotic atmosphere made these roadside "camps" vastly different from the official IDP camp, Mugunga, located on the other side of the city. Mugunga is a sprawling camp "repurposed" from its use sheltering refugees from Rwanda in 1994 to now accommodate IDPs from many areas within the DRC, especially from North and South Kivu, which are notable for ongoing insecurity.

This area closer to Goma is also no stranger to atrocious, severe conflict. But its timing can be sporadic and unpredictable. It is not uncommon for some citizens to flee their villages only to return again within a few months once the immediate danger is over (this is true in other regions of eastern DRC as well). Most flee only far enough to be safe enough, that is, out of range of the immediate threat but close enough to return periodically to check on crops in the fields. This is, of course, done at great risk to one's life, yet the greater risk is for an entire family to go hungry in the long term. These spontaneous settlements along the routes closest to their home villages create a tension between IDPs laying claim to a location that allows them periodic access to their homes, as well as a quick return once the fighting has moved on, and the preferred logistical resources for crisis support already set in place by aid agencies, such as Mugunga.

These are situations without perfect answers that continue to challenge IDPs and humanitarian agencies alike.

Exclusion from Belonging

As a refugee crosses through "no man's land"—that is, the space between borders that is neither *here*, citizen, nor *there*, foreigner—it marks the beginning of a sometimes decades-long journey to negotiate the loss of belonging. An IDP or refugee is perpetually in a state of being an outsider or foreigner. I focus, here, on the category of *foreigner* as a mechanism used by social and political systems to impede, often intentionally, a sense of belonging for refugees and IDPs. Of course, there are displaced persons, including refugees and IDPs, who find communities of belonging outside of their home places, just as there are numerous communities around the world that embrace the displaced. It is not my goal to diminish these successes. Likewise, some category of other is necessary to maintain national borders and to determine to whom each nation is legally accountable as citizens. Nonetheless, the notion of foreigner and all of its negative connotations can and does seep into personal and political infrastructures, conscious and unconscious, creating habitual acts of exclusion against others based solely on difference.

In the United States the concept of the foreigner is used in at least two ways, though both are categories of social exclusion. The first refers to one who does not have the status of citizen—the requirement for legal belonging—nor, consequently, its rights and privileges. This may be applied also to immigrants who have legal permission to be in the country.[18] The second and less formal use is imbued with racist overtones and intended to make ethnic or cultural distinctions that imply one is an undesired and unwelcome outsider.

The ambiguous *foreigner* has become a political target of disdain that threatens the cohesion of the American ideal. This is the underlying thread in ongoing political debate about immigration and how much we are able to control the "path to citizenship." The foreigner that is the object of disdain may be the American citizen for whom an ethnic distinction happens to be apparent, a legal immigrant who chooses to live a life in this country, or one who has crossed borders without permission in hope of feeding his family. The designation of foreigner reveals an ethical and moral failure in our culture to welcome and care for the stranger in our midst.

The Outsider

In the context of IDPs, *outsider* can be a difficult social category, as foreigner is for refugees, and is guided by complex cultural rules of response, frequently complicated further by violence, which can evoke compassion or ridicule and fear. It is often easier to feel one's exclusion as an outsider long before being able to define why one has been labeled as such. Mary, described in the beginning of the chapter, is an excellent example of someone who struggles as an outsider. Like the people of southern Uganda, Mary was a native Ugandan who, with or without a passport, few would deny was a rightful citizen. Uganda was her home place. But violence and social corruption within her country had so invaded the culture as to create a rigid boundary of self and other, insider and outsider. Under these circumstances, even good and caring people can become suspicious and fearful of those who are unfamiliar.

Sexual violence in conflict zones can create particularly tragic boundaries of exclusion. Perhaps one of the most outrageous examples emerged out of eastern Congo, especially in rural areas, where husbands reject wives who have been raped, like Angelique. Many women who are victims of rape by gangs of rebel soldiers are cast out by their husbands and forbidden to see children or extended family. Although it is easy to blame the husbands—and to be sure, they deserve a large portion of it—this custom is so ingrained in the rural culture that even extended family members of both genders may feel obligated to join in the act of rejecting a woman who has been raped. Women become outsiders within their own families.

When we view the notions of foreigner or outsider and their impact on the characteristics for belonging (reciprocity, orienting effect, dynamic quality, and practices of remembrance), we begin to get a sense of the complexity of alienation and rejection with which refugees, immigrants, and other strangers must contend in this country and others.

Failure of Reciprocity

The social notion of foreigner challenges belonging at every point. As we saw in the case of Mary, citizens often resist any sense of *reciprocity* toward foreigners whether refugees, immigrants, or citizens of another ethnicity. In other words, there is no sense of attachment, mutual desire, or even, it seems, responsibility to receive the other in need. Rather, blatant rejection and animosity are more often the response. What has become known as the Australian Papua New Guinea (PNG) Solution is a case in point. In the summer of 2013, Australian Prime Minister Kevin Rudd negotiated an agreement with the prime minister of Papua New Guinea, Peter O'Neill. Australia would send all asylum seekers (most from Iran, Afghanistan, Sri Lanka, and Pakistan), even those determined to be legitimate refugees, to PNG, where they would be held in detention until it was established whether they would be permanently resettled in PNG or returned to their country of origin.[19] There could hardly be a more comprehensive act of rejection than this. Certainly, the matter of men, women, and children—or *boat people* as they have become known—traversing dangerous waters in overfilled boats is complex. The prime minister has focused on the criminal act of "trafficking" refugees and making the distinction between those who arrive as "legitimate" refugees fleeing persecution and economic refugees, leaving by choice, for better economic opportunity. In the final act, though, this distinction is a random one—neither is welcome in Australia.

The United States faces similar challenges with asylum seekers arriving on the coast of Florida in dangerously overfilled watercraft or crossing southern borders in flight from violence and economic hardship. We, too, place men, women, and children in prison-like detention centers until their status can be clarified.

For refugees and IDPs, social and political exclusion can be felt on every level with or without obvious reason or explanation. *Foreigner* may also carry strong political implications as well. National institutions are often strongly vested in defining the boundaries between citizen and foreigner and may, admittedly or not, target certain others with ongoing exclusionary practices. Rather than allowing for integration into a new orienting and stabilizing community, designation as a foreigner attempts to misdirect and deter the refugee or IDP from claiming any sense of belonging.

Denial of the Right to Belong

Citizenship is itself a category of belonging that carries certain legal benefits such as residency, some degree of protection under the law, and the right to expect justice from the nation to which one belongs. Means of determining citizenship vary from nation to nation. The most common criteria include birthright *(jus soli)*—where one is born—or blood inheritance *(jus sanguines)* though some nations sort out issues of citizenship differently. In every case, rules of citizenship are meant to define who belongs and who does not. Post-conflict lands face particular challenges in this regard.

When South Sudan became a new nation in 2011, it determined that both birthright and blood inheritance constituted a right to citizenship.[20] After decades of war, displacement, and repatriation, however, the greater challenge fell to citizens to prove they could meet the criteria.[21] Few in rural South Sudan would have documentation of their birth in South Sudan, such as a birth certificate. Moreover, those fleeing the war or born in locations outside of South Sudan would not likely have much official written evidence of lineage linking them to South Sudanese ancestors. In light of this, South Sudan has made some modifications to their policy such as allowing for testimony of witnesses who can verify one's relationship to a citizen.[22] But even locating these witnesses is a challenge after communities have been dispersed by conflict.

The criteria for who should be excluded, perhaps a particular necessity in formerly occupied post-conflict lands, includes "not 'looking' South Sudanese; originating from outside the capital city Juba; belonging to a small or cross-border tribe; or having lived outside South Sudan during the war against Khartoum."[23] After so many years of war, these criteria are likely to apply to a large section of the population. In its defense, the government states that these demanding criteria are "to prevent foreigners from deceitfully gaining nationality and undermining the state."[24] This is a tragic turn of events for thousands of South Sudanese who survived years of war and exile and who lived to see their homeland become a nation—only to be told that they do not belong.

To make matters even more desperate, South Sudan has withdrawn its agreement to allow dual citizenship with Sudan. And Sudan has nullified the Sudanese citizenship of South Sudanese nationals—even those who have lived in Khartoum for generations. Those in Khartoum with proof of citizenship in South Sudan can obtain appropriate documentation, such as visas, to stay in Sudan. If none can be acquired, these persons are treated as foreign nationals. Bronwen Manby, program advisor for a governance monitoring and advocacy group, observes,

> The loss of Sudanese nationality already carries significant practical consequences. People of South Sudanese origin who have been living in Sudan for decades, or even generations, have now lost the rights and entitlements linked to their Sudanese nationality. Many of these people are in a desperate situation, as they have lost jobs in the public and private sector, and face difficulties in asserting their rights to their homes and other property (the constitution only protects the right to property for Sudanese nationals). Children have been refused entry to schools or treatment by clinics.[25]

Overnight, citizens became foreigners.

Official documentation of one's citizenship is evidence of belonging and the expectation of participation in the rights and laws of a given nation. But few refugees or IDPs, especially from poor, rural areas, have passports or other legal documents, let alone have them on hand when fleeing for their lives. Even in the United States, unless someone has traveled outside the country, and plenty do not, a person would not normally, if asked, be able to produce identity papers or a passport allowing her to legally cross a border. One year after independence, the *Guardian* newspaper reported that the progress of the government toward solving this problem was slow.[26] Progress was interrupted entirely in 2013 when a new conflict erupted, this time a civil war between the Dinka and Nuer tribes. Even with emerging peace accords, the continued threat of instability makes both citizenship and a sense of belonging a vexing problem for all.

Millions of refugees and IDPs around the world invest an immense amount of time and energy waiting for documents that will verify some act of belonging. In lieu of passports and proof of citizenship, refugees and IDPs cling to any type of documentation in the effort to lend authority to their plight. In the refugee camp, identity papers and food vouchers offer assurance that a person has the right to a ration of food. A valuable asset, these vouchers are passed along to others in need when a refugee leaves the camp. So essential are these bequeathed tickets that when I was in Kakuma Refugee Camp, riots erupted just prior to a census in order to prevent the reduction of vouchers. But these vouchers will not help someone cross the border or obtain work in another country.

Management of Unease

There is a reason that most cultures and religions over the centuries have developed customs that strongly encourage and provide instructions regarding the protection and welcome of foreigners. Such traditions tell us that foreigners have long been held as highly suspicious and, as such, strongly distrusted. But since the attacks of September 11, 2001, and the subsequent worldwide war on terrorism led by the United States, the foreigner has had a particularly difficult existence no matter where she goes.

There is no question that the events of 9/11 were pivotal for the United States, which had to that point remained relatively untouched by long-term violence on its homeland. Unlike other countries that live with ongoing monthly death tolls in the hundreds or thousands, the United States had been relatively unscathed. On that fateful morning, the world did not change so much as the people of the United States got a glimpse of violence on a scale that others have had to contend with for some time. This observation is in no way intended to diminish the magnitude of loss endured on that day. Nor does it overlook the loss of thousands more suffered through the wars in Iraq and Afghanistan. But the question I ask is, why did this event not elicit more expressions of empathy with other citizens in countries that have suffered such loss? Instead, the immediate fear and anger were so quickly channeled into public and political discourse that extreme rejection and exclusion of the foreigner became an unstoppable sociopolitical force.

This fear has been capitalized on through what political sociologist Didier Bigo and others call the *management of unease*. This, further complicated by the fluid boundaries of globalization, has led to the securitization of migration.[27] Politicians, Bigo proposes, use the political narrative of national security to problematize the foreigner/immigrant/migrant as a threat in order to gain power that has been lost in other areas. Bigo reminds us of the complex nature of the insider-outsider dialectic that moves beyond the fear provoked by an unknown outsider or a cultural notion of difference. What is at stake for politicians is power. This becomes a strong motivator for a narrative of protection. This narrative is presented, he claims, as a nation conceived of as a body or container, the integrity of which must be protected from harm by outsiders. Bigo writes,

> The concepts of sovereignty, security, and borders always structure our thought as if there existed a "body"—an "envelope," or "container"—differentiating one polity from another. The state justifies itself as the only political order possible as soon as it is accepted that sovereignty, law and order, and a single body are the prerequisite for

peace and homogeneity. It justifies the "national" identity that the state has achieved through territorialization of its order, by a cutting up of borders.

He continues, "The framing of the state as a body endangered by migrants is a political narrative activated for the purpose of political games in ways that permit each politician to distance himself or herself from other politicians, but within the same rules of the game."[28] We see this demonstrated in the United States through use of the term *immigrant*, which has become the acceptable political term to cover all categories of persons deemed the foreign other, including refugees. In Europe and elsewhere, *migrant* is a more familiar term used for the same purpose. This shift in narrative is accomplished by professionalizing securitization through national and international organizations then shaping the political language to the benefit of those in power and to the detriment of those classified as economic, cultural, or physical threats.

The symbolic narrative of a body in need of protection is especially relevant in the United States given the events of 9/11. The images of the airplanes flying into the World Trade Center, arguably the financial center of the United States, or the Pentagon, the military center, leave us with the symbolic image of the foreigner penetrating the American body and psyche. What has now become habitual fear-mongering by political representatives is the attempt to use fear to gain power.

Lack of Remembrance—No Shared History

A designation as foreigner, official or otherwise, is simultaneously a rejection of any claim to a common lineage or heritage and a resistance to making new paths of remembrance. This is an ironic but common political position taken by many in the United States—even with a national history of ancestors who were nearly all foreigners.

When it is not possible for citizens to seek or expect protection from their nation of origin, during times of famine, conflict, or war—declared or undeclared—they also have, according to the UN Universal Declaration of Human Rights, the right to seek protection from other nations. But the practical reality remains that care for the other is always influenced by the resources within particular borders and their particular desire to assist or not. In the absence of protection granted by citizenship, refugees, IDPs, and other immigrants must rely on being a part of the human community as guided by the generally accepted notion of universal human rights.

The concept of universal human rights created by the United Nations in 1948, though couched in terms of the universal, is largely the result of Western ideals that appeal to a particular kind of belonging that its authors believe should transcend traditional borders of place.

Resilience of the Displaced

People have the wonderfully resilient capacity to create pockets of belonging under even the most difficult of conditions. Oddly enough, I think here of trees. I have spent considerable time with elders from South Sudan. In their home villages, when the chief and assorted elder leaders gather, it was always under the nearest tree large enough to provide shade for all. Certainly, the function of such an act is not so deep in meaning—the shade keeps the sun at bay. But it is also a time when they live into their positions of trust and leadership within the community. In Kakuma Refugee Camp, only a few hundred miles from the equator, the continued practice made even more practical sense. And, after more than fifteen years of refugee life, the tree also became a symbol, an unacknowledged talisman, of the extraordinarily ordinary practices of daily life at home in Sudan. It is not surprising, then, that when a small village worth of refugees from South Sudan moved into an aptly named apartment complex in Nashville, Tennessee, called Tennessee Village, the first gathering place was under a tree in the center of the complex. With air-conditioned apartments in plentiful supply, the need to gather here was no longer practical; as a matter of fact, it was often quite impractical in the humid heat of a southern summer. But the sense of belonging it evoked for a new generation of elders embedded in a new culture was profound. This is the difference between Anthony Giddens's modern Western notion of an "I" and the tribal "we" in the lives of refugees.

Authorities, unfortunately, found this public gathering of foreign black men to be a threatening display. Another ethnic group that also occupied a large portion of the apartment complex resented the gatherings and interpreted them as "gang like." This is evidence of both the tragic consequences when contexts of belonging are not shared and the corruption of a just social order besieged by racism and fear.

The Tabitha Center in the Congo is another, though rather different, pocket of belonging that helps women build resilience in the face of daunting odds.[29] Without marketable skills or other means to provide for themselves, women in the Congo who have been rejected by their families due to rape are at risk of further injury or even death. Some make their way to the larger cities where, as outsiders of a different sort, they find compassion and assistance from churches and local aid agencies. I met many such women who had come to the city seeking food and shelter at the church-run Tabitha Center. This center, and others like it, have taken it upon themselves to offer life-skills training or micro-loan programs so that the women can begin to earn a living. For those who come with children, these centers also supplement school support and food when possible. In their efforts to learn and then share these new skills with other women who arrive in need, community forms and many women begin to feel a new sense of belonging.

These same communities can also be, perhaps surprisingly, generous resources toward those fleeing recurring battles in the surrounding region. While I was conducting research in Goma, the capital city of North Kivu, M23, a rebel faction of the Congolese army fighting Congolese government forces for control of Goma, came within fifteen miles of Goma's farthest city edge. IDPs fleeing from the fighting arrived on foot to Kibumba. At first by the hundreds, then thousands, IDPs took up shelter in schoolhouses, churches, and open fields. To my unaccustomed eye, it looked as though every space was equally fair game for squatters' rights. After interviewing several newly arrived folks, I learned that each IDP "community" had an elected leader whose job was to meet with local village elders and negotiate for needed goods like shelter, food, water, and even work. Of course, the villagers themselves were poor and of meager means, but they nonetheless engaged in a process of tending to vital needs with an intention of good will. Instead of treating the new arrivals as outsiders to be rejected, they were received as neighbors in need.

Conclusion

Mary's experience introduces us to the question of belonging—an essential function of the home place. In particular, her experience of rejection reflects the failure of the reciprocal nature of belonging—we claim our places of belonging but they must claim us as well. Belonging orients us toward our sense of identity; without it we can become unmoored, even paralyzed. The hopefulness of belonging can be its dynamic nature; our sense of belonging can change over time, allowing us to move and grow. For refugees this means that a new home place and a new sense of belonging *are* possible. To bind the old and new, the past and the present, belonging depends on practices of remembering to close the gaps.

A sad reality, however, is that far more refugees and IDPs fall victim to the profound social exclusion—rejection—like Mary of being a foreigner. The Age of Terrorism has made the "foreigner" a global enemy, and the situation is only worsening. On the one hand, terrorism has become a vehicle for radical Islamist voices that turn the Western foreigner into an image that is utilized to gain power through fear and violence. On the other hand, ironically, Western politicians use terrorism, the "Age of Terrorism," as a vehicle to turn displaced foreigners into an image that can also be used to invoke fear and garner political power.

In this time and political climate how is a community of faith to respond to the displaced foreigner? We are torn between succumbing to the clamoring of a politically induced god of fear that compels us to reject the others among us who are most in need and embracing the God of invitation, welcome, and neighborly care. In response I borrow liberally when I echo the imperative put before the tribes of Israel in the book of Joshua: "Choose this day whom you will serve" (Josh. 24:15b). We cannot serve both.

six

WAR AND HOME—NO SAFE PLACE

My name is Huerta. I am an American Soldier and I have PTSD.
I refused to admit it to myself even when the Army doctors told
me I had it in 2004. I refused to talk to anyone about it even when
Army health professionals told me I needed to in 2005. I was afraid
how Army leadership would react if I had that on my record. I was a
Soldier, I was tough, I just needed to rub the patch and drive on.[1]
——Major Carlos Huerta

I don't feel comfortable at home anymore. My threat tolerance and
response to perceived threats is so finely tuned that I felt safer in
Iraq. Here, every stranger looks like a possible threat. If I am driving
near my house and a car pulls in behind me, I will take several extra
turns to make sure that I am not being followed. When I am home
I feel like I am being watched. At night I leave the lights off in my
house and the blinds drawn so no one can see inside.[2]
——Anonymous

Like refugees and other civilians exposed to conflict around the
world, few soldiers who participate on the frontlines of combat escape untouched by the experience.[3] Since the end of the Iraq war and
the return of troops from Iraq and Afghanistan, we in the United
States have been confronted with the age-old reality that traumatic
injury, whether physical, psychological, or spiritual, can lead to a
forced displacement of its own kind. If we can resist being distracted
by the politics of war, important though they are, we will be better
able to hear the day-to-day stories of soldiers like Major Huerta who
are returning to find that home is no longer what it once was.

While much about the horror of war never seems to change, doctors and other care providers, even in the military, are realizing new

challenges in the old problem of soldiers struggling to come home from war. For the first time, doctors are becoming aware that even mild blows to the head, once thought to be insignificant, can cause serious brain injury resulting in debilitating, long-term physiological impairment. More soldiers are committing suicide than recorded in past conflicts, raising serious questions about the psychological effects of combat, multiple deployments, and how these are or are not being mitigated effectively. The rise of sexual violence toward women, or at least the rise in reporting such violence, within the ranks of the military reveals the magnitude of violence women face from fellow soldiers—long before they ever meet the enemy in a warzone.[4]

Post-traumatic stress disorder (PTSD) has been a matter of particular concern. Some outside of the military and a few within have begun to question whether PTSD, the emotional and physiological effects of traumatic experiences as designated by the *Diagnostic and Statistical Manual*, the classic diagnosis for combat trauma used since the early 1980s, is sufficient.[5] Some psychologists and now clergy and other spiritual caregivers are introducing the concept of *moral injury* to the conversation in new ways as an alternative or additional aspect of injury resulting from combat. The feeling of remorse, guilt, or shame for having injured or killed another person, moral injury can result not only from acts of military misconduct but also from harm inflicted by soldiers under traditional rules of engagement. This is a response to actions that run contrary to religious and social morals deeply embedded in the meaning framework of an individual. We are faced with the question of whether a "victim"-based psychiatric diagnosis (i.e., PTSD) can remain adequate amid the reality that "perpetrating" the injury or death of another, even when sanctioned as appropriate under rules of engagement for combat, creates its own kind of injury.

After returning home from combat, many soldiers must confront the effects of PTSD and/or moral injury, which can leave them continually facing battles long since fought that rise again to the surface—but this time without any fellow soldiers to help negotiate the battlefield. For some, underlying moral questions arise from harming other persons in the course of battle and can give way to feelings of shame, guilt, and self-judgment. These are emotional, spiritual, and social displacements that can greatly impact veterans' ability to trust once-familiar places and imperil their sense of security in their home places.

To be sure, soldiers must endure other more recognizable forms of displacement as well. Before even reaching the combat zone, soldiers must separate from loved ones. By virtue of joining a volunteer army, theirs is not a forced displacement, but neither is this separation an easy task nor is it without great impact on personnel and families alike.[6] Over time and rather ironically, the combat arena itself becomes a type of home place—though, for most, it is one of necessity rather than desire.[7] This inevitably makes for a difficult separation after a tour of duty ends or when a soldier returns stateside after injury. At that point, a soldier must leave behind this adopted "home place" and especially a "family" of brother/sister soldiers with whom he or she has bonded in intense ways under extraordinary circumstances.

We have looked at the lives of the indigenous Batwa displaced from the mountains of Uganda. Refugees fleeing war in Sudan and the Congo were our focus in chapter 5. In this chapter, I am asking readers to consider expanded and less literal notions of home place and displacement. As we have seen in the opening narratives, the effects of trauma can deeply influence a person's relationship not only to other people but also to places and memories, making it difficult to feel "at home" even in familiar spaces. This prompts me to ask how the home place helps define *safety* or *a sense of security*, and how the multiple forms of displacement faced by American soldiers returning from war impact their ability to accurately comprehend what feels or is safe—particularly as it relates to cases of trauma and moral injury. Ultimately, for some veterans, these physical, emotional, and spiritual effects can become so overwhelming that family relationships break down and the literal loss of home becomes a reality.

Sense of Security as a Function of Home

From the earliest days of life, the home place is essential to developing a sense of security with which to confront the world. A healthy sense of security develops primarily out of trust—trust in, among other things, the reasonable reliability of significant people (or caregivers) and the surrounding environment that constitutes the home place.

A Secure Holding Environment

Psychoanalyst D. W. Winnicott's concept of a *holding environment* as essential to the psychological development of a child, as well as the successful therapeutic relationship, may offer a helpful analogy for understanding the deep sense of security that home provides to many. I turn to Winnicott precisely because of his efforts to hold together the tension between relationships and the environment within a complex theory of human development. It is this same tension we find ourselves attempting to hold together in the effort to understand the home place—which is both relationship and place. The terms he has coined, such as holding environment, are both literally and metaphorically powerful.[8]

Of the holding environment, Winnicott wrote, "The term 'holding' is used here to denote not only the actual physical holding of the infant, but also the total environmental provision prior to the concept of *living with*. In other words, it refers to a three-dimensional or space relationship with time gradually added."[9] Literary scholar Brooke Hopkins makes note of Winnicott's emphasis on the power of space, particularly the home space, to influence one's sense of security in the world. He notes, "Home for Winnicott is not just a physical structure with four walls and a roof. It is a total environment, both physical and psychic . . . which provides protection as well as a space for growth"; this inner security allows a person to enter the "wider framework of the outside world *without ever entirely leaving home behind.*"[10]

Psychologically, the holding environment describes the function of an infant's, then child's, environment to create a sense of security and well-being relevant to the child's recognition of self and others in an expanding world. Beginning inside the mother's body and extending outward to a primary caregiver, then to a second caregiver, and so on, the environment of the growing child continues to nurture and protect. This includes "good enough" care from a primary caregiver and others as well as the relatively predictable built and natural environment of the home. The result of a good enough holding environment is a confident and secure child able to push back, even rebel in appropriate ways, as he or she grows.[11]

Yet, healthy nurturance and protection of children are not the only consideration to bear in mind. Winnicott pointed out that "certainly parents that are over-protective cause distress in their children, just as parents who cannot be reliable make their children muddled and frightened."[12] We see this today in the form of over-parenting, or helicopter parenting, in which parents are overly involved in the activities of a child's life in an effort to ensure the best possible outcomes. The result is, most often, children who grow into overly anxious, entitled, and narcissistic adults.[13] It is a difficult balance, Winnicott observed, to allow enough protection *and* enough freedom such that the child will flourish: "We hope that each child will gradually acquire a sense of security. There must build up inside each child a belief in something[,] not only something that is good but also something that is reliable and durable, or that recovers after having been hurt or allowed to perish."[14] Further, he noted,

> When we offer security we do two things at once. On the one hand, because of our help the child is safe from the unexpected, from innumerable unwelcome intrusions, and from a world that is not yet known or understood. And also, on the other hand the child is protected by us from his or her own impulses and from the effects that these impulses might produce. . . . The infant that has known security will begin to carry the expectation that he or she won't be let down.[15]

In other words, through a secure holding environment, the child learns a certain degree of trust about home, people, and the surrounding world. Winnicott was quick to point out that security does not take away the frustrations that should greet the healthy, exploring child who encounters new and unknown elements of an expanding environment. Rather, it reinforces a sense of confidence and trust in spite of them.

Holding Back the Forces of Chaos

The basic trust that gives a child a sense of security is also foundational in adulthood for sustaining what sociologist Anthony Giddens calls *ontological security*, which he describes as "a sense of continuity and order in events, including those not directly within the perceptual environment of the individual."[16] The notion of ontological security has a long lineage in social theory. Giddens builds on the work of Robert David Laing, a Scottish psychiatrist who used the term "ontological insecurity" to describe the interior world of those with mental illness.[17] Giddens, who also has a background in psychology, suggests that trust in the reliability of human relationships and the surrounding environment plays a fundamental role in the very complex ways humans manage to hold back the existential anxiety that is part and parcel of being creatures of limited power in an unpredictable and unforgiving world.

The fragility of human life and relative helplessness with which we must face the uncontrollable forces of the world leave us perpetually on the threshold of chaos. If, indeed, we were forced to face the full effects of this underlying vulnerability, we would become paralyzed, unable to function in our day-to-day lives. This lurking chaos is largely attributed to an existential awareness of our limited nature—an existential anxiety—and has compelled much conversation among theology, psychology, and sociology, offering theories for just how it is we can hold back this chaos, or existential anxiety, in order to carry on with our lives.

Sociologists Ann Dupuis and David C. Thorns interpret ontological security, the answer to existential anxiety, to have three essential elements: it is felt when persons have a sense of control over their environment and feel "free from surveillance, free to be themselves and at ease, in the deepest psychological sense, in a world that might at times be experienced as threatening and uncontrollable."[18] Interestingly, these are the very things most disrupted for those suffering the effects of trauma and moral injury.

Giddens suggests that one of the factors in creating an ontological security is a practical consciousness through which we bracket the underlying chaos of our daily lives. He notes, "On the other side of what might appear to be quite trivial aspects of day to day action and discourse, chaos lurks. And, this chaos is not just disorganization, but the loss of a sense of the very reality of things and of other persons."[19] He suggests that "natural attitudes in everyday life . . . bracket out questions about ourselves, others and the object world which have to be taken for granted in order to keep on with everyday activity."[20] This bracketing is similar in purpose to psychological defenses, the failure of which can lead to mental breakdowns, which Winnicott described as "theoretically a state of chaos."[21]

These defenses, or this notion of bracketing, may give us at least two ways to understand how we maintain what psychologist Ronnie Janoff-Bulman suggests are the core assumptions that help us negotiate interactions and events in the world around us. Most people, she argues, operate with three core assumptions: the world is benevolent, the world is meaningful, and the self is worthy.[22] Operating within this assumptive framework, we are able to maintain a level of ease with the world—a sense of security about our place in it. Yet, living with these core assumptions requires a certain bracketing of world events or at least of how we understand these events to affect individuals and ourselves in particular. Traumatic events such as those encountered in combat, according to Janoff-Bulman, create a crisis that ultimately shatters these assumptions. This paradigm may be especially apt for soldiers compelled into combat as a patriotic response to 9/11. For these soldiers, entering the warzone was an attempt to bring a just and right force to the fight of good against evil. Such patriotic responses, especially when unexamined, are likely further fueled by national narratives—narratives of empire as pastoral theologian Ryan LaMothe calls them—that promote additional assumptions, those of, "[American] exceptionalism, superiority, and innocence."[23] But the realities of war are seldom clear-cut. Rather, they are unpredictable, senseless, and filled with rough edges. The symptoms of PTSD are the mind's attempt to integrate a new framework through which to interpret these unpredictable and often senseless traumatic experiences that highlight the failure of these closely held assumptions.

Although Janoff-Bulman does not move in this direction, I suggest in addition that for a person of faith, the failure of these assumptions can reveal a spiritual chaos as well as a psychological one. The loss of a belief that the world is trustworthy and good can prompt the question of God's trustworthiness or faithfulness. The loss of a meaningful world throws question on how we understand God if the world is random and without purpose. The question of the self as worthy points to a question of moral agency. If events of this world do not correlate with the good or bad I bring to it, then I have no control. The person of faith is left to ask, is God in control? If so, then bad events can be seen as divine punishment; if not, one must wrestle with the chaos of a world in which neither God nor self is in control and evil is random. These are not necessarily bad questions to ask but they can create a severe crisis of meaning, especially when accompanied by psychological crisis. Psychiatrist Judith Herman in her classic book *Trauma and Recovery* frames it this way: "Traumatic events call into question basic human relationships. They undermine the belief systems that give meaning to human experience. They violate the victim's faith in a natural or divine order and cast the victim into a state of existential crisis."[24] In this state, all defenses and attempts at bracketing the chaos have failed as it spills through into everyday life, making any degree of security impossible. Here, even the once safe home is no longer a familiar place.

Although hers is a particularly Western theory, I find Janoff-Bulman's work especially helpful for two reasons. First, she includes a moral element that, with some adaptation in theory, may become helpful for those struggling with moral injury due to war or other circumstances. Also, she finds the theoretical *purpose* behind symptoms of PTSD, which affects so many combat veterans returning home, to be largely adaptive rather than pathological.[25] This, of course, is far from the actual experience of the symptoms, which she recognizes are painful, difficult—even horrible—and sometimes debilitating. But we may also understand them to function as highly adaptive attempts at integrating difficult experiences that fall outside the framework of our assumptive worlds. In short, they can be signs of resilience. Recognizing this resilience can help shift the paradigm from being victim-centered to survivor-centered. Interestingly, Janoff-Bulman does not fully make this link in her own work as she continues to focus on the nature of the victim. This is more than just a shift in semantics. As we will see shortly, in the life of a veteran, the conceptual shift from victim to survivor of PTSD is profound and can be life-saving.

With all of this said, there remains an important disclaimer. While many soldiers' experiences of combat may be of a traumatic nature, not all result in a diagnosis of PTSD. Some can, indeed, have a memory of traumatic events and not have PTSD. The secular, very popular, and quite overused assumption of PTSD for all things deemed "traumatic" can cause us to overlook signs of natural resilience or even sometimes cloud the very real need for care. Many people living under extreme conditions, including war, have vivid, sometimes reoccurring dreams of fearful moments. These may decrease in intensity and frequency over time, or not. For some, the memories are a visceral reliving of events themselves. There is a spectrum of reactions to the intense emotional, physical, and spiritual experience of combat. But caution should be used in pathologizing what may be a very appropriate response to extreme conditions. Of course, one of the most significant determining diagnostic questions is, to what degrees do the memories or other residue from the experience interfere with daily life?

The psychological and spiritual effects caused by trauma and moral injury are complex, to be sure. But what becomes clear, as demonstrated in the narratives of combat veterans who have returned home, is that primary underlying effects include fear, insecurity, and isolation. The *victim* of PTSD is helpless in a world of unpredictable danger.

Many veterans struggle with having killed or injured others and may have feelings of shame and self-judgment as a *perpetrator* of harm. These individuals know all too well the consequences of no longer believing their act of violence and harm is justified. The consequence for those suffering moral injury is also a type of insecurity in which one can find no moral safe space—no way to be at peace with self, others, or God. For these persons, self-judgment, shame, and fear of judgment from others become the mainstays of day-to-day life, threatening home and relationships, especially with loved ones. Some live on the threshold of both PTSD and moral injury, unable to negotiate what the world has become or to push back the inner chaos that ensues. There is no safe place to turn. In the midst of this, how does one find trust in home again?

Finding a Relatively Safe Space

Even though I was home, I never left the battlefield. . . . The home
I came back to was not the one I left. My Family was not the same,
I was not the same. I felt that something important was stolen from
me and there was nobody I could talk to about it. Nobody except the
guys I was over there with. I would look for combat patches, look
for buddies to talk to, look for the Soldiers who went through what I
went through and felt the same way I did. There were many of us.[26]
—Major Carlos Huerta

At least in Iraq I had an armored vehicle and body armor,
and I carried and operated several weapon systems.
Most importantly, we had skilled soldiers watching each

others' backs. At home, I have none of that. . . . If I had
a choice, I would still be in Iraq or in Afghanistan.[27]
—Anonymous

In combat, soldiers have a unique resource that serves as a powerful "holding community," to draw from Winnicott's language, which
helps mitigate the full effects of living in the reality that no actual
safe space exists on the frontlines. Here, the contested and conflict-
ing categories of victim and perpetrator must be held at bay, or the
full force of all that lies beneath them will come tumbling in, making
effectiveness—and staying alive—difficult.

Other than the sheer practicality of literal protection within a
group of fellow soldiers, such a community often serves as a temporary replacement for the home place—that which defines the *relatively* safe spaces. I have previously described the idea of creating
"relative safety" to mean a lessening of danger through cooperative
participation.[28] Especially in national volunteer armies, the community of soldiers temporarily replaces all other social communities
by establishing a relatively safe holding place in which those with a
moral obligation of care for one another "serve to create a temporary
psychic space, and when possible a physical space, created between
individuals (or a group) out of mutual belief and trust, the result of
which is of positive psychological benefit."[29]

Here I am borrowing a concept developed from my work with a
Sudanese refugee population. I can recall hearing the stories of the
Lost Boy refugees and others, some of whom had also been rebel
fighters, describe the role of their "brothers." While there may be
limits to how we compare the Lost Boy refugees of Sudan with
American soldiers, I think there is a close parallel between the relational brotherhood among the Lost Boys and the incredibly close
bond among American soldiers who have fought together.

A distinct role of this combat family pushes the notion of relative
safety to its extreme. The "buddy" that stands next to a person in
the middle of a firefight defines relative safety by at once watching

the other's flank and also stepping into the same chaos of potential death. The intensity of each combat moment leaves an imprint on participants. Only those standing in that moment can know the specific context—the threats as they emerge, the perceptions and misperceptions, all that goes right and all that goes wrong. It is true that all who have known combat share a certain level of understanding, but those in the same battle have the closest level of knowing. That knowing creates an intense emotional bond, and well it should. For within that bond is a means of holding the traumatic psychological and moral chaos created by war.

With the emergence of women in combat roles in the Iraq War, I hope we will see an explicit shift toward inclusion of women soldiers in this pseudo-family and an appropriate shift in the language to reflect it.[30] Unfortunately, women in the military draw at least one similarity with women in the home place—the rate of sexual assault. While women have been generally accepted in combat units and have absorbed the same expectations of protection from their closest combat companions—that they will "watch each others' backs"— the rate of sexual assault of female military personnel belies any real sense of protection. Yet even in families in the home place, women are least safe among the men in their families. Women are more likely to be assaulted/abused by a member of their own families— brothers, uncles, fathers, and so on—than by a stranger. Hence, the notion of relative safety is particularly challenged for women, both civilian and military.

However much soldiers long to see their families again, they also deeply lament the loss of the tight-knit fighting unit, the unspoken understanding among a fighting unit—combat brothers and sisters— of the emotional challenges with which they are dealing, and perhaps even the intensity itself of living life on the edge. It is difficult for family members who have not seen combat to understand how returned soldiers could lament such a dangerous life, nor does culture as a whole give them permission to speak freely of this. Veterans are forced to live in both worlds, one openly, the other silently. To what extent soldiers are able to hold back the world of combat from the everyday depends on many factors including the level of PTSD and moral injury and the presence of a holding community among veterans.

No Safe Place: PTSD

Even though I was home, I never left the battlefield. . . . The home I
came back to was not the one I left. My Family was not the same;
I was not the same. . . . When I close my eyes at night, sometimes
I still see myself picking up the body parts of my Soldiers. I still
see myself holding my Soldiers as they die in my arms on the
battlefield. I still see the blood of Iraqi children spattered all over
my uniform as they take their last breaths due to no fault of their
own. . . . My mind tells me that I did not cause their pain and grief,
but my heart tells me otherwise. . . . Only a Soldier understands
that physically being home doesn't mean coming home.[31]

—Major Carlos Huerta

PTSD can trap a soldier in a continual battle that has no foreseeable end. It leads the psyche to skim the top of a terrible traumatic experience and glean only the very worst, which it tucks away to replay seemingly without warning again and again. Day-to-day life is caught in the onslaught. The soldier is isolated from the home world of family and friends without the benefit of feeling his or her military buddies engaging shoulder to shoulder in the battle. Veterans are not the only ones impacted by the effects of PTSD. On the contrary, loved ones recognize when something is terribly wrong but are often helpless and frustrated, unable to bring comfort or cure. It is particularly sad for families who have long waited for their loved one to finally return to the safety of home, only to realize that for the soldier, there is no such safe place.

The wars in Iraq and Afghanistan have been particularly devastating in terms of the psychological damage to those who have fought. The RAND Center for Military Health Policy Research estimates that upward of 20 percent of veterans returning from Operation

Enduring Freedom (OEF, Afghanistan) and Operation Iraqi Freedom (OIF, Iraq) suffer from PTSD.[32] Only slightly more than half of those soldiers have sought treatment.

PTSD is written about so frequently these days that it seems redundant to list the clinical symptoms, but briefly, the criteria as listed in the *Diagnostic and Statistical Manual* (*DSM-5*) include exposure to a traumatic event that threatens life or injury to self or other, be it actual or perceived, during which one experiences fear or helplessness; persistent and distressing episodes of re-experiencing the event physiologically or through dreams, flashbacks, and so on; an avoidance of things associated with the event; and hypervigilance or other increased arousal of the senses, all of which interfere with daily life. The *DSM* is the diagnostic plumb line against which symptoms for mental illness are judged. It provides a multi-axial system, meaning that it also takes into consideration other conditions that may affect overall patient function and treatment.[33]

While this chapter addresses PTSD in the context of combat trauma, the diagnosis itself includes a broad category of symptoms that can stem from a variety of traumatic stressors. Regardless, all are high-level fear events, particularly ones in which a person's own life or the lives of others have been at risk *and* in which that person has felt a loss of a sense of control or agency—such as being under fire or encountering an improvised explosive device (IED). So it is not only a *fear*-based diagnosis but also a *victim*-based one. This raises a question in the application of a diagnosis of PTSD in the context of those who have inflicted harm on others, especially when it results in death. Mental and emotional injury resulting from such harming of others falls more often under the rubric of moral injury, not a diagnostic category.[34] In other words, the *DSM* does not address issues of shame, guilt, and self-condemnation associated with moral injury. This is an important factor that I discuss further in a moment.

PTSD can be a tragic condition that causes someone to lose trust in self, family, community, and God. For soldiers who return with PTSD, the fundamental sense of trust in themselves and the world is broken. It is especially difficult for those whose views of the war have shifted over time, from one of defending his or her country, inspired by 9/11, to seeing it as a political conflict without purpose. Assumptions about the world are no longer sure, and all is up for grabs. Janoff-Bulman notes,

> Nothing seems to be as they thought, their inner world is in turmoil. Suddenly, the self- and worldviews they had taken for granted are unreliable. They can no longer assume that the world is a good place or that other people are kind and trustworthy. They can no longer assume that the world is meaningful or what happens makes sense. They can no longer assume that they have control over negative outcomes or will reap benefits because they are good people. The very nature of the world and self seems to have changed; neither can be trusted, neither guarantees security.[35]

From a Western, Christian perspective, this shattering of worldviews also affects assumptions of faith. While soldiers from other Christian cultures may respond very differently, veterans with PTSD can lose trust in a faithful God. This notion strikes at the very heart of the Christian message, that is, that even if we cannot be faithful to God, we can trust that God will always be faithful to us. It is nothing less than the feeling of having been abandoned, forsaken, by the very God whose sacrifice of love was to save all. For the veteran caught in this suffering, it feels as if God abandons her because God is not who she believed God to be. PTSD joins with a heartsick despair to shake a person at the spiritual core.

PTSD: Cautions

In general, I am not a fan of the way trauma and PTSD have been introduced into the American vernacular. On the news, riding the subway, on the train, in the grocery store—everywhere people can be overheard laying claim to the *trauma* in their lives, some even "diagnosing" themselves with PTSD. I concede that this may indicate increasing knowledge and decreasing stigma attached to a mental health issue. However, this comes at the cost of often confusing what may be personally traumatic in the sense of an extremely difficult experience requiring a long period of adjustment with extraordinary events that, after a certain period of time, create clinically significant impediments to daily functioning for an individual.

As I have suggested elsewhere, I urge caution with the universal application of the Western diagnostic category of PTSD without regard to cultural context.[36] This is especially relevant to psychosocial programs led by Western-based nongovernmental organizations (NGOs) in refugee camps near conflict zones. While the *DSM-5* makes the effort to consider some of these differences, relatively few of the diagnostic tools used in the United States and globally have been adapted for other cultures.[37] Combat for civilians and soldiers is certainly likely to have some traumatic effects on individuals in all societies, yet the manifestation of such effects (*symptoms* in Western diagnostic language) is likely to carry very different cultural interpretations. Ignoring these differences in other cultures risks overlooking resources for resilience already at work in communities.[38]

The Social Construction of PTSD

The idea that PTSD as a medical condition first evolved in response to the social need to legitimate otherwise ostracized soldiers returning from Vietnam is not new. Derek Summerfield was among the earliest to offer this critique; he explores the negative ramifications when the diagnosis is applied to refugees in other cultural contexts.[39] More recently, French physician Didier Fassin and colleague psychiatrist Richard Rechtman, both also specialists in anthropology, have offered an in-depth analysis of PTSD and its social context. Fassin and Rechtman focus on the manner in which PTSD as a medical diagnosis has been applied without cultural boundaries and has not only served to validate the social role of victimhood but also made it essential for assistance.[40] In other words, declaring that someone is suffering from PTSD enters that person into the socially acceptable role of victim, thus making him or her eligible for everything from healthcare services to asylum to justice and even compassion.

For military personnel suffering from combat trauma, the diagnosis and classification as victims makes them eligible for military services for themselves and their families.[41] Looking back at the history of Vietnam veterans who were socially ostracized until classified as victims for mental health services, this was a helpful category leading to social acceptance. Today, however, many veterans find it difficult to transition from the self-perception of the strongest and best—essential for combat—to victim. It is contrary to both training and the social image of the hero-soldier, which may be more common today. All of this adds to perceptions of social stigma and personal resistance to seeking treatment. Fassin and Rechtman do not offer an analysis of how the role of victim functions differently among soldiers/veterans in the Vietnam era versus those leaving combat today.

Understanding PTSD as a social construction shines a different light on the notion that it is a strictly biomedical diagnosis that can be universally applied to all humans regardless of cultural context. But this should not be misinterpreted to imply that the terrible psychological effects of war demonstrated by returning soldiers are somehow not real or clinically significant. That is not the intention or purpose behind this discussion. Rather, I wish to expand the ways we understand the implications of the clinical diagnosis specifically when applied to military combat personnel, official or otherwise.

As we see from the opening narrative, soldiers often reject the notion of victimhood, no matter how much permission they have been given to embrace it, because it is a direct contradiction to the conditioning they have received from the military to carry on. Training that depersonalizes killing and makes soldiers "killing machines" that can persevere through even the most daunting enemy onslaught creates soldiers who must never believe they are ineffective or out of control, let alone helpless. It is not a surprise that combat personnel often wait until the last possible moment, when they are at the threshold of unbearable suffering, before seeking help. For them, help means admitting failure. Being an effective soldier is in direct contradiction to being an effective victim. This may be one of the exacerbating elements that has led to such strong resistance to treatment and the excessively high suicide rates among both active personnel and returning troops.[42] Left untreated, soldiers frequently self-medicate with alcohol or other drugs and risk an increase in aggressive behavior. This is the point where the psychological displacement of PTSD begins the slide into literal loss of home and physical displacement.

The Dilemma of Preferred Military Treatment Approaches: Cognitive Behavior Therapy and Exposure Therapy

According to the U.S. Department of Veterans Affairs, cognitive behavior therapy (CBT) is the most effective treatment of combat PTSD in military personnel.[43] CBT is based on the hypothesis that "people's emotions and behaviors are influenced by their perceptions of events," and "when dysfunctional thoughts are subjected to rational reflection, one's emotions generally change."[44] Retraining the mind, or adjusting one's perspective, according to CBT, helps relieve not only the persistent symptoms but also feelings of guilt and remorse. In the beginning stages of CBT, treatment is often combined with exposure therapy in which individuals are led to remember details of the offending traumatic event. This can result in a powerful increase in the intensity of PTSD symptoms for a period of time, thus increasing a soldier's sense of disorientation and insecurity. Unfortunately, for some this period may threaten continuation of treatment or prompt an increase in alcohol or drug use in an effort to numb or otherwise ameliorate the intensity of the symptoms. But with time, the symptoms will theoretically lessen as the memories become integrated and a new cognitive schema is constructed.

More specifically, in the context of combat-induced trauma, CBT is intended to help the veteran recognize that he or she is not responsible for the conditions of a battle. In war a soldier must inflict harm on others or be killed herself; it is self-defense. In the military setting, then, CBT places emphasis on a soldier being a victim, or at least an innocent party, rather than the perpetrator of harm.[45] Looking back at the opening narrative, we see that a soldier does not actually have to harm another in order to be haunted by a sense of guilt.

Chaplain Huerta carries intense feelings of remorse for the death of an Iraqi child killed by an IED—a death that he *witnessed*. CBT might encourage him to consider the ways he was unable to foresee, prevent, or intervene to prevent the child's death—that he was not responsible.

While CBT is seen as an efficient, streamlined treatment that can fit into a reliable timetable, its status as *the* most effective long-term treatment for PTSD, however, remains a point of discussion. For example, a 2005 meta-analysis of therapeutic techniques used to treat PTSD does indicate that CBT and exposure therapy are highly effective in the short term, but few studies follow the results beyond a nominal six to twelve months, nor do they include the effects of coexisting conditions.[46]

My intention here is not to diminish what may be a very effective form of therapy for some soldiers struggling with PTSD. Although I have a slight bias toward the inclusion of supportive talk therapies, especially in the group context among combat soldiers, I have no inherent difficulties with cognitive approaches to treatment. But it does not escape my attention that CBT is yet another cognitive attempt to retrain the way a soldier thinks about combat in order to make it acceptable and to ameliorate rather intense but all too natural feelings that arise in wartime. In other words, basic military conditioning makes effective soldiers by depersonalizing the act of killing other human beings. Military personnel are sent into the military theater where their mental and emotional capacities are pushed to the extreme, especially when multiple tours of duty are required. When the human mind recognizes that combat is really very personal, despite the military's attempts to depersonalize it, that mind can become trapped in a seemingly irreparable conflict.

The treatment then is to, once again, cognitively retrain soldiers that they are not culpable for the killing they have done. While this may be true from certain perspectives, there may be real and significant moral questions and struggles that remain unexplored for the combatant. So, while progress is made toward improved mental health, the spiritual and moral dimensions of healing remain at risk.

Moral Injury

How soldiers are morally and spiritually affected by the act of killing in wartime is not a new question. As early as 1992, Alan Fontana and others began to ask questions about the psychological impact on combat soldiers when their actions violate social moral norms, such as killing. A first study suggested that being "the agent of killing" was significantly related to what the researchers identified as "psychiatric distress and suicide attempts."[47] Seven years later, in a separate study, two of the authors went further to suggest not only that "killing or injuring others had a strong direct effect on PTSD" but also that it increased the tendency toward committing atrocities.[48]

There is an important difference conceptually between what I call *endorsed* killing, that is, killing that occurs within the expected parameters of warfare, and atrocities, which can include the killing of civilians or maltreatment of prisoners. Not all studies make explicit distinctions between the two. For example, a 2011 article interviewed chaplains and mental health providers asking the question, "Can moral and ethical violations be uniquely and lastingly injurious to war veterans?"[49] More specifically, interviewees were asked to define the events that might lead to moral injury. Only events that were considered "disproportionate" to standard wartime events were considered relevant. It appears killing in and of itself is assumed to be a necessary, morally neutral (if not positive) act—certainly not morally injurious.[50] All of those interviewed worked within the U.S. Departments of Veterans Affairs or Defense so we might need to ask, does this close association with the military and combat ethos influence the apparent assumption that killing is morally neutral or just in war?[51]

Current research is revealing that even clinical PTSD symptoms aren't enough to explain the full extent of the damage such violence inflicts on humans. In particular, Kent Drescher and others note that PTSD emphasizes the impact on the one receiving the effects of violence, noting, "Combat is one of the few experiences where trauma exposure comes not only through being the direct or indirect victim of violence and witnessing the aftermath and the human toll of violence but also through inflicting (perpetrating) violence and destruction upon others (generally with societal sanction)."[52]

Moral injury, according to Brett T. Litz and others, "involves an act of transgression that creates dissonance and conflict because it violates assumptions and beliefs about right and wrong and personal goodness."[53] They suggest that the inability to reconcile these violations in an adequate manner results in psychological difficulties including intrusions and avoidance behaviors similar to PTSD.[54] Again, Janoff-Bulman suggests that in addition to personal goodness, assumptions of self-worth, associated with control and outcomes, are violated. This opens the door to a dimension of spiritual crisis in which, rather than being abandoned by God, one is *rejected* by God. It may seem a small difference, but the first places the onus on God, who fails to love, while rejection implies that one is not worthy to be loved. One is unredeemed, the other is unredeemable. Both lead to despair.

Moral injury in soldiers is distinct in that the killing and injuring of the "enemy," whether an opposing army or insurgents, is sanctioned as necessary and acceptable by social systems in a manner to mitigate moral guilt or judgment. How does their training prepare them morally for the act of killing or its psychological and spiritual aftereffects?

Conditioning to Kill

How moral injury in the context of war plays itself out in other cultures is an interesting question. My work with Sudanese refugees, many of whom served as soldiers in the Sudanese Peoples Liberation Movement/Army, had a very different social understanding of killing in battle. Warrior rituals symbolically prepared young men from an early age for the expectation that killing in battle helped mark the transition into manhood. But killing outside of the strict social principles that guided engagement in tribal and personal conflicts, or war, was met with severe punishment. Even the influence of Christian faith in the last decades has not changed these expectations. In Dinka tribal culture, *not* killing under certain circumstances can evoke serious personal and social moral questions—or guilt.

Most conversations about the problem of moral injury at some point include the frequently repeated history of how soldiers came to be trained to kill in the manner they are today. It appears that contrary to the bravado portrayed in Hollywood movies, soldiers have historically been very reluctant to fire at the enemy in battle. Through direct interviews with soldiers after battle in World War II, General Samuel L. A. Marshall, the official historian for the U.S. military at the time, discovered that less than 15 percent of soldiers actually fired at the enemy.[55] Dave Grossman, author of the book *On Killing*, which is endorsed and has been used by the Pentagon for training purposes, suggests that the fear of killing another human (labeled as universal human phobia) was apparently greater than their own fear of dying.[56] This became the impetus behind the development of new training techniques intentionally designed to find a way around this moral aversion to killing. The result was an increased ratio-of-fire to nearly 95 percent by the Vietnam War. Rather than training soldiers to fire at human targets, the military now focuses on reflexive firing. This training serves to ingrain the response of firing a weapon at the enemy so deeply in the physiology of the soldier that it becomes mere reflex—simple muscle memory.

Some within the military recognize that attempting to bypass human moral agency—a perhaps innate human characteristic—leads to disastrous results. Clark C. Barrett, West Point graduate and veteran, writing on combat preparedness strategy observes, "The unwillingness to accept human aggression is what makes combat a particularly distressing event—an event that warps sensibilities to the extent that suicide becomes a solution for eliminating the stressor."[57]

Major Peter Kilner, professor of philosophy and ethics at West Point, agrees that the army's lack of attention to the moral aspects of killing proves detrimental to combat soldiers. It is true that the Geneva Convention and other rules of engagement do provide moral frameworks for war. However, both Kilner and Barrett advocate a military education and basic combat training that provide a more precise positive moral framework for the act of killing in wartime. This, Barrett believes, provides a proactive rather than reactive response to PTSD, thus accomplishing what he considers most necessary for building a resilient army. This, he argues, will "harden the inside as well as the outside of our front-line soldiers."[58] According to him, the goal, using an unfortunate term, to "inoculate" military personnel from the emotional damages of war is paramount for those who design modern military training. Is this possible?

Such "stress inoculation" assumes the contested notion that PTSD and moral injury present interchangeable symptoms. It is also based on the theory that training under high-stress simulations can condition the autonomic response system to maintain optimal levels of concentration and homeostasis under duress.[59] As Grossman points out, this is the same kind of conditioning firefighters and police officers undergo. Yet it has long been established that it is *exactly* this autonomic response system at work when symptoms of PTSD break through in ordinary daily life. The problem of PTSD is that these physiological responses, so finely conditioned as to find relative homeostasis during a firefight, cannot be effectively turned off when the context shifts from the battlefield to the ballpark. Here the crack of a bat, crowds of families, or something as simple as the sun at a particular spot on the horizon can trigger a psychophysiological response. In a state of hyper-arousal, the heartrate increases and the adrenaline begins to flow as if preparing for a fight. Panic attacks, flashbacks, dissociation, or a number of other responses may follow.

Moreover, while survivor's guilt and self-blame are common for those who have been on the receiving end of harm, the diagnosis of PTSD does not take into account the lingering guilt, shame, and self-judgment that accompany moral injury. There remains the question whether even the military's best efforts to create a just-war theory for soldiers will be able to mitigate these deeply human responses prompted by moral beliefs. Camilo Mejia, a former army private in the Iraq War, says this of the day he defended himself against a grenade: "The problem was that as I observed that young man through the sight of my rifle, when he was still alive, there was something inside me, a voice one could say, that was telling me not to squeeze the trigger. And I knew, without a shred of doubt, that I should not disobey that voice, and that if I did, there would be serious consequences to face."[60] For some, perhaps many, there is no inoculation that can defend against the charges of one's own moral conscience.

A Universal Moral Core?

Ongoing research by J. K. Hamlin, K. Wynn, and P. Bloom at the Infant Cognition Center at Yale University suggests that experiments with infants as young as three months old indicate that humans have an innate preference for helpful and good behavior toward one another as well as a basic sense of justice that punishes negative behavior toward another.[61] This is not quite a statement for innate altruism but it does seem to indicate a move in that direction. Second, these researchers suggest, even young infants appear to have an innate sense, if undeveloped, of moral judgment. Bloom notes that this study may indicate evidence of what the researchers call an innate moral sense or *universal moral core*.[62] On a less positive note, their research also suggests that infants in this age range show a positive bias toward those who are similar to themselves and a negative bias of harm toward those who are different.[63] Fortunately, research with school-age children up to age ten shows that the moral arc bends back toward positive behavior toward all. Bloom proposes that this change indicates that eventually social influence can help turn these natural biases back toward more positive behavior more broadly. Might it be that this research from the Yale Child Study Center hints at the underpinnings for the reason that humans might resist killing one another? Even in three-month-old infants, there is evidence of an innate moral sense that helping is preferred over hurting and that punishment is deserved for those who violate this code of behavior.

What draws me toward this research in the context of military personnel in combat is the question of a universal moral core. Much of the trauma that soldiers endure is assumed to be the result of being on the receiving end of live fire—having their own lives at risk for extended periods of time. The diagnosis of PTSD is, indeed, based on the notion of helplessness in the face of threat to one's own life or the life of a loved one. However, when one is the perpetrator of harm, it is a different matter. If this research is right, then even the most effective training to bypass moral decision making in combat and justify killing ultimately, in some soldiers, yields to the universal moral core. The ensuing crisis may prove, for some, more secular, but for many it is a fundamental crisis of faith.

Coming Home

Coming home from battle seemed to be one of the easiest things to do. It seemed that you just get on a plane. After spending hours, weeks and months getting help and talking to someone about my wounds, I am only beginning to understand how to come home.[64]
—Major Carlos Huerta

After a year or more of living with a family of brothers (and sisters) under combat conditions, soldiers receive resiliency training, formerly known as "Battlemind" training, which is intended to help soldiers prepare for reentry into civilian life. It also serves as an all-too-brief goodbye to those with whom one has likely bonded closely through shared intense traumatic experiences. Some instruction is given to assist with transition back to the family soldiers left behind. For most, this is a difficult transition. As happy as the veterans may be to hold loved ones in their arms, no civilian can or ever will truly understand the daily threat endured or difficult choices soldiers have made. The longing for the combat family is intense, but social decorum frames homecoming as about mending the long separation with loved ones. Little attention is given to the heartbreaking separation from the combat family. Nor is attention given to the powerful shift of naming the safe places. This is where traumatic stress shows its force most notably: the return to this society in which rules of what is safe and secure, right and wrong, do not match with the emotional imprint the soldier carries. The combat family that has served to help the soldier adjust expectations of threat and reality has disappeared. The soldier is left alone to make the transition.

Soldiers face both combat and coming home with at least two strikes against them that may impair the resiliency that the military strives for through post-combat programs. First, soldiers have been trained to resist any sense of victimhood so that when symptoms of PTSD become overwhelming, they resist treatment, fearing that it makes them weak and a failure. Second, combat training removes all language and overt discussion that questions a moral framework for the killing of another human being. It is more than the dehumanizing of killing but the perpetuation of moral amnesia as key to the fighting effectiveness of the soldier. Yet there is abundant evidence that ignoring the moral issues faced by combat personnel adds significantly to the despair and suffering they endure post-deployment. This can make for a tragic homecoming for combat personnel who are unprepared for the inner turmoil of recognizing oneself as the perpetrator of killing another human. The combat soldier struggling with understandable physical, psychological, spiritual, and moral effects of combat is put in the untenable situation of being both victim and perpetrator—and neither role is he prepared to accept.

Of all those we have examined in this book, combat soldiers suffer multiple displacements from which many struggle to return. Home can become a distant reality for many who return stateside to struggle with the psychological and spiritual effects of war. The first displacement separates military personnel from the places they call home and those they love—parents, spouses, and children. Although voluntary in nature, the separation still carries a significant impact. The two worlds of the stateside home and the frontlines could not be more different. On the battlefield, considering home as the place and people who name the places that are safe seems a preposterous paradox as the soldier enters a world in which no place is safe.[65] On the frontlines, even fortified compounds with guarded perimeters are under constant threat of attack from insurgents or sniper fire. In very short order, soldiers together must redefine what it means to be safe. Relative safety becomes one's best hope and that can only be accomplished through the cooperative efforts of soldiers, men and women alike, who stand together in defense of one another. In these impossible places and under these impossible conditions, soldiers forge extraordinary relationships of trust, mutual understanding, and moral obligation of care. These relationships and even the combat conditions become familiar, longed-for places of deep knowing—where there is no need to explain fear, pain, and loss because all have suffered it together. There is, likewise, no need to explain the moral choices of killing because it has become a reflex on which each life depends.

Ultimately, every combat soldier will be displaced from these deep relationships forged through the repeated high intensity of battle in one of at least three ways: the end of deployment, injury and evacuation, or death. Imagine the shock and despair of a soldier falling injured among comrades and awaking days later and thousands of miles away in a military hospital in the United States. In this single, abrupt shift, one world is lost for another. There is great rejoicing among family, but it is a devastatingly sudden redefinition of home for the serviceperson. Her allegiance remains with those left on the frontlines.

We have explored the complex dichotomy of being both victim and perpetrator in the context of U.S. servicepeople serving in the wars in Iraq and Afghanistan. But in many of my interviews with refugees and internally displaced persons in Sudan and the eastern Democratic Republic of the Congo, they have shared stories of being forced at gunpoint to harm or kill another person—often a spouse or child. They too suffer horribly from the particularly complex psychological, moral, and cultural effects of simultaneously being traumatically victimized and perpetrating death or injury on another. Each of these contexts has its own complications to address. Still, any response to either the U.S. soldiers or civilians caught in this conundrum must be willing to wrestle with the ambiguity that comes from standing at the threshold of both victim and perpetrator, no matter how unpalatable it may be.

If, at its best, the home place is a primary source of framing what brings security and safety to our world, to be displaced creates a crisis of self and spirit. The question becomes, how does one withstand the forces of an unsafe world, and how does God help us to reimagine what safety is in this unsafe world? Are we willing to hold the stories veterans have to tell?[66] For ultimately, it is up to the community, both the community of faith and the community at large, to create for veterans suffering from PTSD and moral injury a relatively safe place where they can find home.

seven

CHRONIC DISPLACEMENT AND
PERSONS WITHOUT HOME

It was around 2 a.m. when someone knocked on the door to my room at the transitional facility where I served as the live-in staff for overnight crisis care. The frantic resident urged me to come quickly. "Cissy," she said, "is fighting with someone downstairs—she's high." Cissy came to our facility after living on the streets. She was a crack addict who had been clean for almost a year and was the resident who had lived at the facility the longest. Sweet, kind, and always ready to lend an ear, the other women looked up to her as a beacon of hope. . . . If she can do it, so can I.

When I arrived at the downstairs room Cissy was screaming and throwing her belongings across the room. Her clothes were dirty and disheveled and her hair unkempt. She didn't appear to recognize me as I cautiously entered the room—her only acknowledgment of my presence was the long stream of obscenities she yelled in my direction. I had never met this Cissy before.

When the police arrived I explained the situation and the lone officer called for backup. I followed him into the room. Cissy became even more hostile and aggressive at the sight of the police officer so that he was forced to restrain her. She fought mightily against his attempts to put her into handcuffs such that it took two of us to hold her arms and get the cuffs around her wrists. After the struggle, handcuffed face down on the bedroom floor, she was wild-eyed and foaming at the mouth. No longer a danger to herself or the rest of us, I tried to comfort her as we waited. I pushed the hair back from her face and told her everything was going to be okay. When I looked up, the other residents were peering through the doorway—many of them crying. This was not just another relapse. This was their beloved Cissy—a crack addict going to jail and on the streets again after tonight. If it could happen to her . . .

After Cissy got out of jail the following day she returned to the house to collect her belongings. As we talked she said, "I don't remember anything at all about last night . . . except I remember someone stroking my hair and face and telling me everything was going to be okay. I think God was trying to tell me something."

In the spring of 1993 I moved my permanent residence to a single room on the third floor of the Wilson Inn, a transitional living facility for women who were without home.[1] Here, for three years, I served as the staff person in residence. The house accommodated approximately fifteen women—and it was a house. I sometimes refer to the Wilson Inn as a facility, but it was a house, a home really, in the tradition of a southern mansion along a main avenue replete with monuments of Confederate soldiers. It would not be an exaggeration to say that the existence of the Wilson Inn in this upper-class neighborhood was often a challenge for our closest neighbors.

The women who came to the Wilson Inn most often had at least one of three primary challenges contributing to their loss of home. First, a large number were ex-offenders whom we interviewed in prison and who, once accepted, lived at the Wilson Inn as a condition of their parole. Second, a very high percentage of residents were in recovery from alcohol or other addictions. The sale and use of illicit drugs was usually the primary reason for incarceration. Finally, a smaller portion of our residents struggled with mental illness. For many, our facility was, unfortunately, only a brief respite from life on the streets.

I am tempted at times to say that I shared home with the many women who resided there. In some respects I suppose this is true. We went through our day-to-day lives passing each other in the hallway. We all grumbled about the plumbing and the heat. During my first year the Wilson Inn provided one cooked meal a day for the women, and I usually joined them in the dining room. But there was never any mistaking the fact that I was staff and they were "residents." We shared an address but it did not mean that we shared home in the same way. I had the keys and the power.

Still, they taught me more about living without home, the challenges of trying to regain home, and hope against astounding odds than any library ever could. I do not attempt here to define for others what life without home looks like. Rather, in this chapter I join my reflections and stories about life at the Wilson Inn with narratives of persons without home from various published sources and conversations with multiple scholars to explore the question of homelessness.

In particular I want to examine the last of four functions of the home place, that is, to move us toward flourishing through the beneficial ways we create, nurture, and sustain *human relationships*. More specifically, I explore the ways that displacement through what we call in the United States "homelessness" threatens human relationships. Understanding the causal and complicating issues that contribute to homelessness is a complex task. But glimpses into the lives of the women at the Wilson Inn and other published personal narratives help us along the way to put a face on these very difficult issues.

I argue that the conditions of homelessness provoke a rupture in relationships—in terms of both inter-human and human-Divine relations. The deteriorating conditions that can lead an individual (or a family unit) to lose her home place create tremendous strain on emotional as well as tangible resources. Individuals and families become placeless when, among other factors, immediate social systems become compromised. Foremost among them are family and friends who may step in at the beginning stages of economic hardship, illness, addiction, or other forms of crisis to provide emotional, financial, or housing support. Because most families have limited and in some cases scarce resources, there comes a point at which this assistance is no longer viable. When that happens, the loss is critical.

On a larger social scale, to those communities who consider them a social blight and even to social service agencies or churches, persons without home quickly can become a "category." This might be a category of disdain or, just as easily, need—sometimes both. Regardless, the resulting fissure in relationships between those lacking permanent homes and the communities surrounding the streets on which they live is unfortunately deep, abiding, and morally tragic.

Social dislocation and alienation of this nature have serious practical and psychological effects on persons without home, not the least of which are shame, low self-esteem, or depression. Such alienation dehumanizes those without place and threatens the very notion of a morally just community. The spiritual ramifications for a broader society that fails in their relationship to those most in need, those without home, are also quite significant. Spiritually, these embedded social conditions escalate homelessness to placelessness and can cloud human perception of and compromise human ability to participate in God's gifts of love, grace, and redemption. It diminishes the ability to see the face of God in the other. Although God's faithfulness always remains true, the methods by which the poor and those without home are relationally alienated from society impede the opportunities for physical, psychological, and spiritual flourishing for all.

Understanding Homelessness

The United Nations estimates that there are over 200 million persons without home globally—up to 3.5 million in the United States alone.[2] People designated as without home are distinct from refugees or internally displaced persons (IDPs), discussed in previous chapters. Although a global issue, I primarily focus on homelessness in the context of the United States and define it broadly as those who "lack a fixed, regular, and adequate night-time residence" or are living in temporary accommodations because they lack safe, permanent alternatives.[3] I want to be sure we understand just how broad the notion of homelessness can be. It includes those chronically without home, the employed without home, those in shelters and transitional facilities, those fleeing domestic violence, those living in hotels and motels, unaccompanied youth, and others.[4]

It is difficult to isolate a single root cause for homelessness when the mix of complicating factors is so complex. It is reasonable to start, though, with the ugly fact of poverty that threatens lives and displaces millions around the world, including so many in the United States. On the global front, the United Nations set first among its millennium development goals to reduce by half the number of people who earn below the global poverty rate of $1.25 a day. Even with the great success of this effort, nearly one billion people are still living in extreme poverty.[5] In the United States, 16 percent of those without home are chronically so, whereas upward of 44 percent are employed but lack stable housing. There is little dispute that the current minimum wage is insufficient to afford a modest one- or two-bedroom apartment at fair market rent and has been so for some time, but efforts to increase the minimum wage to a living wage continue to meet with resistance.[6] To make matters worse, the economic crisis that began to show its effects in 2008 has further pressed those living in chronic poverty, thrown millions more into new homelessness, and left still others perched perilously on its edge.

Complicating Factors in Homelessness

There is nothing new about the idea that addiction, mental illness, and incarceration are complicating factors in the matter of homelessness. It is a not so simple fact. I have long since surrendered to the idea that in most cases when mental illness, addiction, and incarceration are combined with poverty and lack of affordable housing, efforts to identify the defining element that separates one from the other are arbitrary. The tenacity with which these forces, when so intimately intertwined, can grip someone in the cycle of homelessness is astounding.

I did, however, see the day-to-day impact of addiction, mental illness, and incarceration on our lives at the Wilson Inn. So, before tackling the larger systemic problems, though they all certainly overlap, let me take a minute to look at these three complicating matters. In this section I present an example of each so that we might consider the challenges faced and the outcomes experienced at the Wilson Inn.

Mental Illness

A recent article in the *Economist* highlights the tragic cycle of homelessness and the inclusion of incarceration as a complicating factor in the lives of the severely mentally ill who lack significant housing and perhaps treatment options. In the article, Sheriff Thomas Dart of Cook County, Illinois, shares his experiences and what he sees as a larger pattern of rotating the seriously mentally ill in and out of correctional facilities—arresting them for charges such as "trespassing, prostitution, drugs, disorderly conduct, drinking in public"—until they die.[7] This is because there are simply no other resources available for their care.

Despite Sheriff Dart's assertion, the Wilson Inn offered at least a possible alternative by frequently taking in women with diagnosed mental illness. During my time on staff perhaps 25 percent of the women suffered from mental illness, usually schizophrenia or extreme bipolar disorder that was difficult to stabilize—either because of the condition itself or because the women were not compliant with their medication.[8] Depression was another serious concern. Those who were least able to regulate their illnesses through a strict regimen of medication were the most at risk of losing their space at the facility.

We can speak of mental illness as a "complicating factor" in homelessness, but this does little to capture the frustration and disappointment for those who do everything right and yet still cannot stabilize their illnesses.[9] I recall being awakened in the early morning hours by a phone call from an ambulance waiting outside the residence advising me that someone had called for assistance. When I arrived in the downstairs living room, Sarah, who suffered from schizophrenia, was standing in her robe looking agitated and confused. Suddenly, she took off her robe, opened the front door, and took off running down the street—naked as the day she was born. Twenty-four hours later, Sarah called to say that she was safe and with a friend. I asked her to go to the emergency room, and, after a brief stay in the psychiatric hospital, Sarah returned to our transitional facility. We were able to find some humor in the story later, but underneath was a deep sadness for Sarah that with a new job, and new hope, once again she had taken two steps back. She had awakened in the night knowing that something was wrong and that she needed to get to her psychiatrist, so she called the ambulance. All of her instincts were correct. Her medications, indeed, needed to be adjusted, but the illness took over before she could get help in a reasonable way.

This outcome may seem unimpressive in terms of the disruption to Sarah's life or the resources of the Wilson Inn. But consider the less obvious details. Sarah's episode required the attention of the Wilson Inn staff (me); an ambulance was dispatched; I summoned the police when she became at risk by running through the street without clothes; she was admitted to the emergency room for short-term psychiatric care in order to adjust her medication. Aside from these public resources Sarah missed nearly five days of work. Only after a medical release was obtained was she allowed to resume residence at the Wilson Inn. This type of "treatment first" housing works for those who can maintain a certain degree of functioning, small fluctuations notwithstanding.[10] Returning to the Wilson was not always the outcome if a resident was considered too unstable or had attempted to harm herself or another. Realistically, whether or not it is a *causal* event, mental illness at the very least can be a significant contributing factor to the difficulties of maintaining steady employment, housing, and in some severe cases even basic self-care.

Addiction and Incarceration

The opening vignette for this chapter unfortunately describes a frequent occurrence at the Wilson Inn—addiction relapse. A high percentage of women at the Wilson Inn struggled with addiction. Because addiction was so often also linked to incarceration in the context of the Wilson Inn, I address them together here. Like mental illness, the effects of addiction or incarceration can create a tipping point that leads to a slide into homelessness and severely limits one's ability to climb out of it. Either can interfere with employment, drain financial resources, especially if those are meager to begin with, and stress family relationships.

A year after I began work at the Wilson Inn we changed our policy so that children were allowed to accompany their mothers as residents. It was often the case that women were being reunited with children who had been living with relatives while the mothers were in prison or otherwise unable to care for them because of active addiction. These reunions were both one of the most wonderful aspects of my work and one of the most difficult. In many cases providing a space for mothers and children to come together allowed for the repair of relationships to begin. But when a mother relapsed it was a gut-wrenching time for all.

One evening a woman I call Barbara returned to the house with her two children under the age of ten. She had clearly been drinking. Her impairment was grounds under Wilson Inn rules for a room search. In the back of her closet I found no fewer than a dozen (mostly) empty bottles of alcohol. Barbara denied she had been drinking that night or that the bottles were hers. The children, who were with her, were frightened and crying. They understood that they were going back to a relative's house and their mother was about to lose her home again. If a relative was not available to take the children, staff would be forced to contact local child protective services to take custody until someone could be found. If Barbara had been on parole, both alcohol consumption and loss of residency at the Wilson Inn would have been violations and she would risk a return to prison. These instances certainly challenged me and challenge linear models that promote steady advancement through sobriety (no toleration of relapse) with permanent housing as an ultimate goal.[11]

We have come to understand addiction as a chronic disease and more recently a brain disease. Like other diseases, it is influenced by a combination of biological and environmental factors and choice. But addiction bears the added burden of a long history during which the cause was considered solely a matter of choice—and a moral one at that. Society tends to apply the chronic disease model to those who can afford to treat it as such but the choice model to those who cannot—especially those without home.

Addiction in the context of homelessness reflects the convergence of three issues—poverty, drug use, and racism—all concerns that society at large seeks to obscure rather than confront. This situation becomes most apparent when we consider how the criminal side of addiction has been used in oppressive ways. Research psychologist Gene M. Heyman makes a compelling point: unlike any other disease, regulatory matters concerning addiction have two homes within the federal government—the Department of Justice and the National Institutes of Health. He writes, "We typically do not advocate incarceration and medical care for the same activities. Indeed, addiction is the only psychiatric syndrome whose symptoms—illicit drug use—are considered an illegal activity, and conversely addictive drug use is the only illegal activity that is also the focus of highly ambitious research and treatment programs."[12] Drug use in this country in the latter part of the twentieth century has, indeed, been heavily prosecuted—at least in certain populations, the poor and black among them. In her powerful book *The New Jim Crow*, Michelle Alexander highlights the impact of the War on Drugs and the consequential Anti-Drug Abuse Act of 1986, which has resulted in mandatory minimum sentences for cocaine-related crimes.[13] The extended prison sentences for many of the women at the transitional facility, some for possession of very small quantities of drugs, were directly due to these very same mandatory sentences. Alexander draws a convincing link between the overly high rates of incarceration of African American men in the United States and systemic racism.[14]

Incarceration and, once released, the denial of rights to persons convicted of crimes is a multi-systemic form of oppression that begins with the forced displacement of African American men. Once a black man is convicted of a felony drug crime, the probability of his receiving future housing assistance after release from prison is extremely low, thus making him especially vulnerable to becoming a person without home. Families, in turn, become vulnerable to forced displacement when a father, husband, or boyfriend can no longer provide income because he has been incarcerated *and* then places the family at risk of losing housing benefits if he is present after release. It is a lose-lose situation for all.

How does this play itself out in the lives of those without a home place? Statistics on various characteristics related to the persons who are homeless are notoriously difficult to obtain. Nonetheless, according to various statistics that we do have, more than 60 percent of the homeless population suffer from some type of addiction. In New York City 88 percent of homeless persons are African American or Latino—and more than 60 percent have been incarcerated at least once.[15]

Affordable Housing

When the reality of poverty is coupled with the lack of safe, affordable housing, the outcome is often quite bleak. Lack of affordable housing is one of the greatest contributors to the problem of homelessness in the United States and elsewhere. This is both a common and logical explanation for this tangle of mess we call homelessness. In fact, this is so often the starting point that it seems difficult to find a new perspective from which to examine the complexities behind this challenging global problem. But since we are trying to understand the ways that deeply systemic forces erode the social relationship between those without home and the communities they inhabit, let's begin here.

The hunger for economic gain and the embedded social realities of racism and classism combine to threaten opportunities for safe, affordable housing for the poor in urban centers across the United States. This combination affects private and nonprofit housing ventures such as single-room occupancy (SRO) hotels and residences and public housing, as well as low-income apartments in urban areas that have struggled with serious decline since the late twentieth century.

Loss of SRO housing is often cited as one of the most significant contributors to the rise in homelessness, and to some degree this may certainly be true. In large urban centers, SROs have long been associated with the flophouses that were targeted as "urban blight" by early gentrification efforts. The thriving real estate market in New York City continues to transform the face of formerly undesirable areas. The infamous Bowery, once a dangerous "skid row" for the addicted and most dire of those without home, for example, now showcases new condominiums that have replaced old, dilapidated buildings. While SROs do still exist in New York City, the numbers are greatly reduced from their heyday. Many smaller cities throughout the country, however, no longer have SRO hotels or similar alternatives.[16]

SRO is also the category used for residential hotels that serve a different clientele than what existed in the old Bowery and rarely do we consider their role in matters of homelessness. Rather, these are simple single-room hotels, some specifically for women, that offer safe, affordable housing to members of the working class, the elderly, students, and others who cannot afford the rising apartment rates in large urban areas. These SROs harken back to a time when religious organizations and other nonprofit institutions offered these accommodations as safe and respectable alternatives for young working women. These residences now serve an important function for some low-income women who live from paycheck to paycheck at or below the poverty line and are at risk of losing a home place.

I myself lived in Brandon House, a women's residence operated by Volunteers of America on the Upper West Side of New York City while a student in the early 1980s. Originally intended to house young women coming to New York for study or work in the early 1950s, it was by the time I lived there a home to a wide variety of women and circumstances. Certainly some of us were students, but there were also some long-term elderly residents or working-class immigrants earning low wages who could not afford an apartment in the already competitive New York City market. The $85-a-week rent for a small single room with communal bathrooms on each floor, a shared telephone, and two meals a day was a bargain. Interestingly, the Wilson Inn transitional facility, noted in the opening vignette, was owned by the United Methodist Church and also once served as a women's residence offering a similar model of safety and hospitality for young ladies.

While the Brandon House still exists, the Salvation Army has sold two similar residences—the Ten Eyck and Parkside Evangeline on Gramercy Park. The Parkside, also a women-only residence, offered small single rooms and two meals a day for a thousand dollars a month. Part of the facility was reserved for permanent residents while other rooms were available to visiting guests on a short-term basis. To be sure, given its location on Gramercy Park, the Parkside might seem an extravagant residence, at least by the Bowery standards. Nonetheless, it served those with lower incomes who would have had great difficulty finding alternative housing in New York City. The 100-square-foot rooms have now been renovated into luxury apartments, a 4,707-square-foot penthouse among them. That one penthouse apartment recently sold for $16,575,000.

Federal Housing Assistance

For many of the women at the Wilson Inn, a remarkably positive outcome was qualification for subsidized housing. I can recall the difficulty these women faced waiting for actual Section 8 housing vouchers—for approved private-market housing—to arrive.[17] More than once we stretched the one-year-residency limit for someone nearing the top of the waiting list for housing assistance. Although there is in general a wide variance in wait times from city to city, the U.S. Department of Housing and Urban Development (HUD) states that in 2013, on average, low-income persons waited up to twenty-three months for housing vouchers.[18] Vouchers—or even public housing—were seldom options for our residents with felony records. Public housing authorities across the country have wide permission to deny assistance to anyone convicted of a felony or even suspected of criminal activity.[19] Likewise, a tenant can be evicted if suspected of such activity or if he or she allows a convicted felon to reside, even unofficially, in the home. As Human Rights Watch points out, this all but eliminates second chances, at least in terms of housing, for those felons who wish to improve their lives.[20] Fathers released on parole cannot live in subsidized housing with their families, and children of convicted single parents are all the more likely to be sent to live with other family members or taken into custody by child protective services when housing cannot be maintained. As we have already seen, those arrested and convicted of drug-related crimes are disproportionately black. Statistics from 2007 show that, perhaps consequently, African Americans made up 46 percent of the homeless population but only 12 percent of the U.S. population.

Many of the women in residence at the transitional facility were ex-offenders working to regain custody of their children—a nearly impossible task if they could not stay sober and provide adequate housing. It is not a surprise that excessively long waiting lists and restrictions against those convicted or suspected of a crime can cause families with already strained resources to fall over the edge into losing a home place. Although felons are also excluded from public housing, there are few other options in large urban areas for the poor who are without employment.

I can recall sitting in my car in 1999 riveted to a report on National Public Radio about the infamously violent Cabrini-Green housing project in Chicago and the monumental efforts underway to transform public housing in the city. Chicago's renovation of public housing was part of a larger effort—the Hope VI (Housing Opportunities for People Everywhere) program—by the federal government to overhaul policy on how it houses the poor across the country and, as HUD describes the effort, "to eradicate severely distressed public housing."[21]

The Hope VI program in Chicago sought to reduce violent crime, desegregate public housing, and lessen the overall poverty level of communities in which residents lived. Residents were dispersed among other public housing units, voucher housing, and placement in private market mixed-income housing units. Overall, the Chicago story provides a sad but helpful example of the complex issues facing the poor and the challenges of adequate housing in the United States.

Over the years, I have periodically heard news of the city's progress. Depending on whom you ask, this effort is described as either a grand vision to transform public housing policy or an outright land grab. In reality, there is likely some degree of truth to both views. Citing Cabrini-Green's location on the edge of the even more notable

Gold Coast and the recent construction of condominiums selling for $300,000 to $700,000 on the former public housing project's now-cleared site, sociologist Stephen Steinberg chooses the latter. He likens the displacement of Chicago's poorest and predominately black citizens from this prime real estate to James Baldwin's notion of "Negro Remove" in the early sixties as well as the displacement of Native Americans from their tribal land through Indian removal in the early nineteenth century.[22]

For its part, HUD cites the Move to Opportunity for Fair Housing (MTO) study, results of a "ten-year research demonstration" that examined benefits for moving participants out of problem-plagued public housing programs like Chicago's.[23] They concluded that overall improvements in the lives of residents as a result of these programs are notable. HUD notes that studies

> demonstrate significant improvements in residents' lives, with most residents now living in decent housing located in neighborhoods where they feel substantially safer. More than 75 percent reported that their current housing is in better condition than their original unit. In addition, the proportion of residents reporting shootings and violence as major neighborhood problems declined from more than half in 2001 to about a quarter in 2011. Furthermore, residents' new communities are less segregated and poor than the old CHA developments, which had poverty rates of more than 70 percent and populations that were almost entirely African American. These problems persist in the new communities, but the average poverty rate is 41 percent.[24]

Most studies do agree that, regardless of other outcomes, residents live in communities with less violent crime. What has not been carefully tracked are the number of residents who were left without housing by these large overhauls—in either the short or long term. The Urban Institute, for example, estimates a net loss of up to fourteen thousand housing units in Chicago alone, which is especially dire news for the "hard to house"—those chronically at risk of losing their housing.[25]

Another casualty not tracked was the loss of neighborhood social support when residents were dispersed to housing throughout the city. In this regard, *relocation* might also be understood as *social displacement* for many of the residents. While few debate that the conditions of the former high-rise public housing were violent, even deplorable, it was also a community of poor who knew the faces of their neighbors and cared and depended on each other in ways unmeasured by housing authority evaluations and statistics.[26] Even in violent housing projects, communities such as these are sources of resilience for residents. An interview with one former resident who was relocated to private-market (mixed-income) housing reveals that the social capital among the neighbors in her public-housing building often made the difference between surviving and not. While living in the projects this resident had the support of her mother, who provided childcare without charge; of storeowners, who extended her credit for necessary food and household items; and of neighbors with whom she bartered. She recorded, "Poor people help poor people. They have no one else, so they know how to help each other get by."[27]

She and others likewise depended on local churches for support, either spiritually as part of the congregation or through their food pantries—sometimes both. An ethnographic study conducted through Yale Divinity School of local churches in the surrounding New Haven, Connecticut, area at least anecdotally supports the notion that African American churches are particularly attuned to the needs of the people in their vicinity. Churches in low-income areas tend to respond to the needs of local people.[28] It is a fundamental part of their ministry. If the objective is to move residents from the housing projects like Cabrini-Green into more integrated or "less black" neighborhoods, agencies should be mindful of the great cost to those who depend on the care of neighbors and local churches to make ends meet. It is no wonder that so many of the former residents of Cabrini-Green express a desire to return to their old neighborhoods.[29]

"Nontraditional" Circumstances

"Economic refugees"—that is, those displaced by the economic crisis that began in 2008—are a population of persons without home who largely defy the conventional image of homelessness. Although the term *economic refugee* is most often applied to persons who cross national borders, with or without permission, in search of work when none can be found in their homeland, I use it here to refer to those who have crossed borders of a different type—from middle-class suburbanites to working persons without home. Once living the American Dream, they are now victims of a failed mortgage system that put their homes in foreclosure and left their children hungry. They live in cars and shelters, surprised to count themselves among those without a home place. Never could they have imagined they would find themselves living in two worlds—a daytime of business as usual and a nighttime of trying to find a safe place to sleep.

In 2010–2011, more than one million schoolchildren without home joined their families in trying to find shelter.[30] Further, young adults (18–24) make up one of the fastest growing populations of homeless persons in the United States. Many are college students forced to drop out because of rising costs and a shortage of employment opportunities, largely due to unstable economic conditions. As the *New York Times* points out, boomerang kids who can return home are the lucky ones with families in a financial position to offer assistance.[31] Others must find a way to survive on their own and are now living in shelters across the United States, joining lesbian, gay, bisexual, and transgender (LGBT) youth ostracized by families; young adults who age out of the foster care system; and other young people who struggle without home.

To this point, we have met a few of the faces of those without home, or formerly so, and peeked under the surface to glimpse how addiction, mental illness, and incarceration touched their lives. By the numbers, we can see that those struggling with addiction, mental illness, and incarceration are highly represented among homeless persons. Behind these complicating factors are bigger, more systemic issues of low-paying wages and diminishing sources of affordable housing in this country. We can see that even when large systems like the federal government design housing programs that may indeed have the best of intentions—reducing crime, improving the health of residents, and providing opportunities to rise out of segregated, poverty-ridden areas—racism and classism can seep into the foundations. This is the place where the failure in relationship to our larger social systems begins to show itself.

With the faces of the few we have already met fresh in our minds, our next step is to look at the ways the relationships between those without home and the larger community are fractured or blocked. Only by understanding the how and why behind the gap between those among us whose needs continue to go unmet and our compassionate response as a community of faith can we begin to repair the relationship and close the gap.

Social Alienation of Persons without Home

An insidious rupture of relationship occurs on the social level when both sociopolitical systems and the community at large objectify homeless persons. Someone recently pointed out that calling those without home an *objectified population* is old news. Yes, it is. And isn't that tragic. To social agencies and government protocols, persons without home are still target populations—in best cases, targets of need; in worst, targets of control. They are reduced to numbers, best practices, and outcome projections that validate aid resources. Politically, they become fodder for party politics that seep through in terms like *entitlements*, which turn a compassionate notion of helping those in need into a slur that implies unearned benefits. Communities can barely look into the eyes of those without home for fear that their despair could become their own. Instead, they toss the displaced in a narrow category of "homeless" and surround it with fear and disdain. Little attempt is made by most to meet the displaced as humans with names and personal needs. If we do by chance recognize need, we most often do so from the safety of distance.

On a Saturday not long ago, I stopped in a local shopping center parking lot to talk with a young family that I saw holding a sign, "need food and work." They were hungry and out of resources. I sat with them on the grass writing down telephone numbers of local shelters and food banks. One woman brought over a shopping bag with diapers and other goods. I noticed that cars stopped to inquire about the problem but instead of speaking with the family, most were content to ask *me* what was wrong and how they could help. While the underlying kindness was appreciated, their behavior begged the question: Were they more comfortable with my white, suburban face than the darker, Romanian faces of these people in need? Was it their poverty that gave them pause?

I have been captivated by the power of face-to-face encounters since my work with newly arrived refugee families in 2000. Oddly enough, it was my tendency to *misunderstand* the stories I interpreted behind faces from other cultures that encourages me not to underestimate such encounters.[32] Communication through facial expressions, like spoken language, requires a certain degree of interpretation if we are to be competent in our listening and understanding. We must also be willing to ask the question: how could I be wrong?

Sociologist Alfred Schutz, though clearly reflecting a particular time and Western inclination, asks what makes communication possible in what he calls face-to-face relations. He suggests that humans must come together as subjects of equal importance engaging together in the joint endeavor of human communication.[33] In other words, face-to-face encounters are those in which we are willing to be vulnerable enough to reveal something about ourselves in an encounter with another who trusts us to do the same. In an overly obvious example, this is demonstrated in the difference between seeking a personal conversation with a displaced person and ignoring his or her presence. More subtly, it is the difference between staying behind the "protection" of the serving line in the soup kitchen and stepping out to sit at a table and engage in conversation with someone who is displaced. The two encounters are very different, with the latter requiring an investment of both vulnerability and trust.

When we fail to do this, Schutz argues, we turn away from the opportunity for the fullness of a social encounter and relegate the other (and ourselves) to a social role that allows us to remain anonymous to one another.[34]

Both Giddens, noted in chapter 5, and Schutz use the day-to-day or face-to-face experience, respectively, to draw us into practical, common human experience that is at once simple to recognize and difficult to understand but that sits at the heart of why objectification of the other creates the violence that it does. In place of the face-to-face relationship, objectification requires that we create social generalizations or stereotypes. We do this easily with homeless persons. What we are left to tangle with is the problematic nature of dismissing the desire for, and therefore betraying, the possibility of a face-to-face relationship with those we place in the role of "homeless." I suggest that such a betrayal on the personal level leads to failure in the ethical demand toward care for the other and is a severe rupture in a personal relationship. Once this refusal of the other becomes institutionalized, it is a social betrayal and a failure of communal justice. The just and moral care of the displaced cannot be confined to meeting basic physical needs—*human relationship* must be the starting point of all moral action.

Giddens, as we recall, examines the social shifts that occurred in response to the emergence of modernity and capitalism. He highlights what he calls the *sequestration of experience* as an effect with particular consequences. Certain human experiences that were once common in the personal realm of life—the day to day—have become institutionalized.[35] In other words, we create a protective distancing between our day-to-day life and those experiences that are morally threatening by handing them over to either organized institutions or well-established social patterns of behavior. Giddens writes, "The ontological security which modernity has purchased, on the level of the day-to-day routines, depends on an institutional exclusion of social life from fundamental existential issues which raise central moral dilemmas for human beings."[36] I must stretch a bit to reconcile Giddens's theory with the issue of homelessness (as a matter to be sequestered) until I recall the three main struggles of the women at the Wilson Inn, along with thousands of persons without home on our streets—addiction, mental illness, and incarceration. Many of us would like to believe we no longer consider the root causes of poverty and homelessness to be moral failures. But the objectification of those who live in poverty and without home, along with the systematic exclusion of the displaced from "places" in our cities, indicates otherwise.

Age-Old Categories of Rejection

We create two categories of objects among homeless persons: those worthy of care or aid—the needy victims—and those who are unworthy—the undesirable and morally questionable. These categories reveal social efforts to control behavior and bring order to an otherwise chaotic social problem.

The Needy

Victimhood in the United States has become paradoxical. It is at once a cultural category to which we cling that makes conditions for which we were once morally culpable (e.g., addiction, mental illness, homelessness) tolerable, yet it is also contrary to prevailing cultural narratives, like the soldier's, that we can persevere against all odds to overcome any obstacle (e.g., in pursuit of the American Dream). Socially, we respond to victimhood and moral failure as though they are kissing cousins. The raw vulnerability of victimhood is as equally threatening to our ontological security as the morally deviant. The social sequestering of victims creates objects of need and, in so doing, ironically strips away the very aspects of humanity and dignity that categorization as victim seeks to preserve. For those without home, isolated from family and other loved ones and ostracized by society, human relationship becomes one of the greatest unmet needs.

Who are those eligible for care in shelters, and by what criteria can they maintain this status as *worthy* recipients? Typical requirements for admission to shelters or feeding programs include sobriety (at time of admission), appropriate behavior, adherence to strict rules including arrival and departure times, and like-gendered sheltering (men and women separated). On the surface this seems quite reasonable, and certainly some rules of order are necessary in any gathering space. But let us consider what these rules imply. Those unable to control substance use, that is, those suffering the effects of addiction, are excluded even though addiction is now considered to be a medical disease. Most adults can present appropriate behavior unless they suffer from mental illness, in which case acting out, hearing voices, and outbursts of anger or sadness are often uncontrollable, rendering those persons ineligible for services. Working homeless persons cannot leave work early or arrive late and so must sometimes forego shelter in order to work. It is unusual to find an overnight shelter that allows children; even more rare is a family shelter that allows entire families to stay together. The addicted, mentally ill, working-persons without home, and families—are they all worthy victims? Or do they fall outside the frame for who is considered the orderly, controlled victims worthy and deserving of aid?

Criminalizing the Undesirable

The history of vagrancy, or homelessness, shows an interesting relationship among the upper social classes, those who are poor or without home, and laws enacted to control the movement and behavior of the latter. From feudalism to industrialism, there have been similar efforts to contain the poor and downtrodden in limited geographical areas. "Vagrancy" itself was a crime in most states until 1972, when it was repealed by the Supreme Court because of its vague definition and the breadth of use, which could, and did, lead to inappropriate use.[37] Since then, various other laws have emerged to replace the vagrancy laws, for example, laws against loitering, sleeping in public, panhandling, begging, and so on. Many such laws, especially illegal lodging and disorderly conduct, became a matter of public conversation during the Occupy Wall Street movement in

2011 and 2012 when cities used them to evict protestors encamped in public parks and other spaces.

To make matters more complex, with the demise of vagrancy laws in the late 1970s, there was a subsequent rise in use of drug laws to rid urban areas of undesirables. Here, authorities used the suspicion of drug activity as the undergirding motivation for police action. Laws in *both* categories, vagrancy and suspicion of drug-related behavior, were easily manipulated to target ethnic minorities, especially African Americans. Michelle Alexander notes a particular shift in the political and public focus during this time *from poverty and class to race and crime*.[38] Homelessness did not cease to become a matter of concern but was henceforth categorized as a criminal matter rather than a social response to poverty. In the end, it is no surprise that laws used to bring order and control over space to the benefit of those in economic and social power are often subject to various forms of social corruption—not the least of which is racism.

Anti-Homelessness

Don Mitchell of Syracuse University offers a fascinating glimpse into what are now called *anti-homeless laws*, replacing in function the vagrancy laws of the past. In an article that suggests current anti-homeless laws are the attempt to figuratively if not literally annihilate homeless persons through laws that control public space—thus giving them no space—Mitchell lists numerous such laws across the country, including those against loitering, sleeping in public, blocking a public way, washing car windows, begging near automatic teller machines or storefronts, and sitting on sidewalks. The purpose, he suggests, is "to control behavior and space such that homeless people simply cannot do what they must do in order to survive without breaking laws. Survival itself is criminalized."[39] Harkening to Giddens's notion of sequestering the day to day that threatens our sense with the morally reprehensible, Mitchell suggests that by criminalizing the day-to-day activities of homeless persons, we likewise sequester or remove any space for those who remind us, "Not there but for the grace of God, but rather there but for the grace of downsizing, out-sourcing corporations, go I. So it becomes vital that we re-order our cities such that homelessness is neutralized and the legitimacy of the state and indeed our own sense of agency, is maintained."[40] Thus, through various sociopolitical systems, we contain and remove from view those objects that remind us of our vulnerability by labeling them—the "morally depraved"—as criminals.

Criminalization of Homelessness as a Human Rights Issue

Although I have focused this chapter on issues of homelessness in the United States, American society is hardly alone in its attempts to diminish the presence of undesirable people in places of social import. Globally, individual nation states have enacted similar laws for similar purposes. The news reports prior to political summits or large global events such as the Olympics reveal the struggles of nations to quietly "clean" newly renovated areas of poor and homeless persons in order to maintain a safe, welcoming environment free of the unpleasant realities of poverty. The Chinese government literally erected a wall to hide what we might call low-income housing areas in preparation for the 2008 Olympics, and Brazil paved through slum areas in order to make way for the 2016 Olympic structures.[41] Although the Olympics are events that require long-term preparation and structural changes to any city, other sporting events, such as the FIFA World Cup, or political meetings that draw global media attention, can be cause for using legal means or force, if necessary, to sweep homeless and poor persons from specific areas. These large-scale acts that manipulate the poor for the benefit of nation states, and similar day-to-day acts using measures of force and law against homeless persons, are common. A 2011 report by Magdalena Sepúlveda Carmona, special rapporteur on extreme poverty and human rights for the United Nations, observes that "[penalization] measures are the result of deeply entrenched prejudices and stereotypes that have permeated public policies. . . . While poverty may not in itself be a violation of human rights, often States' actions or omissions that cause, exacerbate or perpetuate poverty amount to violations of human rights."[42]

For its part, in 2012, the U.S. Interagency Council on Homelessness issued a statement suggesting that the criminalization of homelessness risks infringement on the constitutional rights of homeless persons.[43] The opening sentences of the report are significant:

> In recent years, the United States has seen the proliferation of local measures to criminalize "acts of living" laws that prohibit sleeping, eating, sitting, or panhandling in public spaces. City, town, and county officials are turning to criminalization measures in an effort to broadcast a zero-tolerance approach to street homelessness and to temporarily reduce the visibility of homelessness in their communities. Although individuals experiencing homelessness should be afforded the same dignity, compassion, and support provided to others, criminalization policies further marginalize men and women who are experiencing homelessness, fuel inflammatory attitudes, and may even restrict constitutionally protected liberties.[44]

The report highlights that many of these laws restrict natural or life-sustaining activities that must be conducted in public. These laws, for example, make it illegal to distribute food, sleep, sit, urinate, carry open containers, and so on. Don Mitchell points out that these activities are criminal only because they lack private space. In other words, they are activities that each of us also engages in, but because we do so in private space, it is allowable. He writes,

> The sorts of actions we are outlawing . . . are all actions we regularly and even necessarily engage in. What is at question is where these actions are done. For most of us, a prohibition against asking for a donation on a street is of no concern; we can sit in our studies and compose begging letters for charities. So too do rules against defecating in public seem reasonable. When one of us—the housed—find ourselves unexpectedly in the grips of diarrhea, for example, the question is only

one of timing, not at all of having no place to take care of our needs. . . . Similarly, the pleasure (for me) of dozing in the sun on the grass of a public park is something I can, quite literally, live without, but only because I have a place where I can sleep whenever I choose.[45]

He closes by noting that to take away the possibility of conducting life-sustaining actions in a public space when there is no other space is an effort not only to annihilate freedom but to annihilate people; at its heart it is a matter not just of freedom but of "what kind of society we make."[46]

While the intentions behind the interagency report are undoubtedly good, it does not go far enough in its analysis of the break in societal relationships that results from objectifying the homeless through these laws. The report actually reveals how deeply embedded are the ways that the locally displaced, or homeless, persons are objectified not only by the communities in which they live but also by the government agencies who analyze methods of care. The report argues that homeless laws do not help homeless persons, which is true enough. But the laws were never intended to help homeless persons, and arguing thus does not address the real failure that trying to make those without home invisible is harmful to both homeless persons and the community, and morally reprehensible as well. Although the Interagency Council highlights the need for services that treat homeless persons with dignity and respect, subtle nuances reveal that the report nonetheless reduces homeless persons to objects of need even by the agency. For example, in the context of developing community-wide responses to "target" the vulnerable, among the long list of "stakeholders" (consumers, businesses, law enforcement, etc.) in this effort, those without home are nowhere to be found.[47] Readers are left to believe that only the business owners and local communities are stakeholders in the "problem" of homelessness— those without a home place are merely recipients of aid. Indeed, even, or perhaps especially, aid programs focused on outcomes can help perpetuate the harm of a disinterested society that feels homeless persons are themselves to blame for their own misfortunes.

Effects of Objectification

Black theology, womanist theology, and feminist and social theory, among others, have all helped shape perspectives on how dominant social groups reduce people to objects in order to control and dominate them. This gives us a helpful window into the sociological, psychological, and spiritual consequences of objectification. Studies have shown that once these objectifications are internalized, they can perpetuate learned helplessness, depression, shame, and low self-esteem.[48] These effects are demonstrated in the context of homelessness through narratives of homeless persons gleaned from interviews collected by Sisters of the Road, a homeless advocacy organization based in Portland, Oregon.

Sisters of the Road was founded based on an earlier round of interviews with homeless persons conducted by two community organizers in 1979. The organizers sought the opinions of those without home regarding what they needed most.[49] This approach to gathering information was based on the belief that the voices of those without home are the best resources for finding the solutions to care for homeless persons. The result was the establishment of the Sisters of the Road Café, which offers nutritious meals for a nominal fee of $1.25. Customers can use cash, food stamps, or barter work, or receive a meal for free. But the most astounding aspect, and particularly relevant to our conversation, is the informal statement of purpose noted on their website: "Sisters' customers, volunteers and staff have been creating community for more than three decades by *building long term, stable and mutually supportive relationships.* Creating a safe, hospitable space which offers delicious, nourishing food are our priorities in the Café."[50]

Between 2001 and 2004, a second round of over six hundred interviews was conducted. In order to add political gravitas to these efforts, the interviews were shared with the academic community as a resource for research. This material is a rich resource for anyone seeking to understand the needs of homeless persons and communities.

Quotations from these interviews that specifically focus on inter-actions between homeless "clients" and care providers reinforce not only my suggestion that persons without home are objectified by society but that those who are displaced feel these effects most pro-foundly.[51] The objectification is felt as a lack of humanity, care, and relationship. One forty-seven-year old says, "You walk into a food stamp office; I feel that I should be cared about. Show me concern, walk the path . . . with me." Another person says, "As soon as you walk through the door you are not a name or you are not a person, you are a number. . . . They [those running homeless programs] need to understand that we are people, not a number." Yet another adds, "Your self-respect is taken away from you."[52]

After a long period of time on the streets feeling dismissed and objectified, many homeless persons harden to interactions with care providers and others they meet. These interviews indicate that rather than accept such demeaning treatment, many would prefer to forego shelter or aid in exchange for maintaining some degree of self-respect. Indeed, building relationships with the women at the transitional living facility during my tenure there was difficult for very good reasons, not the least of which were the ways that the strict rules of the house were seen as infantilizing the residents. We as staff, I have no doubt, contributed to that, even if unintention-ally. By the time the women had reached our house, most, quite understandably, had hardened to even the most authentic efforts to reestablish trust and communication. Long-term residents—those who had successfully negotiated the maze of sobriety, medications, parole, or whatever other obstacles confronted them—were the most likely over time to risk trusting staff and establishing some level of relationship.

Respect and dignity remain elusive so long as persons without home are objects of disdain—or even objects of need. All service agencies would benefit from considering the displaced persons in these interviews, or any homeless person for that matter, as *stake-holders* in their community rather than as extraneous and irrelevant to the solutions. These women and men have unique views of what respect and dignity mean to those without home. In the Sisters of the Road study, the voices of the displaced describe the most notable experiences when they felt caring, love, and a sense of home as those when they felt most respected and empowered.[53] Ultimately, the study notes, the most positive comments occurred when "they were treated like a full human being."[54]

The Face of God in the Other

Think about the last time you walked past someone you thought was a homeless person. Did you avert your gaze so that you would not risk making eye contact? Or perhaps you couldn't keep yourself from staring—so long as they didn't look back. We avoid the faces of homeless persons. In some respects, it can certainly seem justified—making eye contact often leads to a plea for money. To be honest, in some parts of the United States, we do not make eye contact with *anyone* on the street. Even so, there is something unique about the lengths to which we go not to look into the faces of those without place. When we turn away we become complicit in the suffering of those without home.[55]

The human face is the literal and metaphoric center of human interaction. It is a mysterious and powerful center of expression and knowing. A glance across disciplines reveals the attempt to make sense of this power in the human face. As we have already seen, using social theory, Alfred Schutz locates what he calls the "pure we-relations" in the face-to-face encounter with the other.[56] Likewise, psychologists D. W. Winnicott and Heinz Kohut seize on the parental face that gazes approvingly into the face of a young infant as a source of sustenance, strength, and reflective ego development for the child.[57] In clinical counseling, the face is a vessel of vulnerability and intent. The actual face can be an effective resource for suggesting or even uncovering conflict and emotion along with a plethora of unspoken messages and contradictions at work within an individual.

How does our interaction with the face of the other who is without home bring about the change that transforms the encounter from one of oppression to one of not merely tolerance but liberating relationality for all involved? From a Christian perspective, I suggest a rather unsurprising though not unchallenging way to overcome objectification—by seeking the face of God in the face of the other who is without home. In biblical theology, the face of God is the ultimate location for the Divine-human encounter. Throughout the Hebrew Scriptures, one of the strongest metaphors for the presence of God is the face. Individuals and the community of Israel use the face of God repeatedly to indicate the presence, absence, hiddenness, desire for, or fear of God's presence.[58] Walter Brueggemann proposes that two main themes run throughout the Hebrew texts—Israel's obligation to live as a just community and the obligation to seek the presence of the Holy (God's face). Brueggemann describes it this way: "Israel understands itself as a community of persons bound in membership to each other, so that each person-as-member is to be treated well enough to be sustained as a full member of the community," and "one of the characteristic markings of Israel is . . . to see God, to commune with Yahweh directly, face to face."[59] This is a lovely vision for a more just community.

In the Christian tradition, the face of God becomes incarnate in the person of Jesus Christ. As with Israel, the obligation to offer care and justice to the other is paramount. We, in turn, have extended this presence, from the early church to the present, through the Eucharist that makes the body of Christ symbolically present to the community. Here, the face of God in Christ and the face of the community become one through the sharing of a meal.

Seeing the face of God in the person without home compels us into relationship, which thwarts the immediate impulse to categorize and objectify. It is not, though, a magic shield to protect against such habits. This face of the divine is the basis for enacting the moral obligation of care toward the other and is a mark of a just community. Human relationships are difficult and messy—especially when active addiction, unstable mental illness, or violence is present. But these conditions are a sign of human frailty and brokenness within the family of God, not antithetical to or rejections of it.

Although seeing the divine in the face of those without home makes relationship possible, it doesn't necessarily make it easier. When we recognize God in the other, we are opening ourselves to see deep suffering and can no longer look away from or ignore loneliness and fear any more so than hunger or lack of shelter.[60] This is difficult to sustain. Sometimes all we can manage is a mere glimpse of that divine presence in the other—homeless or not. Yet even that can develop into possibility and open our eyes to seeing resilience in places and forms we might not otherwise recognize. We find real people with stories of triumph and hope in spite of their circumstances. This we might call grace.

Conclusion

Unlike the dramatic stories of natural disasters, large-scale conflicts, or soldiers returning from war that unfold before us in the media, chronic conditions such as homelessness begin with deeply systemic issues that seldom garner much attention from the general public. Poverty and lack of affordable housing—complicated by conditions such as addiction, mental illness, and incarceration—make homelessness into what seems an unsightly, unwieldy, and overwhelming problem.

Relationship, one of the four main functions of the home place, is at risk when one becomes without a home place. Relations with immediate and extended families become strained and often broken. To federal housing programs, private-market real estate companies, police departments, local communities, aid agencies, private citizens, and even communities of faith, people who are without home quickly become the problem. Social (sociopolitical) systems attempt to contain or restrain the "least desirable" among us—those forced to live on our streets and in our parks. Even those agencies and people with the best of intentions often reduce those without home to objects—objects of need.

The failure of relationship with homeless persons compromises the lives and flourishing of the world's most vulnerable and is a failure of a just community. We may not be able to stop the forces of a hurricane or earthquake, but we can change the human forces of social and political systems that oppress. It is a matter of social justice, and it is the responsibility of the community of faith to exercise its obligation of care toward the most vulnerable.

POSTURES OF HOSPITALITY

This is the life we are living; we do not know the end.

—Elected leader, spontaneous IDP camp near Goma

When we consider these chapters collectively, it becomes most apparent that society at large responds to forced displacement with exclusionary practices toward those without home. While we often recognize this tendency in any one of these contexts—homelessness or refugees, for example—it becomes striking when seen in multiple examples. Displacement starts out being about a need for place but quickly becomes about a need for repairing relational woundedness between persons without home and the communities in which they seek shelter.

Colonialism, rejecting the foreigner, narratives of military exceptionalism, and objectification, in turn, target the fundamental functions of home that become compromised in the process of displacement. They are slight variations on the same theme of exclusion. Colonialism imposes foreign, often Western, values on systems of meaning in other cultures, systematically dismissing ancient meaning making, especially that rooted in the natural world. People without financial or political resources who become displaced in times of conflict must yield to the mercy of immigration laws in other nations that determine who among the foreigners belong and who does not. In the United States we have become so convinced of our soldiers' exceptional abilities that we no longer recognize the obvious strains these demands place on our morals or our interactions with the rest of the world, especially in times of war. Soldiers face the inward psychological and spiritual struggle to reconcile these expectations with what they have experienced and the violent actions they have committed. Anti-homeless laws are enacted simply to deny space to those who have already lost any place to call their own. Those who do offer assistance often turn persons without home into objects of need, carefully categorized into type and stereotype. These examples ultimately leave us to ask: how have we failed to enact our moral obligation to care for the displaced other?

The Underlying Moral Obligation of Care

I first introduced my concept of a moral obligation of care among the displaced in my study of the Dinka of South Sudan as a term that joined the traditional communal ethic of care among the Dinka, which seeks to always value the other on a par with the self, together with the idea of compassionate obligation as proposed by Edward Farley.[1] In his theological anthropology Farley defines compassionate obligation as the moral and empathic response that is invoked by the relational encounter with the suffering other. Farley bases the principles of both compassionate obligation and the relational encounter with the other on the work of Emmanuel Levinas and Gabriel Marcel, whom he summarizes in this way: "When we experience the face of the other, or when the face occurs in conjunction with being-together, we experience a summons, and invocation (Marcel), a claim, a call to commitment and responsibility. . . . The summons from the other is something that evokes a response in which compassion and obligation converge."[2] Humans are, of course, also free to reject compassion and respond to the other with a range of negative actions from disregard to utter hatred, even murder. Such neglect impedes a sense of obligation and suffering is magnified. This is, admittedly, an oversimplification of Farley's highly complex theology, but it is enough for our purposes to outline the parameters of how he understands the notion of compassionate obligation and see how it might be helpful as a foundational concept as we consider our moral obligation to care for the displaced.

In addition to the influence of Dinka communal practices and Farley's theological anthropology, the moral obligation of care I present here is significantly influenced by two frequent, and it seems enduring, questions asked of me in my research encounters among the displaced. The first, an inquiry directed toward the world outside of the refugee camp and perhaps toward the community of faith in particular, is, *Don't they know we are suffering?* The second question seems on the surface even more personal: *Will you remember me?* I have come to understand that these questions represent much more than heartbreaking pleas for help from individuals languishing in refugee camps. They represent a deeply ingrained expectation that others in the human family care about our suffering and carry some measure of obligation to respond.

Christian pastoral theology and care is certainly not the only tradition that grounds itself in a moral obligation to care for the displaced. But the suffering and remembering called out in these questions are particularly familiar concepts to us in the Christian faith as acts that frame God's expression of love through the life, death, and resurrection of Christ. The cross is a symbol that reminds those of us in Christian communities of faith, especially displaced Christians, that God is able to hold both loss and hope, suffering and redemption together in a way that opens a horizon of possibility. Pastoral theologian Sharon G. Thornton observes, "The cross acknowledges suffering and untold tragedy. Yet it puts a question mark next to anything that seems to suggest complete understanding or a 'Last word.'" But, she suggests, the cross also speaks to Christians, and pastoral theology in particular, in another way: "The cross simply calls us to take a stand, to break with neutrality and passivity and account for whose side we are on."[3] For Thornton pastoral theology is always on the side of love and justice—a "just love."[4] Pastoral theology grounds itself in God's love as revealed on the cross, which always looks to justice as its plumb line and is the primary condition of its ethic of care.

The refugee's question, "don't they know we are suffering?" challenges those with place to open themselves to the willingness to acknowledge suffering—to actually see the plight of the displaced. Put another way, we must surrender the blinders that buffer the suffering of the displaced around the globe and down our streets so that we can *see* it with eyes wide open. In a very real way this question, and its challenge, asks Christian communities of faith: Are we willing to look at Jesus on the cross or do we turn our heads and shield our eyes? Can we love the stranger enough to care—to see Christ in his suffering?

Likewise, the question of *remembering* is one that asks us to bring into our presence those hidden in the margins of society who suffer. To remember the despairing and shattered conditions in the lives of the displaced compels us to recall Christ's remembrance of us in his broken body. In this body Christian communities of faith share and celebrate the act of communion. We respond to this gift through acts of relational justice.

I return again and again to John Patton's communal contextual paradigm for pastoral theology that moves the caring encounter from the clinical context to that of the larger community.[5] I have suggested that remembering goes beyond the "re-visioning" that Patton suggests toward an act of bringing the fractured community together, especially in contexts of displacement and trauma. I have written, "Re-membering is the heart of the caring ecclesial community but extends beyond to the greater community. It is the root of the moral obligation to care."[6] I expand on this to suggest that the role of remembering is not only a bringing together in mindful relationship but also a just engagement by a community of faith that seeks to repair the exclusionary breech of relationships created by forced displacement.

Both knowing and remembering point us toward a moral obligation of care as an ethic of care grounded in relational practices of hospitality. The idea that practices, especially communal practices of care, have moral underpinnings is not new to pastoral theology. Don S. Browning in his highly influential work *A Fundamental Practical Theology* suggests the notion of "practical moral reasoning" as the process of enacting normative moral assumptions through pastoral practices within the congregational context.[7] Elaine L. Graham offers a feminist critique that challenges Browning's moral assumptions as androcentric and Western, and, if it does not go without saying, white and privileged. She suggests that practical wisdom emerges from *practices* themselves, not from the application of previously determined moral norms. Graham writes,

> Unlike Browning who regarded pastoral practice as the application and enactment of *a priori* moral principles, I have argued for a model of Christian practice which inherits and inhabits traditions of practical wisdom that are realized and re-enacted through the purposeful ordering of the community. . . . Such a model of pastoral practice is thus a refutation of prescriptive pastoral care which seeks to enforce a moral conformity to absolute norms on behalf of controlling and dominating interests.[8]

Graham does not deny that some guiding principles must be at work in such practices—in her case, feminist theory, narrative, and liberation theology—but makes an argument for the ways in which meaning emerges from within the practice itself.

Notions of Hospitality

Before beginning this book, I never imagined that one of the most controversial concepts I would engage would be *hospitality*. Most who have read portions of this text as it was being constructed agreed with its importance in the life of a Christian community and that it is in general a good thing. Many also agreed that the long lineage of philosophers, theologians, ethicists, and others who have written about hospitality have so worn it over the rocks that while a necessary topic, it is likely a redundant one.

Others have been rather ferocious—and in principle, rightly so— in their criticism of Western notions of hospitality steeped in colonialist practices and standards. It is duly noted that in this book I am attempting to negotiate notions of home, God, hospitality, and Christian relationship among all types of peoples, some of whom are quite different from one another—including those from the United States and those from developing countries in central Africa in particular. These are places in which colonialist practices and sentiment remain deeply embedded.

To be honest, I find hospitality a difficult notion with which to contend and have questioned its use here more than once. While it undeniably has deep and important roots in the history of Christian community, in today's world it can conjure thin descriptions of everything from a service industry that caters to the "need" for excess to trite ideas of how the "haves" help the "have-nots." As challenged as I am, however, with using the term *hospitality*, I would be equally if not more unsettled by its absence. It is, after all, what seems the ultimate in generosity and aid to those forcibly displaced from home. On the face of it, the notion of hospitality should be an easy one, but a quick look at the etymology of the word reveals a clue to the potential difficulties just waiting to break through. From the Latin root *hostis* come both *host* and *hostile*—at once the one who welcomes (host) and the one who is unwelcoming or unwelcome (hostile).[9] This may be a foreshadowing of the underlying reluctance to engage in authentic postures of hospitality or even the tensions that arise from failed hospitality.

Jacques Derrida in his foundational work on the philosophy of hospitality notes, "Injustice begins at the threshold of hospitality."[10] This is especially so with the most marginalized and thus most affected by our refusal of care. Derrida introduces the idea of unconditional hospitality, receiving foreigners across borders without regard to choice of who should receive assistance, over and against bounded hospitality, receiving only the strangers who meet certain criteria determined by the nation state.[11]

In this context, our boundaries are just another way of saying "borders" and focus most clearly on the rights and privileges of refugees, internally displaced persons (IDPs), and the nations that offer them safe harbor. Some may be able to depersonalize this negotiation of boundaries in the name of hospitality as a political endeavor so that it becomes the business of diplomats and politicians. Yet to do so risks underestimating the very personal nature of boundaries, recognized usually when they have been encroached upon, and the very intimate nature of spiritual hospitality, the type of which we consider here. As Sharon Thornton and others remind us, "The political is the personal."[12]

Hospitality is, itself, a complex undertaking. In all its forms, hospitality requires negotiating boundaries. On the individual, communal, and political levels, it requires making choices about to whom one extends the intention of hospitality and whom one rejects. Such conversations about the boundaries of hospitality are not new. Hospitality has long been a task of the Christian church from the earliest of days and follows the practice of Jesus in his own ministry through every act that sought to meet the needs of those following him. We understand, or want to believe, that *real* Christian hospitality has no limits or boundaries—there are none who should be rejected from this act of care and love. But the practical reality is that human hospitality always has limits. Resources are never endless. Living in a violent world means that safety and security are everyday concerns. We are left with working toward hospitality that pushes against boundaries, always expanding them, without giving way to idealistic platitudes that do their own kind of harm in lieu of denying hospitality. When humans set limits and make choices, the potential for both justice and injustice is at its greatest.

Hospitality as Welcoming In

For most of us, hospitality is defined by the ways we welcome others into our world, that is, our neighborhoods and home. What are the ways I open what I have to be shared with others? Christians live under the mandate to welcome the stranger and, in some scriptural examples, to offer all that we have to those we welcome. Hospitality becomes the ultimate plumb line by which one's ethic of love for God and other is judged: "I was a stranger and you welcomed me in" (Matt. 25:35).[13] "Truly I tell you, just as you did it to one of the least of these who are members of my family so you did it to me" (Matt. 25:40). The reader is left with little doubt that by enacting hospitality toward the stranger, we welcome Christ. But welcome is not a simple thing. Many needs often accompany the stranger— food, water, clothing, and companionship among them.

Yet, as ethicist Jessica Wrobleski notes, "The ideal image of hospitality is not total openness—which would deny the integrity of the household and therefore the safety and significance of the welcome—but rather a balance between a generous openness and the safety of boundaries."[14] Not only must we choose to whom we offer hospitality, but we must also make choices about how much to offer those we welcome. These limits lead to other limits. If I offer all to you, I have none for the one who comes after. This is the raw truth of limited existence as human creatures. And so, we are left to struggle with boundaries. Who do we welcome, who do we reject, and by what criteria do we make our choices? Derrida reminds us that even the decision to offer welcome can bear subtle acts of rejection. He writes,

> The "acceptor" is the one who receives, makes welcome, has—as is also said—a welcome in store, or who approves, who accepts, the other and what the other says or does. When I said I am at home here speaking my language, French, that also means I am more welcoming to Latin and Latinate languages than to others, and you see how violently I am behaving as master in my own home at the very moment of welcoming.[15]

Derrida reminds us that the decision of how to distribute hospitality, human limitedness notwithstanding, also reflects the power held by the person who controls the threshold. Every acceptance is a conditional one.

"Us" and "Them"

Already in this conversation about hospitality among the displaced, the language of "us" and "them" leads to two questions. Who counts as "us" and who counts as "them"? A practical hospitality seems to point the us toward those who have the means, inclination, and moral fortitude to offer hospitality to those without place. This is a limited concept of hospitality, which tends to lead to the unfortunate idea that

the displaced have no means of offering hospitality. I say unequivo-
cally: I do not believe that to be the case. While I discuss more about
ideas of us and them in a moment, let me reiterate: some of the most
beautiful practices of hospitality have been offered to me by those displaced by war who had very little in the way of material goods to share
with me. If we use a broader vision, or hermeneutic, to understand
hospitality, we discover the many unexpected ways and places that
hospitality emerges.[16] In bombed-out buildings in Sarajevo and the
dusty shelters of the refugee camp, I have been offered the warmest
of hospitality, through giving even in scarcity but most of all in relationship, peace, and sharing of life narratives—learning. Many have
changed and helped shape the way I now understand my home place
and certainly how I understand theirs.

In matters concerning hospitality to the displaced, we offer our
own best version of home. Yet, as we have seen throughout this book,
home can have very different meanings depending on one's own context. Even though it comes from a very generous intention, creating
home for another by offering them our own can be, in a manner of
speaking, asking them to conform not only to our version of home
but to our attempts at hospitality even when they are not understood.
Even our most generous acts can fall into judgments if they are not
appreciated in the ways we expect. Gestures of care and appreciation indicate that the person receiving our hospitality understands
and values the gift we have given. Yet most of us know the sting that
can come when there is an imbalance in gifts offered and appreciation expressed. When we fail to invest in understanding our guest's
notion of home, we are prone to misinterpret this apparent lack of
appreciation.

In the early 2000s when I worked for Catholic Charities' Refugee
Resettlement Program, a local church group conferred with me—
with great exasperation—about a group of refugees they were assisting. While not a part of our church partnership program, this
church insisted on making a home for a group of Sudanese refugees.
This church had clear expectations about what would make a good
home and what the refugees needed to learn in order to maintain

this home. Little effort was made by this church group to learn about home life in Sudan, and they were easily frustrated by small details that went unheeded by the refugees. On one occasion, the church was appalled that the refugees would not put milk in the refrigerator but would, it seemed intentionally, leave it to spoil. This was alternately interpreted as ignorance or noncompliance, either of which signaled a failure of the refugees to appreciate the hospitality of the church. Had the church group taken the time to step outside of their own vision of culture and home, they would have perhaps learned that in rural Sudan there are no refrigerators. Milk is greatly valued but usually reserved for children. Cow's milk requires owning much beloved cattle—which indicates one's wealth and status in the community. If milk is plentiful, in rural areas it is allowed to ferment and put into containers and stored underground.[17] By failing to ask questions and open themselves to learning, this group of volunteers stayed in a relationship of misunderstanding that belittled the refugees' home traditions.[18] This simple example of hospitality, of "welcoming in," even with the best of intentions served to perpetuate colonialist attitudes among the volunteers and resentment among the refugees. This is no way to make home in either tradition.

Hospitality as Opening Outward

To more deeply welcome the other I suggest that we must look outside of our own safe spaces of home and take the risk of learning what home means from the perspective of the person who is displaced. My efforts to articulate the difference between welcoming in and opening outward in hospitality may seem a tedious exercise. But it is this outward action that I suggest more accurately reflects Jesus's own ministry in which he both offers hospitality himself outside of traditional venues and also invites others to more figuratively "step out of place" in order to offer hospitality. This movement outward— literally or figuratively—toward hospitality is fundamental to learning what I introduce here as *postures of hospitality* that can bridge the relational breach created by forced displacement.

In the Gospel narratives, Jesus leaves his own home place behind yet offers a kind of hospitality that sees through to the heart of the need within all those he encounters throughout his ministry. He steps into the everyday places of death and illness to offer needed respite from suffering. He reaches across the margins to liberate women from oppressive conditions, as seen in the story of the woman at the well (John 4:1–30) and the hemorrhaging woman (Mark 5:21–34). Jesus gathers in those physically and socially displaced by illness such as the Gerasene Demoniac (Mark 5:1–20). In the practice of pastoral theology and care, this is the ultimate example of meeting people where they are.

Jesus's mere presence invites others to step out of place through postures of hospitality initiated toward him. One such example often used in discussion of Gospel hospitality is the woman who anoints Jesus's feet in the home of Simon the Pharisee (Luke 7:36–50):

> In the midst of this mildly chaotic moment, a woman silently moves forward. Quite invisible to those present, she kneels behind Jesus. Like the woman with the hemorrhage (Luke 8:43–48), this woman risks dire consequences as she creeps forward to touch Jesus. Then something happens to this unnamed woman. Instead of shaking with fear and trepidation she begins to weep. Bending low, she tends to Jesus' dusty, dirty feet with her tears. She kisses them and then, clutching the costly oil, gently anoints them. The woman does not use a cloth or the hem of her skirt but, in an intimate gesture of deep love, unfolds her hair and dries the teacher's feet.[19]

The Gospel stories are filled with those persons, particularly women, who step out of place to offer hospitality in public displays of devotion. Not surprisingly, these postures of hospitality welcome transformative learning moments discovered when abundant gifts are offered, especially out of the scarcity of one's resources, moments that reveal the deep understanding of need and love for Jesus. This hospitality meets practical needs but is also deeply relational. Pastoral theologian Emma J. Justes likens this hospitality to a kind of *listening* that attunes one to the needs of the other. And, in some respect, I am suggesting a similar posture of moving out of ourselves toward practices of care that open us to discovering the needs of the displaced other, particularly those less tangible needs of meaning, belonging, safety, and relationship that point toward home.

While we may recognize some stories as miracles that demonstrate Jesus's divine power, it is the relational nature of the encounters that helps us glimpse the embedded posture of hospitality from which we might draw. Jesus's own posture of hospitality in ministry, and ours as we follow suit, provides a means with which to break through the wall of social exclusion created by forced displacement.

Postures of hospitality often require discomfort and vulnerability but are encounters with the other that can lead toward nurturing and growth. This means, in a manner of speaking, that we must ourselves become "displaced" from what is ordinary and familiar to see with fresh eyes a world of difference and otherness. It should be no surprise to us that this is where we are sure to meet God in unexpected ways and places.

I stop short of suggesting that opening ourselves outward in hospitality creates a mutual relationship of care. To do so would overlook the level of power always held by one who can return to the safe haven of home over one who cannot. But, Justes suggests, and I agree, there is a degree of reciprocity that keeps each open to learning from the other even if mutual power does not exist. She writes, "The guest comes with a need (for food, shelter, rest), but not without a blessing to give."[20] I suggest this kind of hospitality does open us to a degree of vulnerability that displaces the usual authority of one who arrives on the scene to offer help and aid.

Certainly, there is always a place for welcoming in, but the value of seeking to understand the other makes opening outward a precious, even necessary step. Sharon Thornton uses the image of meeting people at the threshold to describe ministry "on the border":

> God comes in the form of a stranger. . . . The surprising twist in this encounter is that at the same time the host is also the guest who experiences welcome. When this happens we become willing participants

where philoexenia [love of stranger] crosses our given "thresholds" and in the process disrupts our established borders and boundaries, rules and rituals. Such hospitality is the love of strangers grounded in absolute respect. This love greets the stranger and welcomes them unconditionally as someone we do not desire to manage or control.[21]

While the gesture described here remains one of bringing others in toward what is familiar in our own homes, this image rightly reminds us that thresholds and borders too often separate, but when acknowledged can become places of invitation. And the invitation to negotiate the threshold of guest and host is the first step toward the outward movement of hospitality, that is, out of our own comfortable places of belonging, relationship, safety, and meaning.

Postures of Hospitality

Perhaps it helps to begin by tending to the distinction between acts of hospitality and a thick description of what I call a *posture of hospitality*. I suggest that hospitality is not a set of fixed acts alone but regular practices of care that emerge from a particular *posture*. By that I do not mean a sense of false bravado but rather deep-seated attitudes that open the self to genuine invitations of relationship with the other, especially the displaced other. These are more than arbitrary distinctions or mere shifts in semantics. Postures of hospitality are relational. One can provide food without love of other or shelter without justice. While not inhospitable, even these acts alone may not rise to the level of a posture of hospitality and may not necessarily serve to repair the relational fracture created by some social responses to displacement. When postures of hospitality undergird our practices of care, we become better able to move outside of our own mental models and embrace otherness, difference.[22] Yet even as this is so, we must remain vigilant to take into account the ways that power and privilege may distort these postures of hospitality in any given context.

I am by no means the first to suggest the need for a distinction between acts of hospitality and the motivating intentions behind them. But for centuries, written and unwritten rules of hospitality have centered on meeting the basic needs of the stranger—food, water, shelter. The expectation of *relationship* between stranger and host was ambiguous. And so it often remains today when the stranger is the one without home.

We cannot ignore the fact that the displaced do have real, tangible needs, but for the focus of hospitality to overlook the relational possibilities when encountering the displaced other does a disservice to all. We have seen in the previous contextual case studies that social exclusion in one form or another is an underlying element that can actually prevent the needs of the displaced from being met. I don't deny that practices of hospitality in any form that create an authentic encounter between those with place and those without can contribute to relational growth. But building authentic relational care that can begin to repair social exclusion between the displaced and others requires a particular, embedded orientation that turns practice intentionally toward its relational end.

Committing to postures of hospitality opens us to the possibility of change and a deeper relational encounter with the other. These postures of hospitality do not, of course, create a new literal home place, but I suggest here that they may contribute to creating some measure of a *relational home place that can bridge the gaps in meaning, belonging, security, and relationship left by displacement.*[23] While these relational home places may not lean into God in quite the same way as beloved home places, they can move to close the breech of exclusion and invite encounter with the holy.

By looking back at the four functions of home and the forms of social exclusion that result from loss of home in the contexts of displacement we have examined, I suggest four postures of hospitality: sacred place-making, honoring a new sense of "we," willing vulnerability, and love and justice. Although they overlap, I consider them here as separate notions.

Sacred Place-Making

Sacred place-making, even in the absence of a home place,[24] is the conscious effort to recognize the sacred in the relational space created between people who offer care and those who have been displaced. Sacred place-making does not claim the power to create what is sacred but aims to recognize the sacred that is already present when two or more persons invite earnest relationship. Christine D. Pohl reminds us that "because of God's presence . . . when we offer hospitality our relationship with God is deepened. Hospitality helps us to grow because God is already working in the lives of the people who come and in the lives of those who welcome them."[25] Sacred place-making is a posture of hospitality that seeks to recognize the sacred already present and at work in the other. By explicitly bringing the sacred into the forefront, we all begin the process of making meaning from our experiences together.

Renewed Sense of "We"

Millions of refugees and IDPs around the world flee wars, conflict, even camps of refuge in order to cross borders in search of safety and a place to belong. As foreigners they encounter some communities that are hostile and others that are welcoming—but all stand in judgment over which of *them* should become a part of *us*. I suggest that a posture of hospitality toward the displaced must attend to the task of developing a renewed sense of *we*.

The lives of refugees and IDPs are constantly pushing against the barrier of "us," those with place, and "them," those without. At every turn those without home confront both literal and social borders and boundaries reminding the displaced that they are welcome only at the right time, under the appropriate circumstances, and in limited portion. There are few more consistent examples of such boundaries than those regarding food, often a staple of traditional hospitality. In Kakuma Refugee Camp in Kenya, humanitarian workers live in separate compounds and eat from abundant portions of meats and vegetables in their own protected canteens. Admittedly, options are reduced and it is not the highest level of cuisine I have ever experienced. Nonetheless, refugees receive their meager rations of dry grains at food distribution centers under the close watch of volunteer workers to ensure that no one takes more than her share. I make this comparison not because I do not think humanitarian workers should have appropriate meals but to highlight at least one example of the us-and-them division with which displaced persons and camp workers live daily.[26]

I visited a World Food Program (WFP) food center in Mugunga Camp outside of Goma. Here I encountered an elderly woman with painfully swollen bare feet pacing in distress, back and forth across the sharp lava rocks near the food line. She was pleading for assistance. She spoke in a language I could not understand. But the deeper truth was, I feared understanding her words because I knew that I could not help without creating an impression of favoritism in an already tense and hostile crowd. In that moment I was negotiating not only a physical border but also a social one. By keeping the elderly woman relegated to a category of other, I avoided risk but also failed to see the opportunity to relate to her on a personal level. I left wondering, what would I have done if she were my mother instead of someone else's?

The posture of hospitality that lives toward a renewed sense of "we" must negotiate a difficult tension. Just like the rope that cordoned off the food being distributed by aid workers from the hungry crowds, boundaries are necessary. Without them, sometimes even the few who can be helped would be at risk. But we must live within the tension of honoring some boundaries while pushing against others. A vision of we inclusive of those called the foreigner shifts the moral obligation of care from being directed to insiders only to include all—we become one community.

William James Booth observes that the bias for "exclusionary practices" that attempt to close (literal) borders to foreigners comes in part from the perceived need to "reinvigorate a stronger sense of 'we.'"[27] He goes on to question whether this can reflect a sense of justice toward outsiders. Booth is writing from the perspective of political philosophy. He is taking both liberalism and communitarianism to task for clearly defining neither the concept of nor criteria for justice used to determine who belongs as a citizen and who does not.[28] While political philosophy is not our main focus, justice toward the foreigner, or outsider, is. Booth's observations help us reflect on the notion of we narrowly defined, but more importantly how a posture of hospitality might help break through the desire to shut out the other, especially the foreign other. A renewed sense of we responds in welcome to the entire beloved community, to make a place of belonging and bridge the social exclusion uncovered in the concept of the foreigner.

Willing Vulnerability

Making ourselves vulnerable is not easy nor always the wisest thing to do. Nonetheless, though it in no way matches the experience of vulnerability in the lives of the displaced, willingly making ourselves vulnerable in service to creating a posture of hospitality asks that we step into relationship with the displaced by surrendering claims of authority, recognizing our limitations, and naming assumptions. Vulnerability requires that we anticipate leaning into God in order to manage our own fears, which arise from being displaced from our usual level of comfort and sense of authority.

Seeking to engage the displaced—long relegated, literally, to the marginal spaces in towns, cities, shelters, and refugee camps—may require a *physical* vulnerability as well. Like the notion of fear discussed in chapter 2, it is instinctive to resist this risk in an effort to protect our vulnerable places. Nature makes no small degree of investment in "clothing" creatures in the textures and hues of their environment for the very purpose of decreasing vulnerability and increasing survivability. It may be difficult to cover our discomfort and vulnerability the first time we walk into a shelter, refugee camp, or displacement camp. My first visit to a refugee camp was for research, not a gesture of hospitality per se. Even so, it was clear to all that I was out of place and at risk of harm without assistance. Refugees I met gently chided me for my clumsiness in the rough terrain and my apparent inability to notice what was obvious to them. Nonetheless, in an act of hospitable welcome, they walked beside me and guided me. They expressed a deep gratitude for my coming to see where they were forced to live. In so doing I stumbled into offering an accidental hospitality on my part.[29] For those offering a posture of hospitality, literally walking into the marginal spaces is the ultimate opening outward and in itself speaks volumes about our relational willingness to engage difference and open ourselves to the other we encounter there.

As we engage in postures of hospitality with the displaced and begin to cross the divide of otherness, the risk of vulnerability becomes even more complex. True relational exchange—to whatever degree—begins to open avenues of emotional investment and vulnerability on both sides of the encounter. Justes reminds us that "hospitality does not happen without openness to another—opening up to their presence and the impact it may have on our lives."[30] Receiving hospitality is not without its own risks.

A worthy goal though it may be, I make no grandiose claims that such a willing vulnerability will result in a sense of mutuality—socioeconomic and political power differentials make this quite unlikely.[31] But postures of hospitality ask us to recognize that persons without home are more than displaced persons; they, like everyone, have a multiplicity of identities—daughters, brothers, community leaders, and children of God among them. Postures of hospitality invite encounters with the wisdom and resilience in all others, especially those who are displaced.

Acknowledging, examining, and ultimately relinquishing our own assumptions of cultural, economic, or intellectual superiority are necessary first steps. These are substantial challenges to living with a posture of hospitality, especially when we lean across cultures in our relatedness. Letty Russell reminds us that "if we do not examine the assumptions we carry with us, we inadvertently reinforce Western thinking as 'correct' and 'better'; this is an issue not just for those who have benefited from colonization, but for those who were colonized as well."[32]

Love and Justice

The last of our postures of hospitality harkens back to the notion of *just love* introduced at the beginning of the chapter. The social exclusion that results from the numerous ways we, that is, society at large, objectify those among us who are without home requires a radical response. In chapter 7 I proposed that seeing the face of God in the other is a place to start. Yet this work should not be interpreted as the lofty religious ideal it might seem, but as the messy work that it surely is. As a posture of hospitality, love and justice form the moral center that compels us to move toward it.

I realize that more can be said about love and justice and the relationship between the two than is possible to include here. As Gospel mandates they are considered foundational for communities of faith and perhaps the most essential among the postures of hospitality. With that said, we start with the question: what is the relationship between love and justice and how do they, as postures of hospitality, challenge and embolden the community of faith in its acts of care with the displaced? I suggest that as a posture of hospitality, love and justice are inseparable; they bring the displaced and others toward a love characterized by its messy interconnectedness, and function, ultimately, to invite the presence of the Holy.

Surely numerous forms of justice are relevant to the myriad of political, social, and economic issues that affect those without home. The form of justice to which we give our attention at this point, however, is a relational justice deeply bound to the notion of love that moves us toward bridging the relational rupture created by forced displacement.[33] In *Ethics in Light of Childhood*, John Wall examines the moral obligation of care for the vulnerable in relation to the lives of children, not the displaced, but he introduces important concepts shared in regard to both. His is a relational ethic—grounded in responsiveness to the other. He too points to the fundamental connection between love and justice and notes three areas of moral obligation foundational to a relational ethic: interpersonal relations, social justice, and universal love.[34] He observes, "The goal of justice is not simply to oppose power, but to turn destructive social tensions into creative social tensions that are more radically inclusive of difference."[35]

Definitions of love can be as varied as those for justice. Love of parent, partner, spouse, or friend—each is different. Even more so, we have found, is the love of stranger. A particular challenge in articulating attributes of love is that we are often compelled to paint unrealistic and all too positive notions of what it means to love another human being. Agape, or neighbor love, is just such an example.[36] Nonetheless, it is perhaps the closest form of love that comes near to my intent, though I use it with some trepidation. Christian communities in particular frequently identify agape as the foundation for their obligation and practices of care. Yet these attempts often create the very type of objectification of "the needy" that we are seeking to repair. David H. Kelsey complicates the notion of neighbor love and disagrees with my earlier contention that seeing the other as a beloved child of God (or the face of Christ) is sufficient impetus behind our efforts to love the stranger as neighbor. Doing so, according to Kelsey, "suggests that love as neighbor is a response to something inherently attractive and lovable within those fellow human creatures—namely, the Christ within them—rather than a desire to be in communion with them in the concrete particularities of the consequences of our own and their estrangements from God, fellow creatures, and themselves whether they're loveable or not."[37] So, he argues, we end up loving other humans for the sake of God, not because we actually love our fellow humans. It is a fair observation. Frankly, on some practical level I am quite pleased if love emerges for whatever the reason. But as a posture of hospitality we are seeking a love that has the possibility to transform human relationships in such a way that it plants a seed, no matter how small, for larger social change. This is seldom a neat and tidy love characterized by the glow of self-affirmation. Love of the displaced stranger is, as sometimes with our own families, just as likely to be reluctant, challenging, even inconvenient and incomplete. Although this is not necessarily what Wall calls universal love, he rightly frames the moral life to which I think it leads as having a "decentering effect" that "presses the human imagination constantly toward its own beyond."[38]

I champion a love, like hospitality, that steps out beyond the familiar into endless possibility. Yet love of all kinds must acknowledge real boundaries. Again, this brings us to a tension between the ideal of ever-expanding love and the practical necessity of limitation. Wall describes love at the foundation of relational ethic as "the self's unlimited obligation to the other . . . [that] is unending and excessive, constantly revealing new horizons of meaning, drawing selves and societies into journeys of self-transcendence."[39] I am compelled by his image of love that moves us toward this vision of transformation, but within the human condition are ample means to distort the philosophical good of boundless love. When is giving oneself over in unlimited obligation an act of love and when is it an act of harm, even if well-intentioned? When is relative withdrawal an act of harm or itself an act of love? These are the real, difficult, and necessary questions of boundaries related to our moral obligation as well as practices of care in all human relationships—and no less so in those with the displaced.

I hold love and justice as inseparable partners in a relational ethic that compels us to enact a human obligation of care toward the displaced. Sharon Thornton, as we saw earlier, finds love and justice to be so essentially bound together that she uses the term "just love."[40] I stop short of this but find justice and love no less inseparable. Justice serves as the righteous boundary of love, and love as the arbiter of justice. In so doing, together they invite the presence of the Holy. As a posture of hospitality they serve to close the relational distance between those with place and those without and to invite the possibility of movement outward toward transformative, hospitable practice.

Moving Forward

It seems an impossible task to fully repair the loss of home for the millions already without place around the world or the social exclusion that is its result. To the contrary, there is ample evidence that displacement in its varied forms is only becoming of increasing concern. Even as I write these closing words construction of the Nicaragua Grand Canal threatens homes and livelihoods of indigenous people in coastal Nicaragua.[41] Refugees are dying in the desperate attempt to flee war in Syria and elsewhere around the world. Similar conversations in the United States focus on how to care for immigrants who cross from the southern border. Discovered flaws in leadership within the Veterans Administration have highlighted the struggles of combat veterans to obtain psychological and medical assistance for injuries such as post-traumatic stress disorder. New anti-homeless laws are being enacted that serve to remove persons without home from public spaces; punitive actions have even been taken in some cities in the effort to prevent assisting in public those who are without home.[42] The suffering seems to have no end.

In response to this suffering I suggest that living into the postures of hospitality as I have described here invites a community of faith, and others, into a relational home place that enacts moments of meaning, belonging, relationship, and even security with displaced persons. It is my hope that readers will consider these postures of hospitality as only the beginning of the conversation and invite others to expand, reflect, and move into practice these postures and those yet to be defined.

Hospitality to the displaced, nearly regardless of context, is fraught with limitations and difficult choices. We are likely to fail far more than we succeed. Yet part of responding to the displaced with postures of hospitality means trying to learn from our fears and failures, and always remembering that what we discover in relationship together with those without place comes in unforeseen ways by the presence and grace of God in and beyond our actions. When struggle causes us to fall short of leaning into God, we depend on God to again reach across the horizon and pull us into embrace. Far from letting ourselves off the hook, this compels us to tolerate less failure of hospitality by constantly challenging our own limited visions of how we see the world, how we understand home for the other, and what we are willing to offer in comfort, care, and most importantly human relationship to those in our midst who long for a place called home.

NOTES

Introduction

1. Unless otherwise noted, names have been changed or only first names used in order to protect individual identities.

2. I use the terms *home* (singular form) and *home place* synonymously. Because we all have our own visions of what home means, I use the term *home place* as a linguistic device intended to disrupt immediate, unconscious assumptions about home. I hope the disruption leaves just enough wiggle room to allow us to more easily hear beyond our own experience of a home place. As becomes clear, *place*, particularly the home place, is more than a mere physical location.

3. When we discuss the topic of forced displacement and its effects, the use of the word *people* can be complicated. One of the most common and quietly powerful methods of inviting stereotype and bigotry, especially around racism and class, is to group humans under a category of marginalized people: poor people, displaced people, homeless people, and so on. I have used the word *persons* liberally in order to shift away from this, for example, homeless persons, persons without home, and displaced persons.

4. This research adheres to the approved Human Subjects Committee Protocol of Yale University.

5. This research adheres to the approved Human Subjects Committee Protocol of Yale University and was funded in part by a Lilly Research Scholars Grant.

6. Matt. 2:12–23. All biblical quotations are from the New Revised Standard Version.

7. See, for example, Luke 2:29–52, which tells of Jesus's journey to Jerusalem with his family for the Passover celebration during which he became separated from them and was found engaging the teachers in the Temple. Likewise, the apocryphal Infancy Gospel of Thomas tells of his childhood years, though by this account they were far from ordinary nor was Jesus an altogether pleasant child. Nonetheless, these stories indicate a stable home environment from which the young Jesus grew into adulthood. See Reidar Aasgaard, *The Childhood of Jesus: Decoding*

the Apocryphal Infancy Gospel of Thomas (Eugene, OR: Cascade Books, 2009).

8. This life transition largely crosses cultural and class boundaries. Just what the transition looks like, however, differs widely. This particular image of college as the first step outside the home is, in the United States, largely a middle-class ideal. Much variation is found across classes.

9. Many young girls in arranged marriages have parents who honor their right to refuse a marriage. For many others, especially in poor, rural areas, this is not the case. In these situations, the judgment of whether such a marriage is voluntary or forced is largely a cultural one. I suggest we need to consider the laws of that country, traditional customs, and the opinions of the participants (especially those of women) to determine an insider perspective of what is or is not forced in terms of marriage. Those of us from the West must otherwise be cautious of reading such traditions with a colonialist eye.

10. I discuss this at greater length in chapter 7.

11. I use this term in its broadest sense to describe a generation of young adults who returned home, especially during the difficult economic periods in the late 1990s and 2000s, to live with their parents after leaving home to attend college or begin full-time employment. This term is often used synonymously with "Generation Y" and can include children born as early as 1970 and as recently as 2000.

12. In chapter 7, I have added another interpretation of the term *economic refugee* to indicate those people in the United States who have fallen victim to the economic downturn that began in 2008. Here, middle-class families have been evicted from homes and suddenly find themselves living in homelessness. For most it is a shocking event, especially in contrast to a former life that reflects "the American dream."

Chapter One. Notions of Home

1. Alfred Schutz, "Sociological Inquiries," in *Alfred Schutz on Phenomenology and Social Relations: Selected Writings*, ed. Helmut R. Wagner (Chicago: University of Chicago Press, 1970), 296.

2. Yi-Fu Tuan, *Topophilia: A Study of Environmental Perceptions, Attitudes, and Values* (Englewood Cliffs, NJ: Prentice-Hall, 1974), 93.

3. Ibid., 99.

4. I readily acknowledge throughout this book that this vision of the home place is home at its best. In reality, all homes and families attain the level of "best" only in relative terms. Often home is a place of violence and

harm. Even in such home places, however, a person's ability to make meaning, feel a sense of belonging and security, and form lasting relationships is affected.

5. The process of how one comes to distinguish self from others and the expectations of how an individual relates to a larger community, and even what is considered predictable, likely differ from culture to culture.

6. James W. Fowler also uses basic psychoanalytic development theory to propose six states of faith development; see Fowler, *Stages of Faith: The Psychology of Human Development and the Quest for Meaning* (New York: HarperCollins, 1995).

7. Indeed, the environment and objects (including people) in the environment relating to the self are essential to object relations theory, for example. But this is not the same as attention to how space and place influence human development. D. W. Winnicott, *Home Is Where We Start From: Essays by a Psychoanalyst*, comp. and ed. Clare Winnicott, Ray Shepherd, and Madeleine Davis (New York: Norton, 1986), 72.

8. Clare Cooper Marcus, *House as a Mirror of Self: Exploring the Deeper Meaning of Home* (Berkeley, CA: Conari, 1995), 4.

9. Harold M. Proshansky, Abbe K. Fabian, and Robert Kaminoff, "Place-Identity: Physical World Socialization of the Self," *Journal of Environmental Psychology* 3 (1983): 57.

10. Ibid., 59.

11. Ibid., 67, 73, 76.

12. John Dixon and Kevin Durrheim, "Displacing Place-Identity: A Discursive Approach to Locating Self and Other," *British Journal of Social Psychology* 39 (2000): 31.

13. Ibid., 32.

14. Ibid.

15. Yi-Fu Tuan, "Language and the Making of Place: A Narrative-Descriptive Approach," *Annals of the Association of American Geographers* 18, no. 4 (1991): 685.

16. Ibid.

17. Roger Cohen, "In Search of Home," *New York Times*, April 3, 2014, http://nyti.ms/1h6Jadp.

18. Proshansky, Fabian, and Kaminoff, "Place-Identity," 63.

19. Dixon and Durrheim, "Displacing Place-Identity," 36.

20. Yi-Fu Tuan, "Place: An Experiential Perspective," *Geographical Review* 65, no. 2 (1975): 155.

21. Erik H. Erikson's theory of psychosocial development names nine stages ranging from infancy to old age. Concurrent with the psychological development at each stage is a social context of primary importance. Erikson uses the language of stages that progress in a chronological, linear fashion, however, he describes the significant social relatedness in terms of a radius of social relationships. (Joan Erikson suggests that the relationship is best understood as a weaving together; see Erik H. Erikson, *The Life Cycle Completed* [New York: Norton, 1998], 2.) Erikson's model informs my notions of the importance of an expanding relationship between home place and the individual. His is unapologetically a Western theory, yet through my field research I have observed a similar correlation in the social radius of home place and individual growth and development in Sudanese culture. The customary social radius and how it informs growth, of course, has been influenced by the experience of displacement.

22. The Lost Boys are a large group of unaccompanied minors who were refugees from the area that is now South Sudan. As they fled war in the late 1990s and eventually found their way to Kakuma Refugee Camp in Kenya, they became known to the media and were named "Lost Boys." Thousands of these boys, no longer children, were resettled throughout the United States in the early 2000s.

23. James S. Duncan and Nancy G. Duncan, "Sense of Place as a Positional Good: Locating Bedford in Place and Time," in *Textures of Place: Exploring Humanist Geographies*, ed. Paul C. Adams, Steven D. Hoelscher, and Karen E. Till (Minneapolis: University of Minnesota Press, 2001), 41.

24. Studies focusing on urban health support Tuan's early notion that places, particularly the built living environment, influence the humans who inhabit them. Gary W. Evans, an environmental and developmental psychologist, suggests that characteristics of the built environment influence mental health directly, through "housing, crowding, noise, indoor air quality, and light" (536), or indirectly, by the ways the environment impedes or encourages social relationships. Evans, "The Built Environment and Mental Health," *Journal of Urban Health* 80, no. 4 (2003): 536–55.

25. A notable exception, or at least adjustment, to this as a mark of success is seen in highly populated urban areas where apartments are rented or owned.

26. We are embodied creatures who move through this world temporally and always while connected to physical place. Thomas F. Gieryn, "A

Space for Place in Sociology," *Annual Review of Sociology* 26, no. 1 (2000): 463–96.

Chapter Two. Leaning into God

1. South Sudan is rich in the resource of oil—even if not wealthy from its production.
2. Theologian Craig G. Bartholomew observes that the Judeo-Christian creation story "is oriented toward creating a context suitable for human implacement and flourishing." Bartholomew, *Where Mortals Dwell: A Christian View of Place for Today* (Grand Rapids, MI: Baker Academic, 2011), 10. He is particularly interested in the theology of place and place-making in Christian scripture. He emphasizes, as do others, that the two accounts of creation in Gen. 1–2:3 and Gen. 2 likely reflect differing sources each with a distinct focus—Gen. 1 presenting "earth as a potential place for humans" (p. 24) and Gen. 2 offering "a human story [that] must begin in a specific place" (p. 25).
3. Bartholomew notes that "human identity is deeply bound up with place and in Gen. 3 displacement is at the heart of God's judgment." Ibid., 29.
4. Paul Tillich, *Systematic Theology*, vol. 1, *Reason and Revelation, Being and God* (Chicago: University of Chicago Press, 1951), 194–95.
5. Ibid., 195.
6. Space and place are not always considered interchangeable. Sociologist Edward S. Casey distinguishes between the two: "'Space' is the name for that most encompassing reality that allows for things to be located within it. . . . 'Place,' on the other hand, is the immediate ambiance of my lived body and its history, including the whole sedimented history of cultural and social influences and personal interests that compose my life-history. Place is situated in physical space, but then so is everything else, events as well as material things." Casey, "Body, Self, and Landscape: A Geophilosophical Inquiry into the Place-World," in *Textures of Place: Exploring Humanist Geographies*, ed. Paul C. Adams, Steven Hoelscher, and Karen E. Till (Minneapolis: University of Minnesota Press, 2001), 404.
7. Tillich, *Systematic Theology*, I:195.
8. For an example of the discussion of psychoanalysis and meaning of space in the therapeutic setting, see Arie Peled and Hava Schwartz, "Exploring the Ideal Home in Psychotherapy: Two Case Studies," *Journal of Environmental Psychology* 19, no. 1 (1999): 87–94. For a Jungian

perspective, see Clare Cooper Marcus, *House as a Mirror of Self: Exploring the Deeper Meaning of Home* (Berkeley, CA: Conari, 1995).

9. Many in rural South Sudan believe that God *only* blesses women through the bearing of children and caring for family. Nevertheless, years of interaction with humanitarian aid agencies in refugee camps and exposure to the idea of universal human rights, which attempts to mitigate what is interpreted as the oppressed status of women, has created a challenge to this view in some regions. At the same time, ironically, Western feminist theologians have in the last decades attempted to reclaim the spiritual nature of women's roles as mothers and caretakers even as they tend to careers. See, for example, Bonnie J. Miller-McLemore, *Also a Mother: Work and Family as Theological Dilemma* (Nashville: Abingdon, 1994).

10. The notion that God creates calamities in the effort to benefit humans in various ways is one used by many and is often categorized as meaning making. I make the distinction here that the process of meaning making I propose understands meaning to be an active and cooperative effort between self and God in the unfolding of an experience. This presupposes that God does not create pain and suffering for the purpose of creating meaning or any other lesson. Siroj Sorajjakool and Bryn L. Seyle's qualitative study with women suffering from breast cancer reveals three types of meaning-making responses: God caused cancer for a purpose, God does not cause cancer but there is meaning to be found, and there is no cause and no meaning to be found in cancer. Sorajjakool and Seyle, "Theological Strategies, Constructing Meaning, and Coping with Breast Cancer: A Qualitative Study," *Pastoral Psychology* 54, no. 2 (2005): 173–86.

11. Ibid., 174.

12. "O Lord you have searched me and known me; where can I go from your spirit?" (Ps. 139:1, 7).

13. Mary McClintock-Fulkerson, *Places of Redemption: Theology for a Worldly Church* (New York: Oxford University Press, 2007), 184.

14. Ibid.

15. David H. Kelsey, *Eccentric Existence: A Theological Anthropology*, 2 vols. (Louisville: Westminster John Knox, 2009), 1:347.

16. Ibid., 1:350.

17. John Wall, *Ethics in Light of Childhood* (Washington, DC: Georgetown University Press, 2010), 107.

18. The evaluation of individuality, or enmeshment for that matter, is greatly complicated by cultural context. Western family units value individualism more acutely than do more communal cultures thus making enmeshment perhaps a much more prominent failure in the Western context.

19. Barbara J. McClure, *Moving beyond Individualism in Pastoral Care and Counseling: Reflections on Theory, Theology, and Practice* (Eugene, OR: Cascade, 2010), 217. The term *Kin-dom of God* is used by feminist theologians to push against sexist notions of God as male as inferred by the term Kingdom and also to invite an eschatological vision of humans together as "kin," brother and sister. See ibid., 215n3.

20. Kelsey, *Eccentric Existence*, 1:310.

21. McClure, *Moving beyond Individualism*, 217.

22. Ibid., 218.

23. Kelsey notes, "Of course, a healthy human living body is preferable to an unhealthy one. For that matter, for any personal body, thriving in the sense of prospering is preferable to being impoverished." Kelsey, *Eccentric Existence*, 1:317.

24. Ibid., 1:318.

25. Ibid., 1:119.

26. McClure affirms that "contributing to the flourishing of persons" has been at least an "implicit" goal for the practice of pastoral caregivers. She rightly encourages the field to tend to the well-being of those from a broader range of life circumstances. She writes, "[To expand] the goals of flourishing to all—including and especially those outside the white middle class—is, I believe a value among pastoral theologians and practitioners. In order to . . . expand our effectiveness to currently underserved groups, we will need to be more intentional about attending to the experiences and needs of persons outside the historically prevalent demographic." McClure, *Moving beyond Individualism*, 238. This is certainly true if pastoral caregivers are to attend to the well-being of the displaced either in pastoral care centers or in the context of individual displacement.

27. Kelsey, *Eccentric Existence*, 1:315.

28. These "reciprocities of shared meaning" are the essence of social infection. Edward Farley comments, "Idolatrous postures and agendas are never simply sealed off into the interiority of each individual self. They are an aspect of everyday reciprocities and the mutual sharing of

meanings. They, too, find their way into the group's taken-for-granted typifications and presupposed stock of knowledge at hand and thus into its stories and imageries. Thus the individual's absolute enemy becomes also the shared absolute enemy, the symbolic enemy of the group." Farley, *Good and Evil: Interpreting a Human Condition* (Minneapolis: Fortress, 1990), 256.

29. Ibid., 257.

Chapter Three. Crisis and Forced Displacement

1. Resettlement that is not in one's country of origin or host country but in a third country that has agreed to allow legal entry and a provisional status including protection under its laws.

Chapter Four. Breathing Home

1. Cited in Justin Kendrick, "The Batwa of South West Uganda: World Bank Policy on Indigenous Peoples and the Conservation of the Bwindi and Mgahinga National Parks," October 23, 2000, 14, http://www .forestpeoples.org/sites/fpp/files/publication/2010/08/wbipsugand amayooeng.pdf.

2. A statement from the Batwa, from Chibungo and Chogo, Uganda, cited in ibid., 25.

3. The Batwa are known by many local names throughout Central Africa (primarily the Democratic Republic of the Congo [DRC], Uganda, and Burundi). In most written reports, academic articles, and books, the term *Pygmy* is used interchangeably with *Batwa* or other local names for these indigenous persons. In the local contexts Pygmy carries a derogatory connotation that is not explicitly duplicated in most published material. The term *indigenous* is a somewhat contested category, at least on the African continent where there are a vast number of tribes who lay legitimate claim to being indigenous to the land. I use it in connection to the Batwa, who are identified by other Africans in the Congo as the "first people."

4. The Batwa, also known as Twa and by other regional names, can be found in Uganda, Rwanda, DRC, Kenya, Tanzania, and Burundi.

5. Mugunga IDP Camp is divided into three sections, two of which have become long-term settlements for impoverished citizens of Goma including those who have migrated there from surrounding regions. The third section, sometimes called Mugunga III, serves as the primary intake and settlement point for newly arriving IDPs.

6. Jerome Lewis, "The Batwa Pygmies of the Great Lakes Region," Report of Minority Rights Group International, June 2000, 28, http://www.refworld.org/pdfid/469cbf89d.pdf.

7. Kairn A. Klieman, *"The Pygmies Were Our Compass": Bantu and Batwa in the History of West Central Africa, Early Times to c. 1900 C.E.* (Portsmouth, NH: Heinemann, 2003), xvi.

8. Intermarriage between the Batwa and Bantu over generations has resulted in increased physical stature for some Batwa as well as cultural adaptation to the Bantu's agrarian lifestyle. Ibid., 68–69.

9. Both quotations, ibid., 138

10. Ibid., 3.

11. Ibid., xvi.

12. I critique Miriam's perspective with great caution, aware of the complications that arise when Western researchers question the beliefs of those from other cultures. I cannot separate what part of her belief about Pygmies comes from long-held traditions within her own culture or was imported and imposed through colonial occupation.

13. Axel Kohler, "Of Apes and Men: Baka and Bantu Attitudes to Wildlife and the Making of Eco-Goodies and Baddies," *Conservation and Society* 3, no. 2 (2005): 415.

14. The World Heritage Program and World Heritage Sites are under the direction of the United Nations Educational, Scientific, and Cultural Organization (UNESCO). Sites are chosen by a special committee for their "outstanding universal value." There are, at present, 981 such sites around the world. "World Heritage List," UNESCO World Heritage Centre, http://whc.unesco.org/en/list/.

15. Kendrick, "The Batwa of South West Uganda," 14.

16. Lewis, "The Batwa Pygmies of the Great Lakes Region," 17, 20.

17. Fauna and Flora International, "Batwa Cultural Values in Bwindi Impenetrable and Mgahinga Gorilla National Parks, Uganda: A Report of a Cultural Assessment," October 2013, https://www.google.com/search?q=Batwa+Cultural+Values+in+Bwindi+Impenetrable+National+Park+and+Mgahinga+Gorilla+National+Parks&ie=utf-8&oe=utf-8.

18. The original Bwindi Forest in which they lived is now the national park. This legacy site for the Buhoma Batwa sits just adjacent to Bwindi Impenetrable Forest National Park.

19. I pause to note the manner in which colonialism complicates this intercultural learning exchange. The Batwa were displaced by conservation practices set in motion by oppressive political powers. The land

on which this performance takes place was purchased by a Christian organization on behalf of the Batwa. Even though this organization is one of the very few who have actually given ownership of the land over to the Batwa, Missionary Christianity in general has perpetuated what could be considered colonialist evangelistic practices—offering goods in exchange for "right" belief that comes at the cost of traditional religions. Our presence as paying customers to this display of the Batwa's traditional practices might further be seen as a ridiculous cycle of power and privilege being entertained at the expense of the dignity of those who are oppressed. I continue to struggle with these dynamics and my participation in them. My hope is to not see this experience as "fun entertainment" but as an opportunity to learn about the richness of Batwa life from a generous group of people.

20. Our visit on this day was to a piece of land purchased on behalf of the Batwa by the Kellermann Foundation to help the Batwa create a cultural learning experience, the Batwa Experience. The Kellermann Foundation's mission is "to provide resources for sustainable development, health, education, and spiritual outreach for the benefit of the Batwa pygmies and adjacent communities." Scott and Carol Kellermann served in Uganda as medical missionaries associated with the Episcopal Church, though the foundation is not directly connected to the church. One of the foundation's partner programs, the Batwa Development Program, facilitates the Batwa Experience, a historical performance event intended to pass on cultural traditions to younger generations as well as to educate tourists. http://www.kellermannfoundation.org/index.html.

21. Yi-Fu Tuan, "Language and the Making of Place: A Narrative-Descriptive Approach," *Annals of the Association of American Geographers* 81, no. 4 (1991): 684–96. See also John Dixon and Kevin Durrheim, "Displacing Place-Identity: A Discursive Approach to Locating Self and Other," *British Journal of Social Psychology* 39 (2000): 27–44.

22. Kohler, "Of Apes and Men," 411.

23. We cannot overlook the fact that the performative nature of the Batwa Experience is to tell a story that teaches and entertains. To what degree the story is molded, if at all, toward audience expectations, often Western, cannot be determined.

24. Fauna and Flora International, "Batwa Cultural Values."

25. Emmanuel Turyatunga, "Social Exclusion, Marginalization and the Threat of Extinction of Ethnic Minorities: A Case of the Batwa Com-

munity in Uganda," *International Journal of Sustainable Development* 2, no. 3 (2010): 60.

26. While I find this report problematic for the ways it interprets many of the Batwa responses and circumstances through a Western development-oriented lens, some of the direct information provided from the Batwa is quite helpful. Agrippinah Namara, "GEF Impact Evaluation. Case Study: Impacts of Creation and Implementation of National Parks and of Support to Batwa on Their Livelihoods, Well-Being and Use of Forest Products," September 2007, https://www.thegef.org/gef/sites/thegef.org/files/documents/Impact_Eval_Infodoc10.pdf.

27. Nurit Bird-David et al., "Beyond 'The Original Affluent Society': A Culturalist Reformulation," *Current Anthropology* 33, no. 1 (1992): 29–30. Bird-David coined the phrase in the context of understanding the economy of sharing among animist hunter-gatherers. For Westerners he hopes that "sharing" can become a "primary metaphor which can help us to loosen slightly the bonds of our own Western ways of viewing the world." He notes of the hunter-gatherer relationship to the natural world, "For them nature seems to be a set of agencies, simultaneously natural and human-like. . . . They view their world as an integrated entity."

28. Kohler, "Of Apes and Men," 413.

29. Nurit Bird-David, "Tribal Metaphorization of Human-Nature Relatedness: A Comparative Analysis," in *Environmentalism: The View from Anthropology*, ed. Kay Milton (New York: Routledge, 1993), 121.

30. Many Christian organizations also offer food, clothes, medicine, and other much-needed goods, which lead some to question the motivation for changes in religious commitment.

31. Klieman, *"The Pygmies Were Our Compass,"* 140.

32. Lewis, "The Batwa Pygmies of the Great Lakes Region," 8.

33. Ibid.

34. Stephen R. Kellert, "The Biological Basis for Human Values of Nature," in *The Biophilia Hypothesis*, ed. Stephen R. Kellert and Edward O. Wilson (Washington, DC: Island Press, 1993), 42.

35. The substantial advances of the industrialized and technological world tempt me to make the judgment that such development or progress is a social good, though not exclusively so. Those few who continue to live their lives closely bound to nature without use of technology, by choice or circumstance, offer other wisdom and resources to the collective progress of the world that should be considered of equal value.

36. The nine valuations are Utilitarian, Naturalistic, Ecologistic-Scientific, Aesthetic, Symbolic, Humanistic, Moralistic, Dominionistic, and Negativistic; see Kellert, "The Biological Basis for Human Values of Nature," 56.

37. Roger S. Ulrich, "Biophilia, Biophobia, and Natural Landscapes," in Kellert and Wilson, eds., *The Biophilia Hypothesis*, 75.

38. Joseph Conrad, *Heart of Darkness* (New York: Penguin, 2007), 43.

39. Klieman, *"The Pygmies Were Our Compass,"* 1.

40. Adam Hochschild, *King Leopold's Ghost: A Story of Greed, Terror, and Heroism in Colonial Africa* (Boston: Houghton Mifflin, 1998), 175–76.

41. Lewis, "The Batwa Pygmies of the Great Lakes Region."

42. Environmental psychology, for example, has attempted to understand the impact of the natural and built environments on humans. For the effects of exposure to the natural world on the cognitive abilities of children, see Nancy M. Wells, "At Home with Nature: Effects of 'Greenness' on Children's Cognitive Functioning," *Environment and Behavior* 32, no. 6 (2000): 775–95.

43. I choose here to capitalize the God of the Batwa (as introduced in the creation myth) in the same manner as I capitalize the Judeo-Christian God. Missionary Christianity most prevalent in Central Africa would likely demand that the Judeo-Christian notion of God be held as supreme over the Batwa one. In my work in several African nations, however, I frequently experienced a comfort among the people to merge traditional religious beliefs with Christian ones. I afford them equal levels of respect here in order to honor both ways of believing.

44. Sally Balenger et al., "Between Forest and Farm: Identifying Appropriate Development Options for the Batwa of Southwestern Uganda," Report for First Peoples Worldwide, 2005, http://citeseerx.ist.psu.edu/viewdoc/download?doi=10.1.1.332.4290&rep=rep1&type=pdf.

45. Andrew D. Lester, *Hope in Pastoral Care and Counseling* (Louisville: Westminster John Knox Press, 1995), 62.

46. Jonathan Lear, *Radical Hope: Ethics in the Face of Cultural Devastation* (Cambridge, MA: Harvard University Press, 2006), 2. Lear writes about the cultural demise of the Crow Nation, which seems to me quite relevant to the loss endured by the Batwa. He picks up on one line from the story of Plenty Coups, the last chief of the Crow Nation. In the telling of his life story, Plenty Coups tells nothing of the many years after the Crow Nation was driven from its land and placed on a reservation; instead, he writes, "But when the buffalo went away the hearts

of my people fell to the ground, and they could not lift them up again. *After this nothing happened*" (emphasis added). Ibid., 2. Lear goes on to help the reader understand that Plenty Coups was a remarkable man of courage who was able to comprehend that he had experienced the end of life as the Crow had known it. All the markers and frames by which they made meaning in the world—such as the buffalo—were either destroyed or taken from them.

47. Ibid., 76.

48. In spite of these challenges, I do think Lester's work remains helpful to our discussion of the Batwa in regard to the following concepts: the importance of a future story to the ability to hope, the notion of a core narrative (though perhaps a core communal narrative would be an appropriate modification), and, though I say this with a degree of caution, the theological vision of a hopeful future that lives into God's faithful promise.

49. Lear, *Radical Hope*, 118.

50. The difficulty of being displaced from Bwindi Forest notwithstanding, this rural setting is relatively stable compared to many others throughout the Great Lakes region. As is often the case, displacement in poor urban areas is especially brutal and devastating, especially for the Batwa population.

Chapter Five. Fleeing Conflict and Disaster

1. Nira Yuval-Davis, "Belonging and the Politics of Belonging," *Patterns of Prejudice* 40, no. 3 (2006): 199, http://www.tandfonline.com/doi/abs/10.1080/0031322060076933I#preview.

2. Amon Eddie Kasambala, "The Impact of an African Spirituality and Cosmology on God-Images in Africa: A Challenge to Practical Theology and Pastoral Ministry," *International Journal of Practical Theology* 9, no. 2 (2005): 313.

3. Some developmental theories, such as those of Erik H. Erikson do consider multiple stages of simultaneous psychological and psychosocial development (including eight cycles during life from infancy through old age with a ninth added later). It is not quite the same, however, as considering the impact of internal psychic development of an infant in the context of the ever-present extended African family, community, and cosmic world (ancestors spirits and God). See Erikson, *The Life Cycle Completed* (New York: Norton, 1998), and Augustine Chingwala Musopole, "On Being Human in Africa: A Critical Evaluation of an

African View of Humanity in the Writings of John Mbiti," Ph.D. diss., Union Theological Seminary, 1991.

4. Margaret S. Mahler, Fred Pine, and Anni Bergman, *The Psychological Birth of the Human Infant: Symbiosis and Individuation* (New York: Basic Books, 1975), 15.

5. Harold P. Blum, "Separation-Individuation Theory and Attachment Theory," *Journal of the American Psychoanalytic Association* 52, no. 2 (2004): 542.

6. John S. Mbiti, "A Change in the African Concept of Man," in *For the Sake of the Gospel*, ed. Gnana Robinson (Mysore, India: T. T. S. Publications, 1980), 56–57.

7. Musopole, "On Being Human in Africa," 103.

8. Mbiti, "A Change in the African Concept of Man," 104.

9. John Bowlby, *Attachment and Loss*, vol. 1, *Attachment* (London: Hogarth Press and Institute of Psycho-Analysis, 1969), xi.

10. John Bowlby, *Attachment and Loss*, vol. 2, *Separation: Anxiety and Anger* (London: Hogarth Press and Institute of Psycho-Analysis, 1973), 146–47.

11. Roy F. Baumeister and Mark R. Leary, "The Need to Belong: Desire for Interpersonal Attachments as a Fundamental Human Motivation," *Psychological Bulletin* 117, no. 3 (1995): 497.

12. Anthony Giddens, *Modernity and Self-Identity: Self and Society in the Late Modern Age* (Cambridge, MA: Polity Press, 1991), 53.

13. Like home at its best, we are speaking here of a best vision of a community of faith. It is important to acknowledge, however, that a community of faith, like home gone wrong, can be a place that causes great harm and leaves persons feeling rejected and alienated. Some churches in rural parts of eastern DRC, for example, excommunicate women who have been raped thus sanctioning their rejection not only from the religious community but also from social and familial communities.

14. *Immigrant* and *migrant* are other familiar terms used to indicate those who cross national borders, leaving one home place in search of another. Both categories may imply a voluntary action with permanent relocation as the goal. As noted elsewhere, the line between voluntary and involuntary displacement is sometimes a difficult one to define. Refugees certainly fall under the category of *forced* migration. *Forced migration* is an alternate term for forced displacement.

15. Only approximately 1 percent of refugees who apply for resettlement through the UNHCR after seeking long-term shelter in a host country

receive it. In these cases refugees are assisted in moving their entire families and are given some degree of assistance, financial and otherwise, to begin new lives in a new country.

16. "Refugees," UNHCR, http://www.unhcr.org/pages/49c3646c125.html.

17. George Orwell, *Animal Farm* (New York: Harcourt, Brace, 1954), 148: "All animals are equal but some animals are more equal than others."

18. In the United States foreigners of illegal standing (in the country without legal permission) are frequently referred to by the even more socially denigrating term *illegals*. Interestingly, in the public sphere, Latino/a immigrants are more frequently named as illegals than other foreign-born nationals. Certainly a shared border with Mexico and the close proximity to other Central American countries increases the likelihood that Latino/a immigrants can gain access illegally.

19. "The PNG Solution," *Economist*, July 27, 2013, http://www.economist .com/news/asia/21582320-shadow-looming-election-falls-desperate -asylum-seekers-png-solution; Matt Siegel, "Australian Premier Seeks to Slow Tide of Refugees," *New York Times*, July 2, 2013, http://www .nytimes.com/2013/07/04/world/asia/Australian-Premier-Kevin-Rudd -Seeks-to-Slow-Tide-of-Refugees.html?pagewanted=all.

20. South Sudan grants citizenship to those who were born in South Sudan, those who are members of an indigenous ethnic group in South Sudan, or those who qualify by inheritance (a proven descendent of any one of three generations, that is, parent, grand-, or great-grandparent— maternal or paternal—born or residing in South Sudan since 1956). Bronwen Manby, *International Law and the Right to a Nationality in Sudan*, African Government Monitoring and Advocacy Program (AfriMAP), Open Society Foundations, 2011, 11.

21. Bronwen Manby, *The Right to a Nationality and the Secession of South Sudan: A Commentary on the Impact of the New Laws*, AfriMAP, Open Society Initiative for Eastern Africa, 2012, 2.

22. Ibid., 4.

23. Sarnata Reynolds, "South Sudan: Millions Wait for Proof They Are Citizens of New Nation," *Guardian*, July 10, 2012, http://www.guardian .co.uk/global-development/poverty-matters/2012/jul/10/south-sudan -proof-citizens-nation.

24. Ibid.

25. Sudanese citizenship can be reinstated only through a presidential decision; see Manby, *Right to a Nationality*, 5.

26. Reynolds, "South Sudan."

27. Didier Bigo, "Security and Immigration: Toward a Critique of the Governmentality of Unease," *Alternatives: Global, Local, Political* 27, no. 1 (2002): 63–92.

28. Ibid., 67, 68.

29. Tabitha Center in Goma is a small center that focuses on helping women who have been rejected from their families gain marketable skills. The center was started by Pastor Othniel Mweniyamba, who is an ordained minister in the Church of the Nazarene. Programs at the center include microloan projects, agricultural training and sale of produce, soap making, sewing, and a primary school for children of women associated with the center. Tabitha Center in Goma is associated with the Tabitha Center Ministries of the Evangelical Free Church in America (EFCA) located in Kinshasa, DRC, and was at one time supported in part by ASSIST (Aid to Special Saints in Strategic Times), a Canadian Christian ministry.

Chapter Six. War and Home—No Safe Place

1. Chaplain (Major) Carlos C. Huerta, U.S. Army, "Leaving the Battlefield: Soldier Shares Story of PTSD," April 25, 2012, http://www.army .mil/article/78562/Leaving_the_battlefield__Soldier_shares_story_of _PTSD/. This and all subsequent quotations from this work are used with permission, courtesy of Chaplain (Major) Carlos C. Huerta, U.S. Army.

2. "Haunted by 40 Months in Iraq," http://www.anothersource.org/ haunted_2.html.

3. The term *soldier* is used here as a generic term to refer to all members of the armed forces, commissioned and noncommissioned, specifically in the U.S. Army, Marine Corps, Navy, and Air Force (including National Guard members of each branch called to active duty). When discussing issues relating to the soldier returning home, I use *veteran* and *soldier* interchangeably.

4. Pastoral theologian Kristen Leslie, along with Marie Fortune and Jane Frederickson of the FaithTrust Institute, were contracted with the Department of the Navy to provide sexual assault incident training for Navy chaplains beginning in 2014. The program was titled "Fiscal Year 14 Professional Development Training Course for the U.S. Navy Chaplain Corps on the Chaplain's Role in Sexual Assault Incidents."

5. The most current revision of the *Diagnostic and Statistical Manual of Mental Disorders*, the 5th edition (*DSM-5*), was released in 2013 after a

lengthy vetting process. Any direct references I make to the *DSM* are to this version. I do note, however, that some references, depending on their dates of publication, may have relied on earlier versions. I highlight any relevant changes brought forth in the *DSM-5* that might have significant impact on quoted resources using an earlier version.

6. Loosely defined to include family of origin or family of choice, partner with or without children.

7. Much of the focus concerning PTSD and moral injury highlights how the effects interfere with a soldier's ability to continue to perform duties in combat or to return to day-to-day life at home. However, it is important to note that not all soldiers are diagnosed with PTSD, and others find the resources to negotiate the moral dimensions of actions taken in combat. Some, for a variety of reasons, choose to redeploy instead of returning home. For them, the combat arena is a home place of choice.

8. Holding occurs from the time of "inter-uterine life" to handling in infanthood to family life, and even in the therapeutic setting. D. W. Winnicott notes, "In an environment that holds the baby well enough, the baby is able to make personal development according to the inherited tendencies. The result is a continuity of existence that becomes a sense of existing, a sense of self, and eventually results in autonomy." Winnicott, *Home Is Where We Start From: Essays by a Psychoanalyst*, comp. and ed. Clare Winnicott, Ray Shepherd, and Madeleine Davis (New York: Norton 1986), 27–28.

9. D. W. Winnicott, "Theory of the Parent-Infant Relationship," *International Journal of Psycho-Analysis* 41 (1960): 588.

10. Brooke Hopkins, "Winnicott and Imprisonment," *American Imago* 62, no. 3 (2005): 277, emphasis added.

11. D. W. Winnicott, *Deprivation and Delinquency* (London: Tavistock/Routledge, 1984).

12. D. W. Winnicott, *The Family and Individual Development* (London: Tavistock, 1965), 30.

13. Michelle Givertz and Chris Segrin, "The Association between Overinvolved Parenting and Young Adults' Self-Efficacy, Psychological Entitlement, and Family Communication," *Communication Research*, August 20, 2012, http://crx.sagepub.com/content/early/2012/08/16/009 3650212456392.

14. Winnicott, *Family and Individual Development*, 30.

15. Ibid., 31.

16. Others explore ontological security in relation to whether home owner-ship provides greater security than tenancy. For example, see Ann Du-puis and David C. Thorns, "Home, Home Ownership and the Search for Ontological Security," *Sociological Review* 46, no. 1 (1998): 24–47; Rosemary Hiscock et al., "Ontological Security and Psycho-Social Benefits from the Home: Qualitative Evidence on Issues of Tenure," *Housing, Theory and Society* 18, nos. 1–2 (2001): 50–66; Hazel Easthope, "A Place Called Home," *Housing, Theory and Society* 21, no. 3 (2004): 128–38; and Anthony Giddens, *Modernity and Self-Identity: Self and Society in the Late Modern Age* (Cambridge, MA: Polity Press, 1991), 243.

17. R. D. Laing, *The Divided Self* (New York: Pantheon Books, 1960), 40; Giddens, *Modernity and Self Identity*, 53. See also Deborah K. Padgett, "There's No Place Like (a) Home: Ontological Security among Per-sons with Serious Mental Illness in the United States," *Social Science and Medicine* 64, no. 9 (2007): 1925–36.

18. Dupuis and Thorns, "Home, Home Ownership and the Search for On-tological Security."

19. Giddens, *Modernity and Self-Identity*, 36.

20. Ibid., 37.

21. D. W. Winnicott, *Maturational Processes and the Facilitating Environment: Studies in the Theory of Emotional Development* (New York: International Universities Press, 1965), 131.

22. Ronnie Janoff-Bulman, *Shattered Assumptions: Towards a New Psychology of Trauma* (New York: Free Press, 1992).

23. Ryan LaMothe, "Empire, Systemic Violence, and the Refusal to Mourn: A Pastoral Political Perspective," *Journal of Pastoral Theology* 23, no. 2 (2013): 1.2–1.26.

24. Judith Herman, *Trauma and Recovery: The Aftermath of Violence—From Domestic Abuse to Political Terror* (New York: Basic Books, 1992).

25. I call this resilience; it has been referred to more specifically as post-traumatic growth.

26. Huerta, "Leaving the Battlefield."

27. "Haunted by 40 Months in Iraq."

28. This notion of relatively safe places is in part influenced by Edward Farley's understanding of the *social world*, which "is a people's shared way of understanding the places that are safe, the home place, the familiar in contrast to the dangerous, the alien, and the strange." Likewise, the broader notion of a holding environment, in psychoanalytic terms dis-

cussed by D. W. Winnicott and others, has influenced the idea that the community can function to create a relatively safe space that invites a similar kind of psychological, and perhaps physical, holding space. Farley, *Good and Evil: Interpreting a Human Condition* (Minneapolis: Fortress Press, 1990); M. Jan Holton, *Building the Resilient Community: Lessons from the Lost Boys of Sudan* (Eugene, OR: Cascade Books, 2011), 125n25.

29. Holton, *Building the Resilient Community*, 125, see also n27.

30. Women have long served in various capacities on the frontlines of war and have been particularly effective and visible in the wars in Iraq and Afghanistan. Only in 2013 were they granted permission to officially serve in combat positions.

31. Huerta, "Leaving the Battlefield."

32. Invisible Wounds of War Project, "Site-Wide Navigation," http://www.rand.org/multi/military/veterans.html.

33. The *DSM-5* focuses specifically on mental disorders and is endorsed by the American Psychiatric Association. The International Classification of Diseases (ICD-10), which also includes mental health disorders though not exclusively, is endorsed by the World Health Organization and was originally a codification system for international statistical purposes. The criteria for PTSD diagnosis differ between the two, leading some to question the accuracy in statistical analysis of PTSD prevalence. Rita Rosner and Steve Powell, "Does ICD-10 Overestimate the Prevalence of PTSD? Effects of Differing Diagnostic Criteria on Estimated Rates of Post Traumatic Stress Disorder in War Zone Exposed Civilians," *Trauma and Gewalt* 3, no. 2 (2009), http://www.researchgate.net/publication/220039528_Does_ICD-10_Overestimate_the_Prevalences_of_PTSD_Effects_of_Differing_Diagnostic_Criteria_on_Estimated_Rates_of_Posttraumatic_Stress_Disorder_in_War_Zone_Exposed_Civilians.

34. Many victims of non-combat-related PTSD also struggle with shame and guilt, seen especially in cases of sexual assault, believing that they themselves are somehow culpable for the violence they have suffered. Even so, this guilt is generally not associated with the infliction of harm on others, nor is it a specific diagnostic factor.

35. Janoff-Bulman, *Shattered Assumptions*, 62.

36. See Holton, *Building the Resilient Community*, chap. 4.

37. Ibid., 91.

38. Ibid., 86.

39. Derek Summerfield, "The Invention of Post-Traumatic Stress Disorder and the Social Usefulness of a Psychiatric Category," *British Medical Journal* 322, no. 7278 (2001): 95–98.

40. Didier Fassin and Richard Rechtman, *The Empire of Trauma: An Inquiry into the Condition of Victimhood* (Princeton, NJ: Princeton University Press, 2009), 240.

41. While currently military personnel are, indeed, made eligible for mental health (and other) services by the diagnosis of PTSD, access to these services remains cumbersome and inadequate.

42. A recent study on suicide risk factors for military personnel disputes that there is a direct correlation between combat in Iraq, Afghanistan, or both and current rising suicide rates. Rather, it points to male gender, depression, manic-depressive disorder, and alcohol abuse as having direct links to suicide. Yet several items should be noted: by the study authors' own admission, their research ended in 2008 before the sharpest rise in suicides, and the eighty-three suicides counted during the study period may be statistically too low to draw a robust conclusion. I would add that the focus of the study does not interpret the correlation between increased depression and alcohol use and combat or long-term deployment. Instead, the researchers conclude that "suicide risk was independently associated with male sex and mental disorders but not with military-specific variables." I suggest that more research is needed before dismissing the effects of combat. Cynthia A. LeardMann et al., "Risk Factors Associated with Suicide in Current and Former US Military Personnel," *Journal of the American Medical Association* 310, no. 5 (2013): 496 (quotation), 502, http://jama.jamanetwork.com/article.aspx?articleid=1724276.

43. The U.S. Department of Veterans Affairs (VA) provides treatment to veterans for medical needs, including those related to mental health, regardless of their origin. In other words, veterans may also be treated for PTSD caused by events or circumstances other than combat. "PTSD: National Center for PTSD," http://www.ptsd.va.gov/public/pages/treatment-ptsd.asp#.URz6YtodPqg.email.

44. Judith S. Beck, *Cognitive Therapy: Basics and Beyond* (New York: Guilford Press, 1995), 14–15.

45. "VA Website Maintenance," http://www.ptsd.va.gov/public/pages/treatment-ptsd.asp. The website states, "For example, a soldier may feel guilty about decisions he or she had to make during war. Cognitive

therapy, a type of CBT, helps you understand that the traumatic event you lived through was not your fault."

46. Rebekah Bradley et al., "A Multidimensional Meta-Analysis of Psychotherapy for PTSD," *American Journal of Psychiatry* 162, no. 2 (2005): 214–27.

47. Alan Fontana, Robert Rosenheck, and Elizabeth Brett, "War Zone Traumas and Posttraumatic Stress Disorder Symptomatology," *Journal of Nervous and Mental Disease* 180, no. 12 (1992): 748–55. Results of this study indicate that being a target of aggression and threat is a more significant indicator of clinical PTSD symptomology. This conclusion was refuted in a subsequent research project by two of the same authors in 1999. Alan Fontana and Robert Rosenheck, "A Model of War Zone Stressors and Posttraumatic Stress Disorder," *Journal of Traumatic Stress* 12, no. 1 (1999): 111–26.

48. Fontana and Rosenheck, "Model of War Zone Stressors," 123.

49. Kent D. Drescher et al., "An Exploration of the Viability and Usefulness of the Construct of Moral Injury in War Veterans," *Traumatology* 17, no. 1 (2011): 9.

50. Ibid., 11.

51. Drescher et al. acknowledge that future research should include care providers outside these systems, including those who do not offer care to veterans. Ibid., 12.

52. Ibid., 8.

53. Brett T. Litz et al., "Moral Injury and Moral Repair in War Veterans: A Preliminary Model and Intervention Strategy," *Clinical Psychology Review* 29 (2009): 698.

54. Soldiers are not the only ones to suffer moral injury or to struggle with being on both sides of receiving and inflicting harm. Individuals forced under threat of death to inflict harm on others as an act of torture, for example, also suffer in this way. Individuals responsible for unintentional acts or negligence that result in the death of another, such as vehicular homicide or injury while driving under the influence of drugs or alcohol, may suffer a similar moral injury.

55. Samuel L. A. Marshall, *Men against Fire: The Problem of Battle Command in Future War* (Norman: University of Oklahoma Press, 2000), 54.

56. The notion of universal human phobia (resistance to killing one of one's own species) put forth in Lt. Col. Dave Grossman's book *On Killing: The Psychological Cost of Learning to Kill in War and Society*, rev. edn. (New

York: Little, Brown, 2009), is contested by some, including the clinical psychiatrist credited with coining the term *moral injury*, Dr. Jonathan Shay, author of *Achilles in Vietnam: Combat Trauma and the Undoing of Character* (New York: Scribner, 1994), and *Odysseus in America Combat Trauma and the Trials of Homecoming* (New York: Scribner, 2002). Shay says, "I do not actually believe that there is an inherent injury to a human being or any other mammal or fish from killing another of one's own species. This is an idea that was put forth by Dave Grossman, and unfortunately, it just isn't well-founded. I think that a lot of people do suffer very much when they believe they have killed the wrong people for the wrong reason. In the lingo of the people who are currently there, somebody who didn't need to be killed." Dr. Jonathan Shay, Tyler Boudreau, and Reverend Rita Brock, interviewed by Neal Conan, ©2012 National Public Radio, Inc. NPR news report "Moral Injury: The Psychological Wounds of War" was originally broadcast on NPR's *Talk of the Nation* on November 21, 2012, and is used with the permission of NPR. Any unauthorized duplication is strictly prohibited.

57. Clark C. Barrett, "Unarmed and Dangerous: The Holistic Preparation of Soldiers for Combat," *Ethical Human Psychology and Psychiatry* 13, no. 2 (2011): 100.

58. Ibid., 95.

59. Ibid., 101.

60. Quoted in Rita Nakashima Brock and Gabriella Lettini, *Soul Repair: Recovering from Moral Injury after War* (Boston: Beacon Press, 2012), 88.

61. J. K. Hamlin, K. Wynn, and P. Bloom, "Social Evaluation by Preverbal Infants," *Nature* 450 (2007): 557–59.

62. Howard Bloom, "The Moral Life of Babies," *New York Times Magazine*, May 5, 2010, http://www.nytimes.com/2010/05/09/magazine/09 babies-t.html?_r=0. For an interesting glimpse into reactions of infants at the Yale Child Study Center, see "Born Good? Babies Help Unlock the Origins of Morality," CBS News, June 28, 2013, http://www.cbsnews.com/videos/born-good-babies-help-unlock-the-origins-of-morality/, and Hamlin, Wynn, and Bloom, "Social Evaluation by Preverbal Infants."

63. J. K. Hamlin, K. Wynn, and P. Bloom, "Three Month-Olds Show a Negativity Bias in Their Social Evaluations," *Developmental Science* 13 (2010): 923–29.

64. Huerta, "Leaving the Battlefield."

65. This notion that naming the places that are safe is a communal task harkens back to the theological anthropology of Farley, *Good and Evil*, 47.

66. I hold up here the work of the Soul Repair Center for Moral Injury Recovery at Brite Divinity School as just such a place and community willing to hear these difficult stories.

Chapter Seven. Chronic Displacement and Persons without Home

1. Please note my usage of two terms: First, *transitional facility* is used here to indicate a place that meets an intermediate housing need between a short-term shelter and long-term permanent housing. This facility allowed residents to stay for up to one year under conditions of sobriety and those specifically related to parole where applicable. It was owned and operated by the United Methodist Church and located in a moderately sized southeastern city. This facility closed in the late 1990s, and the property was eventually sold. I use the singular form of *home* (where otherwise the plural would be grammatically appropriate) as I have elsewhere to indicate both the physical structure, a place for living, as well as those elements of a home place, such as the psychological and spiritual, not necessarily represented by the traditional use of the word *homes*.

2. National Law Center on Homelessness and Poverty, "Homelessness and Poverty in America: Overview," 2008, http://www.nlchp.org/hapia.cfm.

3. In this definition I refer to only part of the definition of homeless as stated in the Stewart B. McKinney Act, 42 U.S.C. § 11301, et seq. (1994). See National Coalition for the Homeless, "Who Is Homeless," 2007, http://www.nationalhomeless.org/publications/facts/Whois.pdf.

4. I have found the following to be the most helpful resources for terms and statistics concerning homelessness in the United States: Department for Housing and Urban Development, http://portal.hud.gov/hudportal/HUD?src=/program_offices/comm_planning/homeless; National Coalition for the Homeless, http://www.nationalhomeless.org/; and National Law Center on Homelessness and Poverty, http://www.nlchp.org/.

5. The UN Millennium Goals' topics include poverty/hunger, education, gender equality, child mortality, maternal health, HIV/AIDS and other diseases, environmental sustainability, and development. For information regarding evaluation and progress of the goals set for the year

2015, see http://www.un.org/millenniumgoals/. See also information on the post-2015 sustainable development goals at http://www.un.org/sustainabledevelopment.

6. The current federal minimum wage is $7.25 per hour and was set on July 24, 2009. Many states also have minimum wage laws, and some provide a higher wage that the federal standard. See http://www.dol.gov/whd/minimumwage.htm.

7. "Locked In: The Costly Criminalization of the Mentally Ill," *Economist*, August 1, 2013, http://www.economist.com/news/united-states/21582535-costly-criminalisation-mentally-ill-locked.

8. The Substance Abuse and Mental Health Administration estimates that upwards of 25 percent of persons without home suffer from some form of mental illness. Add addiction as a complicating condition and the numbers climb much higher. "Current Statistics on the Prevalence and Characteristics of People Experiencing Homelessness in the United States," November 2011, http://homeless.samhsa.gov/ResourceFiles/hrc_factsheet.pdf. See also the U.S. Department of Housing and Urban Development's report on homelessness: "213 AHAR: Part I-PIT Estimates of Homelessness in the U.S.," November 2013, https://www.hudexchange.info/resource/3300/2013-ahar-part-1-pit-estimates-of-homelessness.

9. See also Craig Rennebohm and David W. Paul, *Souls in the Hands of a Tender God: Stories of the Search for Home and Healing on the Streets* (Boston: Beacon Press, 2008).

10. Deborah K. Padgett, "There's No Place Like (a) Home: Ontological Security among Persons with Serious Mental Illness in the United States," *Social Science and Medicine* 64, no. 9 (2007): 1925–36.

11. Since at least the late 1990s, however, at least a few alternative efforts have been made to serve the addicted homeless with programs that do not require abstinence. These programs focus on harm reduction and positive life improvement. See Deborah Kraus, Michael Goldberg, and Luba Serge, "Homelessness, Housing and Harm Reduction: Stable Housing for Homeless People with Substance Use Issues," *The Social Planning and Research Council of British Columbia* (SPARC BC), July 2005, http://www.raincityhousing.org/wordpress/wp-content/uploads/2008/02/homeless-housing-and-harm-reduction.pdf.

12. Gene M. Heyman, *Addiction: A Disorder of Choice* (Cambridge, MA: Harvard University Press, 2009), 1.

13. Michelle Alexander, *The New Jim Crow: Mass Incarceration in the Age of Colorblindness* (New York: New Press, 2010), 53.

14. Ibid., esp. 97–139.

15. Addiction: Homelessness Resource Center, Substance Abuse and Mental Health Services Administration, "Current Statistics on the Prevalence and Characteristics of People Experiencing Homelessness in the United States," November 2011, http://homeless.samhsa.gov/ResourceFiles/hrc_factsheet.pdf.; race: National Coalition for the Homeless, "Basic Facts about Homelessness: New York City," September 2015, http://www.coalitionforthehomeless.org/basic-facts-about-homelessness-new-york-city/; and incarceration: Stephen Metraux, Caterina G. Roman, and Richard S. Cho, "Incarceration and Homelessness," http://www.huduser.org/portal//publications/pdf/p9.pdf.

16. To their credit, some cities have recognized the need for a similar low-income SRO option and have created so-called supportive housing options. In Richmond, Virginia, Clay House started as an SRO but was recently renamed Virginia Supportive Housing. This facility offers single rooms for rent but also provides various social services to help residents break the cycle of homelessness.

17. Section 8 housing vouchers allow residents meeting income and legal immigrant or citizenship status to rent preapproved apartments on the private housing market. The federal government subsidizes rent in these apartments, which must meet minimum safety standards. See U.S. Department of Housing and Urban Development, "Section 8 Assistance for Public Housing Relocation/Replacement," http://portal.hud.gov/hudportal/HUD?src=/programdescription/phrr.

18. U.S. Department of Housing and Urban Development, "Report: Picture of Subsidized Households" (data from 2009–2013), http://www.huduser.org/portal/datasets/picture/about.html.

19. Felony convictions, depending on the crime, may compromise a person's ability to qualify for section 8 or public housing. Even suspicion of committing a crime (regardless of conviction) is grounds for eviction. U.S. Department of Housing and Urban Development, "Tenancy Addendum, Section 8 Tenant-Based Assistance Housing Choice Voucher Program, Exp. 09/30/2017," http://portal.hud.gov/hudportal/documents/huddoc?id=52641-a.pdf.

20. Human Rights Watch, "No Second Chance: People with Criminal Records Denied Access to Public Housing," November 17, 2004, https://

www.hrw.org/report/2004/11/17/no-second-chance/people-criminal
-records-denied-access-public-housing.

21. "The Move to Opportunity: A Random Assignment Housing Mobility Study"—a social experiment studying the effects of mixed-income
housing in five U.S. cities—came out of this initiative and has provided
significant information. See U.S. Department of Housing and Urban
Development, "HOPE VI—Public and Indian Housing," http://portal
.hud.gov/hudportal/HUD?src=/program_offices/public_indian
_housing/programs/ph/hope6.

22. Stephen Steinberg, "The Myth of Concentrated Poverty," in *The Integration Debate: Competing Futures for American Cities*, ed. Chester
W. Hartman and Gregory D. Squires (New York: Routledge, 2010),
213–27.

23. The complete data for MTO can be found at "Neighborhood Effects of
the Long-Term Well-Being of Low-Income Adults from All Five Sites
of the Moving to Opportunity Experiment," 2008–2010 [Public Use
Data] (ICPSR 34563), http://www.icpsr.umich.edu/icpsrweb/ICPSR/
studies/34563.

24. PD&R Edge Home, "Lessons from Chicago's Public Housing Transformation," http://www.huduser.org/portal/pdredge/pdr_edge_featd_
article_052013.html.

25. People who are "hard to house" are defined as "those at risk of los-
ing their housing for reasons that go beyond affordability," such as
multiple-barrier households, the disabled, the elderly, grand-families
(grandparents raising children), large families, or felons. See Mary K.
Cunningham, Susan J. Popkin, and Martha R. Burt, "Public Housing
Transformation and the 'Hard to House,'" *Metropolitan Housing and
Communities Center* 9 (June 2005): 1–8, http://www.taxpolicycenter.org/
UploadedPDF/311178_Roof_9.pdf.

26. Lawrence J. Vale and Erin Graves, "The Chicago Housing Authority's
Plan for Transformation: What Does the Research Show So Far?" June 8,
2010, https://www.macfound.org/media/article_pdfs/VALEGRAVES
_CHA_PFT_FINAL-REPORT.PDF.

27. Cited in Sudhir Venkatesh and Isil Celimli, "Tearing down the Community," *Shelterforce Online* 138 (November–December 2004), National
Housing Institute, http://www.nhi.org/online/issues/138/chicago.html.

28. The final report, based on interviews with a variety of pastors and
other religious leaders in the New Haven area, highlights the following: "African American and Immigrant-serving congregations focused

their time and resources on the people and places in their immediate surroundings. Many of these congregations served members and communities with numerous unmet needs. These churches focused the bulk of their energies on serving the spiritual, social, and economic needs of their members and neighborhoods." Although originating in a different city, the findings of this study support the narratives of community members in the Venkatesh and Celimli study. See Vida Maralani et al., "New Haven Mapping Project Report," Yale Sociology, submitted to Yale Divinity School and the Jessie Ball DuPont Fund, June 2013.

29. Venkatesh and Celimli, "Tearing down the Community," 6.

30. United States Interagency Council on Homelessness, "Public Schools: Counting and Caring for Children Experiencing Homelessness," http://usich.gov/member_agency/department_of_education/public_schools_counting_and_caring_for_children_experiencing_homelessness/.

31. Susan Saulny, "After Recession, More Young Adults Are Living on Street," *New York Times*, December 18, 2012, http://www.nytimes.com/2012/12/19/us/since-recession-more-young-americans-are-homeless.html?_r=0.

32. My early mistakes in communication with those arriving from other cultures included misinterpreting emotional responses—or no emotional response—from certain facial gestures. Others from the same culture could clearly interpret the anger, fear, and concern appropriately. I had the same experience in Kakuma Refugee Camp. Young Sudanese refrained from looking directly into the faces of those they considered elders—by age or knowledge (authority). For more on the value of tending to these misunderstandings as moments of learning and growth, see Melinda A. McGarrah Sharp, *Misunderstanding Stories: Toward a Postcolonial Pastoral Theology* (Eugene, OR: Pickwick, 2013).

33. "The persons participating in the communicative environment are given one to the other not as objects but as counter-subjects, as consociates in a societal community of persons." Alfred Schutz, *Alfred Schutz on Phenomenology and Social Relations*, ed. Helmut R. Wagner (Chicago: University of Chicago Press, 1970), 165.

34. Ibid., 298; Richard M. Zaner, "Theory of Intersubjectivity: Alfred Schutz," *Social Research* 28, no. 1 (1961): 71–93.

35. Anthony Giddens, *Modernity and Self-Identity: Self and Society in the Late Modern Age* (Cambridge, MA: Polity Press, 1991), 160.

36. Ibid., 156: "In each case [of institutional sequestration] they have the effect of removing basic aspects of life experience, including especially

moral crises, from the regularities of day-to-day life established by the abstract systems of modernity. The term 'sequestration of experience' refers here to connected processes of concealment which set apart the routines of ordinary life from the following phenomena: madness; criminality; sickness and death; sexuality; and nature. In some cases such sequestration is directly organizational; this is true of the mental asylum, the prison and the medical hospital. In other instances, sequestration depends more on more general characteristics of the internally referential systems of modernity."

37. Andrew J. Liese, "We Can Do Better: Anti-Homeless Ordinances as Violations of State Substantive Due Process Law," *Vanderbilt Law Review* 59, no. 4 (2006): 1413–55.

38. Alexander, *The New Jim Crow.*

39. Don Mitchell, "The Annihilation of Space by Law: The Roots and Implications of Anti-Homeless Laws in the United States," *Antipode* 29, no. 3 (1997): 307.

40. Ibid., 321.

41. Simon Romero, "Slum Dwellers Are Defying Brazil's Grand Design for Olympics," *New York Times*, March 4, 2012, http://www.nytimes.com/2012/03/05/world/americas/brazil-faces-obstacles-in-preparations-for-rio-olympics.html?pagewanted=all&_r=0; Jake Hooker, "Before Guests, Beijing Hides Some Messes," *New York Times*, July 29, 2008, http://www.nytimes.com/2008/07/29/sports/olympics/29beijing.html?emc=eta1.

42. United Nations General Assembly, Sixty-Sixth Session, "Extreme Poverty and Human Rights," submitted by Magdalena Sepúlveda Carmona, August 4, 2011, http://www.ohchr.org/Documents/Issues/EPoverty/A.66.265.pdf.

43. The United Nations recognized this report as a groundbreaking move on the part of the United States to rectify violations against some of its most vulnerable citizens. Nonetheless, at a forum at the United Nations in 2013, various human rights advocacy groups continued to call into question current laws and practices of discrimination against homeless people as violations of human rights.

44. U.S. Interagency Council on Homelessness, "Searching out Solutions: Constructive Alternatives to the Criminalization of Homelessness," 2012, http://usich.gov/resources/uploads/asset_library/RPT_SoS_March 2012.pdf.

45. Mitchell, "The Annihilation of Space by Law," 310.

46. Ibid.
47. U.S. Interagency Council on Homelessness, "Searching out Solutions," 11.
48. Barbara L. Fredrickson and Tomi-Ann Roberts, "Objectification Theory: Toward Understanding Women's Lived Experiences and Mental Health Risks," *Psychology of Women Quarterly* 21, no. 2 (1997): 173–206.
49. The outcome was the creation of the Sisters of the Road Cafe in Oregon, which offers meals for a nominal charge and allows alternative means for "paying" if one is without money. Lisa Hoffman and Brian Coffey, "Dignity and Indignation: How People Experiencing Homelessness View Services and Providers," *Social Science Journal* 45, no. 2 (2008): 207–22.
50. Ibid., emphasis added; Sisters of the Road, "The Cafe at Sisters of the Road," http://sistersoftheroad.org/what-we-do/cafe/.
51. Hoffman and Coffey, "Dignity and Indignation."
52. Ibid., 214–15.
53. Ibid., 217.
54. Ibid., 218.
55. Brita L. Gill-Austern names knowing home as the first step of practical solidarity, by which she means, I think, know the place you come from. While this can be parsed at great length, she in part means to know our "assumptions about the poor, about why poverty exists. . . . We cannot reach out to the other . . . without examining our own complicity." Gill-Austern, "Engaging Diversity and Difference: From Practice of Exclusion to Practices of Practical Solidarity," in *Injustice and the Care of Souls: Taking Oppression Seriously in Pastoral Care*, ed. Sheryl A. Holbrook and Karen Brown Montagno (Minneapolis: Fortress Press, 2009), 37.
56. Schutz, *Alfred Schutz on Phenomenology and Social Relations*, 298.
57. See the term *mirroring* in Heinz Kohut, *Does Analysis Cure?* ed. Arnold Goldberg, in collaboration with Paul E. Stepansky (Chicago: University of Chicago Press, 1984), 23.
58. Hermann Gunkel and Joachim Begrich, *Introduction to Psalms: The Genres of the Religious Lyric of Israel*, trans. James D. Nogalski (Macon, GA.: Mercer University Press, 1998), 127.
59. Walter Brueggemann, *Theology of the Old Testament: Testimony, Dispute, Advocacy* (Minneapolis: Fortress Press, 1997), 421, 425.
60. See Sharon Thornton's research on St. Mark's Episcopal Cathedral's efforts to care for persons without home in Seattle, Washington. This congregation is notable for its efforts to engage in the earnest challenge

to recognize (I would add recognize the face of the other) and welcome the stranger through the building of relationships. Sharon G. Thornton, "Homeless in Seattle: A Lived Religion of Hospitality in Pastoral Bearings: Lived Religion and Pastoral Theology," in *Pastoral Bearings: Lived Religion and Pastoral Theology*, ed. Jane F. Maynard, Leonard M. Hummel, and Mary Clark Moschella (Lanham, MD: Lexington Books, 2010), 91–118.

Chapter Eight. Postures of Hospitality

1. M. Jan Holton, *Building the Resilient Community: Lessons from the Lost Boys of Sudan* (Eugene, OR: Cascade Books, 2011).
2. Edward Farley, *Good and Evil: Interpreting a Human Condition* (Minneapolis: Fortress Press, 1990), 41.
3. Sharon G. Thornton, *Broken yet Beloved: A Pastoral Theology of the Cross* (St. Louis: Chalice Press, 2002), 61.
4. Ibid., 112.
5. John Patton introduced this idea in *Pastoral Care in Context: An Introduction to Pastoral Care* (Louisville: Westminster John Knox, 1993), 5. Pastoral theologian Nancy J. Ramsay notes, "The communal contextual paradigm, as Patton conceived it, includes ecclesial communities of care and the importance of cultural and political contexts shaping persons' lives. It retrieves the earlier awareness that care is a ministry of the church or faith community rather than solely a clerical responsibility. It also reclaimed the importance of social context from the influence of the social gospel on the field in the early twentieth century and the contemporary influences of issues related to difference posed by asymmetries of power such as gender, race, and class." Ramsay, ed., *Pastoral Care and Counseling: Redefining the Paradigms* (Nashville: Abingdon Press, 2004), 11.
6. Holton, *Building the Resilient Community*, 20.
7. Don S. Browning, *A Fundamental Practical Theology: Descriptive and Strategic Proposals* (Minneapolis: Fortress Press, 1991).
8. Elaine L. Graham, *Transforming Practice: Pastoral Theology in an Age of Uncertainty* (New York: Mowbray, 1996), 208.
9. Kevin D. O'Gorman, "Dimensions of Hospitality: Exploring Ancient and Classical Origins," in *Hospitality: A Social Lens*, ed. Conrad Lashley, Paul Lynch, and Alison J. Morrison (Oxford: Elsevier, 2007), 17–32.
10. Jacques Derrida, *Acts of Literature*, ed. Derek Attridge (London: Routledge, 1992), 55.

11. Jacques Derrida, *Of Hospitality: Cultural Memory in the Present*, trans. Anne Dufourmantelle and Janet Bowlby (Stanford, CA: Stanford University Press, 2000).

12. "The personal is the political" is a long-used phrase introduced into theological conversation by feminist theologians. I draw specifically from Thornton's work in its use here because it points us toward reimagining pastoral theology from a particular frame of justice making. See Thornton, *Broken yet Beloved*, 7.

13. Matt. 25:35 is considered here in the context of verses 34 to 40.

14. Jessica Wrobleski, *The Limits of Hospitality* (Collegeville, MN: Liturgical Press, 2012), xii.

15. Jacques Derrida, "Hospitality," *Angelaki: Journal of the Theoretical Humanities* 5, no. 3 (2000): 7.

16. Letty M. Russell, *Just Hospitality: God's Welcome in a World of Difference*, ed. J. Shannon Clarkson and Kate M. Ott (Louisville: Westminster John Knox, 2009), 24. See also Russell's use of "Hermeneutic of Hospitality," 43.

17. In the United States we are more familiar with cultured buttermilk, which is similar to traditional fermented milk common in poor, rural regions around the world.

18. For more about how we can learn across difference through our misunderstandings, see Mindy A. McGarrah Sharp, *Misunderstanding Stories: Toward a Postcolonial Pastoral Theology* (Eugene, OR: Pickwick, 2013).

19. M. Jan Holton, "Luke 7:36–8:3, Pastoral Perspective," in *Feasting on the Word: Preaching the Revised Common Lectionary*, Pentecost and Season after Pentecost 1 (Propers 3–16), Year C, vol. 3, ed. David L. Bartlett and Barbara Brown Taylor (Louisville: Westminster John Knox Press, 2009), 140, 142.

20. Emma J. Justes, *Hearing beyond the Words: How to Become a Listening Pastor* (Nashville: Abingdon Press, 2006), 4.

21. Sharon G. Thornton, "Homeless in Seattle: A Lived Religion of Hospitality in Pastoral Bearings: Lived Religion and Pastoral Theology," in *Pastoral Bearings: Lived Religion and Pastoral Theology*, ed. Jane F. Maynard, Leonard M. Hummel, and Mary Clark Moschella (Lanham, MD: Lexington Books, 2010), 104.

22. Letty Russell proposes a similar notion when she speaks of a "hermeneutic of hospitality," which she proposes to replace a dualistic language of otherness. She writes, "I want to look within the Christian tradition for ways to affirm the key importance of difference while sharing in

God's hospitality and welcome for all and for the whole creation." Russell, *Just Hospitality*, 24.

23. I have named the relational encounter as necessary for enacting postures of hospitality. This is not to say that relationship is the most important of the four functions of home that I have proposed. I do not believe we can place a higher value on any one of the four, meaning, belonging, security, or relationship. Rather, the relational aspect of communal engagement within society at large is fundamental to creating postures of hospitality.

24. This may seem a strikingly different context for many, but even in the West, relationship with the sacred often begins in the home place. Home is where children often first encounter religious language or traditions and devotional icons and other material.

25. Christine D. Pohl, *Making Room: Recovering Hospitality as a Christian Tradition* (Grand Rapids, MI: Eerdmans, 1999), 187.

26. Humanitarian workers I met in Kakuma struggled with the knowledge that while they ate plentifully, thousands outside the staff compound struggled with starvation. There are no easy solutions to problems such as this. Working with this reality from day to day is part of what makes humanitarian aid work so very difficult.

27. William James Booth, "Foreigners: Insiders, Outsiders and the Ethics of Membership," *Review of Politics* 59, no. 2 (1997): 263.

28. Ibid., 259–92.

29. I offer this example not as a model for vulnerability as a posture of hospitality, per se, or to imply that I somehow offer remarkable hospitality through my research. I am reflecting on my encounters in my fieldwork and the often accidental moments when refugees or other displaced persons have helped me learn something valuable.

30. Justes, *Hearing beyond the Words*, 9–10. Justes points to biblical accounts of hospitality including Abraham and Sarah welcoming the strangers (Gen. 18), the woman who anoints Jesus's feet (Luke 7:36–50), and the more recent history of sheltering Jews during the Holocaust and opening homes to people escaping slavery in America as examples of the ways that hospitality makes both host and guest vulnerable, though often in different ways.

31. Sharp, *Misunderstanding Stories*, 106. Sharp notes the importance of "shared vulnerability" as a fundamental aspect of justice-oriented care toward the other.

32. Russell, *Just Hospitality*, 33.

33. Thornton proposes a political theology of the cross in which love and justice—just love—are inseparable; see Thornton, *Broken yet Beloved*, 112. Likewise, in her sexual ethic, Margaret A. Farley uses the term *just love* to mean "a love [that] is right and good insofar as it aims to affirm truthfully the concrete reality of the beloved." Farley, *Just Love: A Framework for Christian Sexual Ethics* (New York: Continuum Press, 2010), 200.

34. John Wall, *Ethics in Light of Childhood* (Washington, DC: Georgetown University Press, 2010), 100.

35. Ibid., 104.

36. There is no shortage of biblical narratives to guide the community of faith in rich discussions about what determines a compassionate response toward one another, especially the marginalized. In the Christian context we can turn to the Good Samaritan and the Great Commandment as frequent instructors; the Golden Rule serves similarly in traditions around the world.

37. David H. Kelsey, *Eccentric Existence: A Theological Anthropology*, 2 vols. (Louisville: Westminster John Knox Press, 2009), 2:711.

38. Wall, *Ethics in Light of Childhood*, 106.

39. Ibid., 106.

40. Thornton, *Broken yet Beloved*, 112.

41. Mark Anderson, "Nicaragua Canal Will Wreak Havoc on Forests and Displace People, NGO Warns," *Guardian*, September 30, 2014, http://www.theguardian.com/global-development/2014/sep/30/nicaragua-canal-forest-displace-people.

42. Peter Holley, "After 90-Year-Old Is Arrested, Florida Judge Halts Law That Restricts Feeding the Homeless," *Washington Post*, December 3, 2014, http://www.washingtonpost.com/news/post-nation/wp/2014/12/03/after-90-year-old-is-arrested-florida-judge-halts-law-that-restricts-feeding-the-homeless/.

INDEX

addiction, 139, 141–44, 155

Afghanistan, war in, 58, 107, 119–20

African-Americans, 9, 143–44, 147, 148, 149, 156

agape, 185

Alexander, Michelle, 143, 156

alienation, 137–38, 151–62. *See also* exclusion, rejection

altruism, 130

American Dream, 27–28, 29, 150

ancestors, 70, 71, 90, 103

Anti-Drug Abuse Act (1986), 143

Arou, Mading, 32

Australia, 62, 97

Baldwin, James, 148

Bantu, 63, 64

Barrett, Clark C., 128–29

Batwa, 59–72, 75–80, 196n3. *See also* Pygmy

Batwa Experience, 76–77, 80, 197n18, 197n19, 198n20, 198n23

Baumeister, Roy F., 87

belonging: compromised, 42–44; creation of, 12–13, 15, 17, 103–5; exclusion from, 95–103; and God, 37–39, 43–44, 88–90; lack of, 42–43, 90–91; nature of, 81–88; need for, 25

Bigo, Didier, 101–2

Biophilia Hypothesis, 72–73

biophobia, 73

Bird-David, Nurit, 70

Bloom, P., 130

Blum, Harold P., 85

boat people, 97

Booth, William James, 181–82

Bor, South Sudan, 1, 29, 32

border: between "us" and "them," 180–81; economic, 150; fluidity of, 8, 10, 101; and hospitality, 177–78; national, 23, 95, 102

boundary: definition of, 98; and home, 22, 30; in hospitality, 171–72, 173, 180–82, 186

Bowlby, John, 15–16, 86–87

Brazil, 157

Browning, Don S., 169

Brueggemann, Walter, 163

Buhoma, Uganda, 57, 66, 67, 71, 76

Bwindi Impenetrable Forest National Park, 57, 65, 67

Cabrini-Green housing project, 147–48, 149

camp: hospitality in, 174, 182; and identity papers, 100; Kakuma Refugee Camp, Kenya, 81, 83, 84, 100, 103–4, 180–81; Mugunga Camp, Goma, 61, 94, 181, 196n5; Nakivale Refugee Camp, Uganda, 89; and preservation of home, 83–84; time in, 56–57, 58; spontaneous, 56, 94–95; Western presence in, 122 care, moral obligation of, 3–4, 41, 117, 163, 167–70, 181, 184–86

Carmona, Magdalena Sepúlveda, 157

categorization: of the displaced, 65, 82, 91–99, 102–3, 167, 180–82; of the homeless, 137, 154–57, 163; as victim/perpetrator, 117, 122–24, 126–27, 132, 133–34

Chicago, 147–48

childhood: and home place, 15–16, 18–19, 20, 21–23, 25; of Jesus, 7, 189n7; and moral judgment, 130; and security, 111–12; and separation, 84–87

children: displacement of, 9–10, 150; and gaze, 162; support for, 84, 104, 141–42, 155

China, 157

Christ, 163, 169, 172

church: as center of community, 89; "failure of," 202n13; and hospitality, 172; Pygmy, 61; support from, 104, 149, 174–75

citizenship, 95–96, 98–100

class: middle, 10, 12, 27, 29, 150; upper, 136, 155; working, 145

classism, 30, 144, 151, 156

cognitive behavior therapy (CBT), 124–25

Cohen, Roger, 18–19

collusion, 48–49

colonialism, 64, 72, 74–76, 77, 166, 170, 175

combat zone, 109, 205n7

communication, 152–53, 161, 162, 215n32

communion, 169. See also Eucharist

community: conceptions of, 8, 86; functioning of, 105, 149; as home, 20–23; as just, 41, 71–72, 138, 163; loss of, 149; need for, 84–85; single, 180–82; for soldiers, 117–19

community of faith: care by, 3–4, 134, 165, 169, 174–75, 184; disruption of, 53–54; role in displacement, 89–90

compassion, 167

Congo: and colonialism, 64, 74–75; creation of community in, 104–5; displacement in, 50, 51, 53, 54, 90, 94, 96–97; home-place in, 27; security in, 26, 39

conversion, 61, 76–77, 80

Creation narrative, 18, 32–33

criminalization, 97–98, 143, 155–59

cross, 168–69

Crow Nation, 200n46

dance, 66, 84

Dart, Thomas, 140

depersonalization, 171

Derrida, Jacques, 171, 172

Dinka: and cultural preservation, 84; and displacement, 1; ethic of care, 167; and home, 21, 32, 86; and killing, 128

displaced, 167–68, 174

displacement: of Batwa people, 57–58, 59–62, 65–66, 76–78, 80; definition of, 19; and exclusion, 95–103, 166–67; forms of, 4–5, 7–11, 90–95; longing for home, 83–84; and moral obligation of care, 167–70; narratives of, 19–20; as ongoing, 187; and relationship, 137–38, 149, 151–65; and resilience, 103–6; responses to, 47–48, 50–51; in scripture, 7–8, 32–33; stages of, 51–57; as subject, 2–4; veterans' experience of, 58, 107–9, 118–20, 131–34. *See also* homelessness

Dixon, John, 17–20

documentation, 99–100

Drescher, Kent, 126

Duncan, James, 23

Duncan, Nancy, 23

Dupuis, Ann, 112–13

Durrheim, Kevin, 17–20

Eden, Garden of, 33, 48

eligibility, 66, 92, 122–23, 154–55

Erikson, Erik H., 16, 192n21, 201n3

Ethiopia, 93

Eucharist, 90, 163. *See also* communion

exclusion: of Batwa, 61–66, 74–76; by community, 47–49; of the displaced, 166–67; of the outsider, 95–103, 105–6, 181–82; of Pygmies, 61. *See also* alienation, rejection

Exodus, 33

face, 162

faith: as challenged, 49, 54, 114, 121, 131; in displacement, 1; as framework for interpretation, 24

family: of Christ, 90, 163; displacement of, 9–10; and home, 21, 22, 87; and homelessness, 141–42, 143, 146–47, 155; as human right, 48; rejection from,

39, 90, 97; in scripture, 7–8, 172; for soldier, 109, 117–118, 131–32; as support, 51, 56, 137, 168

Farley, Edward, 48–49, 167

Fassin, Didier, 122–23

fear: of absence of God, 38; coping with, 182, 187; in displacement, 53, 96; exploitation of, 101–2, 106; forms of, 39–40; of nature, 73–74; of persecution, 91–92; and PTSD, 120, 132

first peoples, 59, 61–63, 72, 77, 79

flourishing, 44–47, 48

Fontana, Alan, 126

foreigner, 10, 81, 95–106, 166, 180–82, 203n18

future, 78–79

Geneva Convention, 128

Giddens, Anthony, 88, 104, 112–13, 153, 156

globalization, 8–9, 101

God: and Batwa, 71–72, 76; face of, 163–64; and future, 78–79; leaning into, 11, 12, 35–49, 179, 182; and meaning making, 24, 25, 43; presence of, 12, 54, 180, 187–88; questioning of, 114, 120–21; rejection by, 127; relationship with, 33–35, 86, 88–90, 106, 138

Goma, the Congo, 53, 55–56, 60, 94, 99, 104–5, 196n5

gorilla, 65, 72

government: and Batwa, 75; Chinese, 157; and homelessness, 147, 151, 159; and language, 92; response to crisis, 50, 93; of South Sudan, 99–100

grace, 42, 43, 45–56, 164
Graham, Elaine L., 169–70
Grossman, Dave, 128–29

Hamlin, J. K., 130
health, 26, 45–46, 69,192n24;
  mental, 86–87, 119–25, 143,
  207n33, 208n41, 208n43, 212n8
Herman, Judith, 114
Heyman, Gene M., 143
holding community, 110–11, 117,
  206n28
home: for Batwa, 65–66, 67–70;
  circles of, 20–23; cultural con-
  structions of, 29–31; and death,
  70; definition of, 14, 110; dual,
  83; "failure," of 42–44; and
  flourishing, 44–47; function of,
  2, 23–26, 35–36, 82–83; and God,
  12, 32–49; idealized, 26–28; and
  identity, 15–20; as just, 71–72;
  and love, 40–42; and meaning
  making, 12–14, 36–37; memory
  of, 83–84, 91; and nature, 60,
  65–70; new, 77–78, 83, 103–5,
  108, 174–75, 179; psychology
  of, 34–35; and security, 39–40,
  107, 109–12, 117–19; Western
  understandings of, 48. See also
  homelessness
homecoming, 32, 131–34
homelessness, 2, 30, 58, 136–51;
  criminalization of, 51–59
home place. See home
homesickness. See longing
hope, 78–80, 105
Hope VI (Housing Opportunities for People Everywhere),
  147–48

Hopkins, Brooke, 110
hospitality, 7, 11, 30, 169–88,
  220n30
housing, 56, 139, 144–49, 151, 164
Huerta, Carlos, 107, 116, 118, 125, 131
Hurricane Sandy, 53, 54

identity, and place, 16–20
illegals, 203n18
immigrant, as designation, 92, 102,
  202n14
incarceration, 139, 141–43
Infant Cognition Center, Yale
  University, 130
insecurity, 112–16
internally displaced person (IDP),
  definition, 90, 92–95
Iraq, war in, 58, 107, 116–17, 118,
  119–20, 129, 208n42
Israel, 79, 106, 163

Janoff-Bulman, Ronnie, 113–15,
  121, 127
Japan, 55, 91
Jesus, 7–8, 169, 172, 175–77, 189n7
Justes, Emma J., 176, 177, 183,
  220n30
justice, 72, 130, 163, 168, 169,
  184–86

Kakuma Refugee Camp, Kenya.
  See camp
Kasambala, Amon Eddie, 84
Katrina, hurricane, 50, 53
Kellermann, Scott and Carol,
  76–77, 198n20
Kellert, Stephen R., 72–73
Kelsey, David H., 41, 45–47, 185
Kibumba, Goma, 56, 94, 105

killing, 116, 123–33, 209n56
Kilner, Peter, 128–29
Klieman, Kairn A., 62–64, 71, 74, 75
Kohler, Axel, 64, 68, 70
Kohut, Heinz, 162

Laing, Robert David, 112
LaMothe, Ryan, 114
Latinos, 144, 203n18
law, 155–59, 166
leaning in, 11, 12, 35–49, 179, 182
Lear, Jonathan, 78–79
Leary, Mark R., 87
Leopold, king of Belgium, 64, 74
Lester, Andrew D., 78, 79
Levinas, Emmanuel, 167
Lewis, Jerome, 72, 75
Litz, Brett T., 127
longing, 14, 25, 28, 33–34, 83–84, 91, 131
Lost Boys of Sudan, 22, 117, 192n22
love, 26, 37–38, 40–41, 88, 168–69, 178, 184–86

Mahler, Margaret, 15–16, 85
Manby, Bronwen, 99–100
Marcel, Gabriel, 167
Marcus, Clare Cooper, 16
marriage, 9, 190n9
Marshall, Samuel L. A., 128
Mbiti, John S., 86
McClintock-Fulkerson, Mary, 38
McClure, Barbara J., 44, 45
meaning, 15, 23–26, 36–37, 63, 68–70, 114, 194n10
media, 27
Mejia, Camilo, 129
memory. See remembering
mental illness. See health: mental

migrant, 92, 102, 202n14
Miriam, Apostle, 61, 63–65, 76–77
Mitch, hurricane, 50
Mitchell, Don, 156, 158–59
moral injury, 108, 116,120, 126–31, 132, 209n54
moral obligation of care. See obligation of care
mother, 85–87, 141–42, 194n9
Mugunga Camp, Goma. See camp
Musopole, Augustine Ching-wala, 86

Nakivale Refugee Camp, Uganda. See camp
narcissism, 40–41
Nashville, TN, 104
Native American, 72, 148
natural disaster, 50–51, 52–53, 54, 55, 93
New Orleans, 50
New York City, 143–46
Nicaragua, 50, 51, 85, 187
9/11, 100, 101, 102, 113
nomad, 21, 70
nostalgia, 28
Nyamata Church, Kigali, Rwanda, 89

objectification, 151–62, 163, 185
obligation of care, 4, 41, 117, 133, 163, 167–69, 184–86
Olympics, 157
opening outward, 175–78, 183
Orwell, George, 92
outsider, 95–97, 101–2

Papua New Guinea, 97
parent, 111, 162

Parkside Evangeline, NYC, 145–46
patriotism, 23, 113–14, 121
Patton, John, 169
place identity, 14, 18–19
Pohl, Christine D., 180
post-traumatic stress disorder (PTSD), 58, 107–8, 114, 115–16, 119–27, 129, 131–32
postures, of hospitality, 175–80
poverty, 10, 50, 138–39, 146–51, 157–58, 164
Proshansky, Harold M., 17–20
Pygmy, 61–65, 70, 71, 74–77, 196n3. See also Batwa

racism, 49, 96, 143–44, 151, 156
rape. See sexual violence
Rechtman, Richard, 122–23
reciprocity, 82, 88–89, 97–98, 105, 177
refugee, 7, 58, 83–84, 90–106, 133, 174–75, 180–81; conservation, 65–66, 76–77, 91; economic refugee, 10, 98, 150.
refugee camp. See camp
rejection, 30–31, 81–82, 88–90, 127. See also alienation, exclusion
relationship: in Africa, 86; with the Divine, 33, 35, 40–42, 88–90, 138, 162–64; with fellow soldiers, 132–33; and home place, 15–17, 19–23, 26, 31; through hospitality, 172–86; human, 161–64; as love, 40–41, 43; as ruptured, 137–38, 151–62, 164–65; troubled, 42–44
remembering, 23, 28, 83–84, 90–91, 115, 169

resilience, 43–47, 78–80, 103–5, 115, 122, 149, 164
resources, 50–51
Richmond, VA, 22
ritual, 27, 70, 77, 84, 90, 127
Rudd, Kevin, 97–98
Russell, Letty, 183, 291n22
Rwanda, 61

sacredness, 24, 35, 37, 48, 79–80, 180
safety. See security
Salvation Army, 145
Sandy, hurricane, 53, 54
Sarajevo, 174
Schutz Alfred, 13, 152–53, 162
scripture: and belonging, 37, 88; displacement in, 7–8; face of God in, 163; and future, 79; and home place, 32–33; hospitality in, 172, 176–77, 220n36
security, 25–26, 39–40, 101–2, 109–21, 132–34
self-medication, 124
separation, 84–88, 109
sexual violence, 39, 40, 90, 96–97, 104, 108, 118, 207n34
Seyle, Bryn L., 37
shelter, 51, 56–57, 105, 150, 154–55, 161
single room occupancy (SRO), 144–45, 213n16
Sisters of the Road, Portland, OR, 160
social exclusion. See exclusion
soldier, 58, 90, 107–9, 113–34, 166, 204n3, 205n7
Somalia, 93
Sorajjakool, Siroj, 37

sources, 5–7, 60, 137, 160
space, control of, 33–34, 50, 68,
    155–59, 166–67, 180; distin-
    guished from place, 193n6
stages, of displacement, 51–57
stakeholder, 159, 161–62
Steinberg, Stephen, 148
students, 145, 150
Sudan (South Sudan), 22, 93,
    98–100, 174–75, 203n20
suffering, response to, 164,
    168–69
suicide, 75, 108, 124, 128, 208n42
Summerfield, Derek, 122
Syria, 187

Tabitha Center, Congo, 104–5,
    204n29
terrorism, 100–101, 105–6
Thorns, David C., 112–13
Thornton, Sharon G., 168, 171,
    177, 186
Tillich, Paul, 33–34
topophilia, 13, 23
trauma, 108, 109, 112–26, 130–31
tree, 103–4
trust: early childhood, 15; in God,
    35, 78, 114, 121; for the home-
    less, 161; lack of, 43, 101; and
    PTSD, 120–21; and security,
    110–12
Tuan, Yi-Fu, 13–14, 18, 20, 23, 68
Turyatunga, Emmanuel, 69
Twa. See Batwa

Ulrich, Robert, 73
United Methodist Church, 145
United Nations, 138

United Nations High Commis-
    sioner for Refugees (UNHCR),
    58, 91, 93
United States: and crisis, 50, 52,
    55, 56; diagnostic constructs of,
    122; economy, 9; and foreigner,
    95–96, 98, 101–3, 203n18; home-
    lessness in, 138–39, 144, 150,
    158; home place in, 25–26, 29
universal human rights, 48, 92,
    103, 194n9
"us" and "them," 180–82
U.S. Interagency Council on
    Homelessness, 158–59

vagrancy, 155–56
veterans. See soldier
victimhood, 123–24, 132, 133–34, 154
victim/perpetrator, 117, 122–24,
    126–27, 132, 133–34
Vietnam War, 123, 128
vulnerability, 152, 154, 177, 182–84

Wall, John, 41, 184–85, 186
welcoming, 172–75
Wilson, Edward O., 72
Wilson Inn, 136–37, 139–42, 145,
    146
Winnicott, D. W., 15–16, 110–12,
    113, 117, 162
women, 1, 40, 96–97, 104–5, 108,
    118, 136–37, 176, 194n9
worthiness, 154–55
Wrobleski, Jessica, 173
Wynn, K., 130

young adults, 9, 150
Yuval-Davis, Nira, 83